Whillans Tax Tables 2025–26

Budget Edition

2025

Edited by
Kevin Walton MA
Shilpa Veerappa ATT

LexisNexis® UK & Worldwide

United Kingdom	RELX (UK) Limited trading as LexisNexis®, 1-3 Strand, London WC2N 5JR and 9–10 St Andrew Square, Edinburgh EH2 2AF
LNUK Global Partners	LexisNexis® encompasses authoritative legal publishing brands dating back to the 19th century including: Butterworths® in the United Kingdom, Canada and the Asia-Pacific region; Les Editions du Juris Classeur in France; and Matthew Bender® worldwide. Details of LexisNexis® locations worldwide can be found at www.lexisnexis.com

First published in 1948

© 2024 RELX (UK) Limited

Published by LexisNexis®
This is a Tolley title

All rights reserved. No part of this publication may be reproduced in any material form (including photocopying or storing it in any medium by electronic means and whether or not transiently or incidentally to some other use of this publication) without the written permission of the copyright owner except in accordance with the provisions of the Copyright, Designs and Patents Act 1988 or under the terms of a licence issued by the Copyright Licensing Agency Ltd, Saffron House, 6–10 Kirby Street, London EC1N 8TS. Applications for the copyright owner's written permission to reproduce any part of this publication should be addressed to the publisher.
Warning: The doing of an unauthorised act in relation to a copyright work may result in both a civil claim for damages and criminal prosecution.

Crown copyright material is reproduced with the permission of the Controller of HMSO and the King's Printer for Scotland. Parliamentary copyright material is reproduced with the permission of the Controller of His Majesty's Stationery Office on behalf of Parliament. Any European material in this work which has been reproduced from EUR-lex, the official European Communities legislation website, is European Communities copyright.
A CIP Catalogue record for this book is available from the British Library.

ISBN for this volume: 9781474331029

Printed and bound by CPI Group (UK) Ltd, Croydon, CR0 4YY

Visit LexisNexis® at www.lexisnexis.co.uk

Foreword

Since 1948, when George Whillans produced the first edition of his tax tables this publication, which still bears his name, has provided tax practitioners with concise, quick and easily accessible information about rates, allowances and other useful information across all the main taxes. This Budget edition includes all relevant measures announced in the Budget on 30 October 2024 and other changes since the 2024–25 Finance Act edition was published in August 2024. In particular, this edition includes changes to capital gains tax rates and the reduction in the lifetime limit for investors' relief, increased employers' NIC and increases to SDLT for certain residential property transactions.

Andrew Hubbard

Editor-in-chief *Taxation Magazine*

Disclaimer

In the preparation of this guide, every effort has been made to offer current, correct and clearly expressed information. However, the information in the text is intended to afford general guidelines only. This publication should not be regarded as offering a complete explanation of the tax matters referred to and is subject to changes in law and practice. No responsibility for any loss occasioned to any person acting or refraining from action as a result of any material included in or omitted from this publication can be accepted by the authors or publishers. This work does not render legal, accounting or tax advice. Readers are encouraged to consult with professional advisers for advice concerning specific matters before making any decision.

Administration

Bank base rates

[T1.101]

Period	Rate
from 7 November 2024	**4.75%**
1 August 2024–6 November 2024	5.00%
3 August 2023–31 July 2024	5.25%
22 June 2023–2 August 2023	5.00%
11 May 2023–21 June 2023	4.50%
23 March 2023–10 May 2023	4.25%
2 February 2023–22 March 2023	4.00%
15 December 2022–1 February 2023	3.50%
3 November 2022–14 December 2022	3.00%
22 September 2022–2 November 2022	2.25%
4 August 2022–21 September 2022	1.75%
16 June 2022–3 August 2022	1.25%
5 May 2022–15 June 2022	1.00%
17 March 2022–4 May 2022	0.75%
3 February 2022–16 March 2022	0.50%
16 December 2021–2 February 2022	0.25%
19 March 2020–15 December 2021	0.10%
11 March 2020–18 March 2020	0.25%

Due dates for tax

Capital gains tax

[T1.102]

Gains generally — Normally 31 January following end of tax year. (TMA 1970 s 59B).

Disposals of UK residential property by UK residents and by UK branch/agency of non-residents
For disposals after 5 April 2020, 60 days after date of completion of sale (30 days for disposals that completed before 27 October 2021).

Disposals of UK land by non-residents and by UK residents in the overseas part of a split tax year
60 days after date of completion of sale (30 days for disposals that completed before 27 October 2021).
(See also *Extended due dates* under **Income tax**, see **T1.104**.)

Corporation tax

[T1.103]

SEE TOLLEY'S TAX COMPUTATIONS 115.1.
Must be paid electronically.

Generally (TMA 1970 s 59D)
9 months and 1 day after end of accounting period.

Instalments for large and very large companies (TMA 1970 s 59E; FA 2021 Sch 1 paras 13, 33; SI 1998/3175)

A '**large company**' is any company whose augmented profits (see **T4.108**) for the accounting period exceed £1.5m (but from 1 April 2019, do not exceed £20m, see below), both thresholds being proportionately reduced for accounting periods of less than 12 months and divided by 1 plus the number of any active associated companies. Any company which pays the bank levy is also a large company unless it exceeds the £20m threshold resulting in it being a very large company (see below). A company is not a large company in respect of an accounting period if its total liability for that period is not more than £10,000, or if its profits for an accounting period are £10m or less (both limits proportionately reduced for accounting periods of less than 12 months) and it was not a large company or a very large company in the 12 months preceding that accounting period. For most large companies (those with no ring fence profits) the amount of each instalment for a 12 month accounting period will be one quarter of its total liability. The amount of each instalment for any accounting period longer than 3 months but shorter than 12 months is calculated using the formula 3 x CTI/n where CTI is the amount of a company's total liability for that accounting period, and n is the number of months in the accounting period. The due dates of instalments are as follows:

   1st instalment: 6 months and 13 days from start of accounting period (or date of final instalment if earlier);

2nd instalment: 3 months after 1st instalment, if length of accounting period allows;
3rd instalment: 3 months after 2nd instalment, if length of accounting period allows;
Final instalment: 3 months and 14 days from end of accounting period.

Earlier payment dates apply to a '**very large company**' which is one whose augmented profits exceed £20m (proportionately reduced for accounting periods of less than 12 months and divided by 1 plus the number of any active associated companies). A company is not a very large company in respect of an accounting period if its total liability for that period is not more than £10,000 (proportionately reduced for accounting periods of less than 12 months). The due dates of instalments are as follows:
1st instalment: 2 months and 13 days from start of accounting period (or date of final instalment if earlier);
2nd instalment: 3 months after 1st instalment, if length of accounting period allows;
3rd instalment: 3 months after 2nd instalment, if length of accounting period allows;
Final instalment: 3 months after 3rd instalment, if length of accounting period allows.

Close companies: tax on loans or benefits to participators

9 months and 1 day after the end of the accounting period. To be included in instalment payments for large and very large companies (see above) (TMA 1970 s 59E(11)).

Income tax
[T1.104]

SEE TOLLEY'S TAX COMPUTATIONS 26.1.

Payments on account (TMA 1970 s 59A; SSCBA 1992 ss 11A, 16; SI 1996/1654)

A payment on account is required where a taxpayer was charged to income tax in the immediately preceding tax year to an amount exceeding the amount of tax deducted at source in respect of that year (subject to a de minimis limit, see below).

The payment on account (which includes Class 4 NIC) is made in 2 equal instalments due on:
 (a) 31 January during the tax year, and
 (b) 31 July in the following tax year.

This is subject to relaxations as part of the Government's assistance to taxpayers during the COVID-19 pandemic. The second self-assessment payment on account for the **2019–20** tax year could be deferred from 31 July 2020 to 31 January 2021. No interest was applied for the period between 31 July 2020 and 31 January 2021. In addition, the first 5% late payment penalty was not charged for any tax due for 2019–20 where it was paid before 2 April 2021, or a time to pay arrangement was set up before that date. There was no deferral of payments on account for **2020–21** or later years. However, as for 2019–20, the first 5% late payment penalty was not charged for any tax due for 2020–21 where it was paid before 2 April 2022, or a time to pay arrangement was set up before that date.

No payments on account are required where either:
 (a) the aggregate of the liability (including Class 4 NIC) for the preceding year (net of tax deducted at source) is less than £1,000; or
 (b) more than 80% of the taxpayer's income tax and Class 4 NIC liability for the preceding year was met by tax deducted at source (including PAYE).

Payments on account are not required for Class 2 NIC.

Final payment (TMA 1970 s 59B, Sch 3ZA)

Balance of income tax due for a tax year (after deducting payments on account, tax deducted at source if any) is due on:

31 January following end of tax year, but see above for details of the relaxation of late penalty provisions for 2019–20 and 2020–21 (TMA 1970 s 59B(4)).

Class 2 NIC is also due through the self-assessment system no later than 31 January following end of tax year.

Extended due dates:
 (a) If a taxpayer has given notice of liability within 6 months of the end of the tax year, but a notice to make a return is not given until after 31 October following the end of the tax year, the due date is 3 months after the notice is given (TMA 1970 s 59B(3)).
 (b) If tax is payable as a result of a taxpayer's notice of amendment, an HMRC notice of correction or an HMRC notice of closure following enquiry, in each case given less than 30 days before the due date (or the extended due date at (a) above), the due date is on or before the day following the end of a 30-day period beginning on the day on which the notice is given (TMA 1970 s 59B(5), Sch 3ZA).
 (c) If an assessment other than a self-assessment or simple assessment is made, tax payable under the assessment is due on the day following the end of a 30-day period beginning on the day on which notice of the assessment is given (TMA 1970 s 59B(6)).

The extensions under (b) and (c) do *not* alter the due date for *interest purposes* (see **T1.106**).

Final tax payable under simple assessment:
- (a) If a taxpayer is given notice of the simple assessment after 31 October following the end of the tax year, the due date is 3 months after the notice is given (TMA 1970 s 59BA(4)).
- (b) In any other case, due date is no later than 31 January following end of tax year (TMA 1970 s 59BA(5)).

Harmonised interest regime see **T1.108**.
Interest on overdue tax see **T1.109**.
Interest on overpaid tax see **T1.115**.
Penalties see **T1.137**.
Remission of tax see **T1.122**.

Inheritance tax

[T1.105]

(IHTA 1984 s 226)

Chargeable transfers other than on death, made between:

6 April and 30 September	–	30 April in next year.
1 October and 5 April	–	6 months after end of month in which chargeable transfer is made.

Relevant property settlements periodic and exit charges

– 6 months after end of month in which chargeable event occurs.

Chargeable events following conditional exemption for heritage etc property and charge on disposal of trees or underwood before the second death:

– 6 months after end of month in which chargeable event occurs.

Transfers on death:

Earlier of	(a)	6 months after end of month in which death occurs, and
	(b)	delivery of account by personal representatives.

Tax or extra tax becoming payable on death:
Chargeable transfers and potentially exempt transfers within 7 years of death.

– 6 months after end of month in which death occurs.

PAYE and NIC

[T1.106]

(SSCBA 1992 ss 11A, 15; SI 2001/1004; SI 2003/2682)

Employer's tax and Class 1 NIC payable under PAYE	In-year payments – 17 days after end of tax month or quarter to which it relates (14 days where payments are not made by electronic means). Final payment for tax year – 22 April following deduction year (19 April where payments are not made by electronic means).
Class 1A NIC	22 July following year in which contributions due (19 July where payments are not made by electronic means).
PAYE settlement agreement and Class 1B NIC	22 October following year to which agreement relates (19 October where payments are not made by electronic means).
Class 2 NIC	Contributions based on an annual liability are due through the self-assessment system no later than 31 January following the tax year[1].
Class 4 NIC	See under income tax at **T1.104**.

---

[1] For 2023–24 and earlier years, those who do not pay through self-assessment will be sent a bill by HMRC. Voluntary payments could be made. For 2024–25 onwards, payment of Class 2 NIC is entirely voluntary; see **T8.107**.

Paying HMRC

[T1.107]

HMRC have a number of bank accounts. The respective accounts to which payments should be made from UK bank accounts for the main taxes are as follows:

Tax	Account name	Sort code	Account number
Self-assessment/ capital gains tax	HMRC Shipley	08 32 10	12001020
Self-assessment/ capital gains tax	HMRC Cumbernauld	08 32 10	12001039
Corporation tax	HMRC Shipley	08 32 10	12001020
Corporation tax	HMRC Cumbernauld	08 32 10	12001039
PAYE/ Class 1/ Class 1A NIC	HMRC Cumbernauld	08 32 10	12001039
Class 2 NIC[1]	HMRC NIC Receipts	08 32 20	12001004

[1] If taxpayer does not pay through self-assessment.
[2] Where both Shipley and Cumbernauld can apply and a taxpayer does not know which accounts office they normally pay, generally the payment should be sent to Cumbernauld. For details of other taxes see the list of taxes at www.gov.uk/topic/dealing-with-hmrc/paying-hmrc.

Harmonised interest regime

[T1.108]

SEE TOLLEY'S TAX COMPUTATIONS 13.1, 222.1.
(FA 2009 ss 101–104, Schs 53–54A; SI 2011/701; SI 2011/2391; SI 2013/280; SI 2013/2472; SI 2014/992; SI 2014/3269; SI 2015/974, SI 2019/918, SI 2019/921, SI 2020/979, SI 2021/445, SI 2023/997)

A harmonised interest regime currently applies to:
— income and capital gains tax self-assessment amounts including penalties from 31 October 2011,
— CIS late return penalties from 6 October 2011,
— tax agent dishonest conduct penalties from 1 April 2013,
— annual tax on enveloped dwellings and penalties from 1 October 2013,
— PAYE and CIS in-year amounts for 2014–15 onwards from 6 May 2014 (including penalties),
— stamp duty reserve tax and penalties from 1 January 2015,
— diverted profits tax and penalties from 1 April 2015,
— Class 2 NIC from 6 April 2015,
— capital gains tax on disposals of UK land (where not included in a self-assessment) from 6 April 2019,
— various DOTAS penalties from 1 June 2019,
— penalties for offshore evasion from 6 September 2019,
— loan charge from 5 October 2020,
— recovery of deemed employer NIC debts from 6 April 2021,
— VAT from 1 January 2023,
— economic crime (anti-money laundering) levy from 30 September 2023,
— electronic sales suppression from 4 March 2024.

For annual PAYE payments such as Classes 1A and 1B NIC HMRC charge interest on any amount which remains unpaid after the due date.

Appointed Day Orders will be made in due course to align the treatment of interest and penalties for inheritance tax purposes with other taxes (F(No 2)A 2015 s 15).

Differential interest rates are charged and paid by HMRC, based around the Bank of England base rate. The government announced at the Autumn Budget 2024 that late payment interest rates will be increased by 1.5 percentage points from 6 April 2025. The current late payment rate is:

Late payment interest	Rate
from 26 November 2024	**7.25%**
20 August 2024–25 November 2024	7.50%
22 August 2023–19 August 2024	7.75%
11 July 2023–21 August 2023	7.50%
31 May 2023–10 July 2023	7.00%
13 April 2023–30 May 2023	6.75%
21 February 2023–12 April 2023	6.50%
6 January 2023–20 February 2023	6.00%
22 November 2022–5 January 2023	5.50%
11 October 2022–21 November 2022	4.75%
23 August 2022–10 October 2022	4.25%
5 July 2022–22 August 2022	3.75%
24 May 2022–4 July 2022	3.50%
5 April 2022–23 May 2022	3.25%

The current repayment rate is:

Repayment interest	Rate
from 26 November 2024	**3.75%**
20 August 2024–25 November 2024	4.00%
22 August 2023–19 August 2024	4.25%
11 July 2023–21 August 2023	4.00%
31 May 2023–10 July 2023	3.50%
13 April 2023–30 May 2023	3.25%
21 February 2023–12 April 2023	3.00%
6 January 2023–20 February 2023	2.50%
22 November 2022–5 January 2023	2.00%
11 October 2022–21 November 2022	1.25%
23 August 2022–10 October 2022	0.75%

Late payment interest runs from the start date to the date of payment. The start date is generally the date on which the amount becomes due and payable, but special rules apply as follows:

Where an amount is due as a result of—
- (a) an amendment or correction to an assessment or self-assessment; or
- (b) an HMRC assessment in place of, or in addition to, an assessment made by the taxpayer; or
- (c) an HMRC assessment in place of an assessment which ought to have been made by the taxpayer,

the start date is the date it would have been if the original assessment or self-assessment had been complete and accurate and made on the date (if any) by which it was required to be made, and the tax had been due and payable as a result of the original assessment or self-assessment.

Repayment interest runs from the start date until the date the payment or repayment is made. The start date in the case of an amount paid to HMRC is the later of—
- (i) the date the amount was paid to HMRC; and
- (ii) the date on which the amount became due and payable to HMRC (in a case where the amount has been paid in connection with a liability to make a payment to HMRC, and it is to be repaid by them).

The start date, in the case of an amount which has not been paid to HMRC and which is payable by virtue of a return or a claim having been submitted, is the later of—
- (1) the date (if any) on which the return or claim was required to be submitted; and
- (2) the date on which the return or claim was submitted.

The start date in the case of the carry back of losses or averaging claims is 31 January following the *later* tax year in relation to the claim.

Interest on overdue tax

[T1.109]

See **T1.108** regarding the **harmonised interest regime** and the taxes to which this currently applies. The provisions on interest on overdue tax continue to apply to taxes where the harmonised interest regime does not yet apply, and applied to other taxes before the transition to the harmonised regime. The government announced at the Autumn Budget 2024 that interest rates on late payments will be increased by 1.5 percentage points from 6 April 2025.

NICs Class 1A, 1B, 4, stamp duty and stamp duty land tax

[T1.110]

Interest runs from the due date (see **T1.104** for income tax and **T1.102** for capital gains tax) to the date of payment, on the amount outstanding. Interest is payable gross and is not tax deductible.

Period	Rate
from 26 November 2024	**7.25%**
20 August 2024–25 November 2024	7.50%
22 August 2023–19 August 2024	7.75%
11 July 2023–21 August 2023	7.50%
31 May 2023–10 July 2023	7.00%
13 April 2023–30 May 2023	6.75%
21 February 2023–12 April 2023	6.50%
6 January 2023–20 February 2023	6.00%
22 November 2022–5 January 2023	5.50%
11 October 2022–21 November 2022	4.75%
23 August 2022–10 October 2022	4.25%
5 July 2022–22 August 2022	3.75%
24 May 2022–4 July 2022	3.50%
5 April 2022–23 May 2022	3.25%

Corporation tax

[T1.111]

SEE TOLLEY'S TAX COMPUTATIONS 110.1.

Interest runs from the due date (see **T1.103**) to the date of payment. For instalment payments by large and, for accounting periods beginning on or after 1 April 2019, very large companies, a special rate of interest runs from the due date to the earlier of the date of payment and nine months after the end of the accounting period (after which the normal rate applies).

Period	Normal rate
from 26 November 2024	**7.25%**
20 August 2024–25 November 2024	7.50%
22 August 2023–19 August 2024	7.75%
11 July 2023–21 August 2023	7.50%
31 May 2023–10 July 2023	7.00%
13 April 2023–30 May 2023	6.75%
21 February 2023–12 April 2023	6.50%
6 January 2023–20 February 2023	6.00%
22 November 2022–5 January 2023	5.50%
11 October 2022–21 November 2022	4.75%
23 August 2022–10 October 2022	4.25%
5 July 2022–22 August 2022	3.75%
24 May 2022–4 July 2022	3.50%
5 April 2022–23 May 2022	3.25%

Period	Special rate for instalment payments (except where still unpaid nine months after end of accounting period)
from 18 November 2024	**5.75%**
12 August 2024–17 November 2024	6.00%
14 August 2023–11 August 2024	6.25%
3 July 2023–13 August 2023	6.00%
22 May 2023–2 July 2023	5.50%
3 April 2023–21 May 2023	5.25%
13 February 2023–2 April 2023	5.00%
26 December 2022–12 February 2023	4.50%
14 November 2022–25 December 2022	4.00%
3 October 2022–13 November 2022	3.25%
15 August 2022–2 October 2022	2.75%
27 June 2022–14 August 2022	2.25%
16 May 2022–26 June 2022	2.00%
28 March 2022–15 May 2022	1.75%

Income tax on company payments

[T1.112]

Period	Rate
from 26 November 2024	**7.25%**
20 August 2024–25 November 2024	7.50%
22 August 2023–19 August 2024	7.75%
11 July 2023–21 August 2023	7.50%
31 May 2023–10 July 2023	7.00%
13 April 2023–30 May 2023	6.75%
21 February 2023–12 April 2023	6.50%
6 January 2023–20 February 2023	6.00%
22 November 2022–5 January 2023	5.50%
11 October 2022–21 November 2022	4.75%
23 August 2022–10 October 2022	4.25%
5 July 2022–22 August 2022	3.75%
24 May 2022–4 July 2022	3.50%
5 April 2022–23 May 2022	3.25%

Digital services tax
[T1.113]

Interest runs from the due date to the date of payment.

Period	Rate
from 26 November 2024	7.25%
20 August 2024–25 November 2024	7.50%
22 August 2023–19 August 2024	7.75%
11 July 2023–21 August 2023	7.50%
31 May 2023–10 July 2023	7.00%
13 April 2023–30 May 2023	6.75%
21 February 2023–12 April 2023	6.50%
6 January 2023–20 February 2023	6.00%
22 November 2022–5 January 2023	5.50%
11 October 2022–21 November 2022	4.75%
23 August 2022–10 October 2022	4.25%
5 July 2022–22 August 2022	3.75%
24 May 2022–4 July 2022	3.50%
5 April 2022–23 May 2022	3.25%

Inheritance tax
[T1.114]

Interest runs from the due date (see **T1.105**) to the date of payment.

Period	Rate
from 26 November 2024	7.25%
20 August 2024–25 November 2024	7.50%
22 August 2023–19 August 2024	7.75%
11 July 2023–21 August 2023	7.50%
31 May 2023–10 July 2023	7.00%
13 April 2023–30 May 2023	6.75%
21 February 2023–12 April 2023	6.50%
6 January 2023–20 February 2023	6.00%
22 November 2022–5 January 2023	5.50%
11 October 2022–21 November 2022	4.75%
23 August 2022–10 October 2022	4.25%
5 July 2022–22 August 2022	3.75%
24 May 2022–4 July 2022	3.50%
5 April 2022–23 May 2022	3.25%

Interest on overpaid tax
[T1.115]

See **T1.108** regarding the **harmonised interest regime** and the taxes to which this currently applies. The provisions on interest on overpaid tax continue to apply to taxes where the harmonised interest regime does not yet apply, and applied to other taxes before the transition to the harmonised regime.

NICs Class 1A, 1B, 4, stamp duty and stamp duty land tax
[T1.116]

Calculated as simple interest on the amount of tax repaid. The supplement is tax-free.

Repayment interest	Rate
from 26 November 2024	3.75%
20 August 2024–25 November 2024	4.00%
22 August 2023–19 August 2024	4.25%
11 July 2023–21 August 2023	4.00%
31 May 2023–10 July 2023	3.50%
13 April 2023–30 May 2023	3.25%
21 February 2023–12 April 2023	3.00%
6 January 2023–20 February 2023	2.50%
22 November 2022–5 January 2023	2.00%
11 October 2022–21 November 2022	1.25%
23 August 2022–10 October 2022	0.75%

Inheritance tax

[T1.117]

(IHTA 1984 s 235)
Repayments of inheritance tax or interest paid carries interest *from* the date of payment *to* the date on which the order for repayment is issued.

Repayment interest	Rate
from 26 November 2024	**3.75%**
20 August 2024–25 November 2024	4.00%
22 August 2023–19 August 2024	4.25%
11 July 2023–21 August 2023	4.00%
31 May 2023–10 July 2023	3.50%
13 April 2023–30 May 2023	3.25%
21 February 2023–12 April 2023	3.00%
6 January 2023–20 February 2023	2.50%
22 November 2022–5 January 2023	2.00%
11 October 2022–21 November 2022	1.25%
23 August 2022–10 October 2022	0.75%

Corporation tax

Normal rates

[T1.119]

SEE TOLLEY'S TAX COMPUTATIONS 109.1.
Rates on overpaid corporation tax in respect of periods after normal due date (SI 1989/1297 reg 3BB).

Period	Rate
from 26 November 2024	**3.75%**
20 August 2024–25 November 2024	4.00%
22 August 2023–19 August 2024	4.25%
11 July 2023–21 August 2023	4.00%
31 May 2023–10 July 2023	3.50%
13 April 2023–30 May 2023	3.25%
21 February 2023–12 April 2023	3.00%
6 January 2023–20 February 2023	2.50%
22 November 2022–5 January 2023	2.00%
11 October 2022–21 November 2022	1.25%
23 August 2022–10 October 2022	0.75%

Special rates

[T1.120]

For instalment payments by large and, for accounting periods beginning on or after 1 April 2019, very large companies and early payments by other companies, a special rate of interest runs from the date the excess arises (but not earlier than the due date of the first instalment) to the earlier of the date the repayment order is issued and nine months and one day after the end of the accounting period, after which the normal rate of interest (as above) applies.
Rates on overpaid instalment payments and on corporation tax paid early (but not due by instalments).

Repayment interest	Rate
from 18 November 2024	**4.50%**
12 August 2024–17 November 2024	4.75%
14 August 2023–11 August 2024	5.00%
3 July 2023–13 August 2023	4.75%
22 May 2023–2 July 2023	4.25%
3 April 2023–21 May 2023	4.00%
13 February 2023–2 April 2023	3.75%
26 December 2022–12 February 2023	3.25%
14 November 2022–25 December 2022	2.75%
3 October 2022–13 November 2022	2.00%
15 August 2022–2 October 2022	1.50%
27 June 2022–14 August 2022	1.00%

Digital services tax

[T1.121]

Where a payment in respect of digital services tax liability for an accounting period is made before the due date, the payment carries interest at the applicable rate from the later of—
(a) the date the payment is made, and
(b) 6 months and 13 days from the start of the accounting period,
until the due date.

Period	Rate
from 26 November 2024	**3.75%**
20 August 2024–25 November 2024	4.00%
22 August 2023–19 August 2024	4.25%
11 July 2023–21 August 2023	4.00%
31 May 2023–10 July 2023	3.50%
13 April 2023–30 May 2023	3.25%
21 February 2023–12 April 2023	3.00%
6 January 2023–20 February 2023	2.50%
22 November 2022–5 January 2023	2.00%
11 October 2022–21 November 2022	1.25%
23 August 2022–10 October 2022	0.75%

Direct recovery of debt

[T1.122]

(F(No 2)A 2015 Sch 8)
HMRC can secure payment of tax and tax credit debts directly from debtors' bank and building society accounts (including funds held in cash in Individual Savings Accounts) that have a minimum aggregate credit of £5,000. HMRC will only take action against debtors who owe over £1,000 of debt, and will only put a hold on the funds in the affected account up to the value of the debt. Safeguards in place include a face-to-face visit with an HMRC officer, a specialist unit to deal with cases involving the vulnerable, and availability of appeal to the County Court.

Remission of tax

[T1.123]

(Concession A19)
By concession, arrears of tax may be waived if they result from HMRC's failure to make proper and timely use of information supplied by the taxpayer or, where it affects the taxpayer's coding, by his or her employer. The concession also applies to information supplied by the Department for Work and Pensions affecting the taxpayer's entitlement to a retirement, disability or widow's pension. The concession only applies where the taxpayer could reasonably have believed that his or her affairs were in order and (unless the circumstances are exceptional) where the taxpayer is notified of the arrears more than 12 months after the end of the tax year in which HMRC received the information indicating that more tax was due.

Special relief

[T1.124]

(TMA 1970 Sch 1AB para 3A; FA 1998 Sch 18 para 51BA)
A statutory 'special relief' is available which allows HMRC to give effect to a claim for repayment or discharge of an amount of tax that a person is liable to pay, but which the person believes is not due or, if it has been paid, was not due, where the usual time limits for such relief have expired. Relief is only available to taxpayers in receipt of an income tax or corporation tax self-assessment determination made by HMRC in the absence of a self-assessment return being submitted, and where the following specific conditions are met: (a) it would be unconscionable for HMRC to seek to recover the amount or to refuse to repay it if it has already been paid; (b) that the person's tax affairs are otherwise up to date, or arrangements have been put in place to HMRC's satisfaction, to bring them up to date as far as possible; and (c) the person has not previously claimed special relief, or its concessionary predecessor equitable liability, whether or not such a claim was successful. This latter condition may be waived in exceptional circumstances. There is no time limit for claiming the relief.

Certificates of tax deposit

[T1.125]

From 23 November 2017 the scheme is closed for new purchases, but existing certificates were honoured until **23 November 2023**. Any certificates remaining after this date should be submitted to HMRC for refund. HMRC have indicated that they will try to repay the balance of any certificate remaining unpaid and unclaimed. If they are unable to contact the current certificate holder after reasonable effort the balance will be forfeited.

Certificates were available to purchase by individuals, partnerships, individual partners, trustees, personal representatives and companies for the payment of income tax, Class 4 NIC, capital gains tax, inheritance tax, or petroleum revenue tax, but not payment of corporation tax, PAYE liabilities, or tax payable by companies etc on disposals of high value UK residential property, see **T4.109**. Interest is paid gross and is chargeable to tax. It will only be paid for the first six years of a deposit. A deposit bears interest for the first year at the rate in force at the time of the deposit and for each subsequent year at the rate in force on the anniversary of the deposit. HMRC provide an interest calculator tool on their website.

Date of deposit	Amount	Held for (mths in yr)	Pay't of tax %	Cashed %
6.3.09–	Under £100,000	No limit	0.00	0.00
	£100,000 or over	under 1	0.00	0.00
		1–under 3	0.75	0.25
		3–under 6	0.75	0.25
		6–under 9	0.75	0.25
		9–12	0.75	0.25

Student loan deductions

Plan 1

[T1.126]

	Percentage of income above the threshold	Threshold
2025–26	**9%**	**£26,065 per year** **£2,172.08 per month** **£501.25 per week**
2024–25	9%	£24,990 per year £2,082.50 per month £480.57 per week
2023–24	9%	£22,015 per year £1,834.58 per month £423.36 per week
2022–23	9%	£20,195 per year £1,682.91 per month £388.36 per week
2021–22	9%	£19,895 per year £1,657.91 per month £382.59 per week
2020–21	9%	£19,390 per year £1,615.83 per month £372.88 per week

Plan 2

	Percentage of income above the threshold	Threshold
2025–26	**9%**	**£28,470 per year** **£2,372.50 per month** **£547.50 per week**
2024–25	9%	£27,295 per year £2,274.58 per month £524.90 per week
2023–24	9%	£27,295 per year £2,274.58 per month £524.90 per week
2022–23	9%	£27,295 per year £2,274.58 per month £524.90 per week
2021–22	9%	£27,295 per year £2,274.58 per month £524.90 per week
2020–21	9%	£26,575 per year £2,214.58 per month £511.05 per week

Plan 4

Plan 4 is a redesignation of Plan 1 loans taken out by students who studied in Scotland and applied for the loans through the Student Awards Agency for Scotland. The redesignation applies from 6 April 2021 in order to allow for the increase to the repayment threshold introduced by the Scottish Government.

	Percentage of income above the threshold	Threshold
2025–26	**9%**	**TBA**
2024–25	9%	£31,395 per year £2,616.25 per month £603.75 per week
2023–24	9%	£27,660 per year £2,305 per month £531.92 per week
2022–23	9%	£25,375 per year £2,114.58 per month £487.98 per week
2021–22	9%	£25,000 per year £2,083.33 per month £480.76 per week

Plan 5

Plan 5 applies in England only where the course started on or after 1 August 2023. Repayments are due to begin from April 2026.

	Percentage of income above the threshold	Threshold
2026–27	9%	£25,000 per year £2,083.33 per month £480.76 per week

Postgraduate loans

	Percentage of income above the threshold	Threshold
2019–20 onwards	6%	£21,000 per year £1,750 per month £403.84 per week

Filing dates

Corporation tax

[T1.127]

SEE TOLLEY'S TAX COMPUTATIONS 118.2.

(FA 1998 Sch 18 paras 14, 15; SI 2003/282 reg 3(2A))

The return must be filed on the latest of the following dates—
- (a) 12 months from the end of the period for which the return is made;
- (b) where the company makes up its accounts for a period not exceeding 18 months, 12 months from the end of that period;
- (c) where the company makes up its accounts for a period exceeding 18 months, 30 months from the start of that period;
- (d) 3 months from the date of issue of the notice requiring the return.

All company returns must be filed online. Computations and, in most cases, accounts must be submitted in iXBRL format. Micro-entities have the option to file simplified accounts.

Income tax and capital gains tax

[T1.128]

(TMA 1970 ss 8, 8A, 12AA; SI 2003/2682 reg 186)

Self-assessment returns[1]

Basic position for paper returns.	On or before 31 October following end of tax year.
Basic position for electronic returns.	On or before 31 January following end of tax year.

Paper return and notice to file return issued after 31 July but on or before 31 October following end of tax year.	Within 3 months of date of notice.
Electronic return and notice to file return issued after 31 July but on or before 31 October following end of tax year.	On or before 31 January following end of tax year.
Paper or electronic return and notice to file return issued after 31 October following end of tax year.	Within 3 months of date of notice.
Paper return and taxpayer wishes tax underpayment of less than £3,000 to be coded out.	On or before 31 October following end of tax year.
Electronic return and taxpayer wishes tax underpayment of less than £3,000 to be coded out.	Before 31 December following end of tax year.
Returns relating to disposals of UK land	
Returns relating to disposals of UK residential property by UK residents / UK branch or agency of non-residents	For disposals after 5 April 2020, 60 days after date of completion of sale (30 days where completion is before 27 October 2021).
Returns relating to disposals of UK land by non-residents and by UK residents in the overseas part of a split tax year	For disposals after 5 April 2019, 60 days after date of completion of sale (30 days where completion is before 27 October 2021).

[1] This is subject to relaxations as part of the Government's assistance to taxpayers during the COVID-19 pandemic. If the 2019–20 return was filed by 28 February 2021 no £100 late filing penalty was issued. Likewise, if the 2020–21 return was filed by 28 February 2022 no £100 late filing penalty was issued.

[2] Making tax digital (MTD) for income tax will apply to unincorporated businesses with turnover over £50,000 for 2026–27 onwards and to those with turnover over £30,000 for 2027–28 onwards. Taxpayers meeting certain criteria can sign up to operate MTD early. The government plans to extend MTD to unincorporated business with income over £20,000 by the end of the current Parliament. MTD requires businesses to keep records digitally and submit tax return data directly from those records using MTD compatible software. Under MTD, a report of the business's trading or property income, allowable expenditure and claims for allowances or reliefs against such income must be submitted in relation to each tax year and interim reports must be submitted quarterly on fixed dates (5 August, 5 November, 5 February and 5 May). MTD for VAT applies to all VAT registered businesses from April 2022.

Capital gains tax on UK land

[T1.129]

(FA 2019 Sch 2)
Direct disposals of UK residential property by UK residents and by UK branch/agency of non-residents
For disposals after 5 April 2020, 60 days after date of completion of sale (30 days for disposals that completed before 27 October 2021).
Direct or indirect disposals of UK land by non-residents and by UK residents in the overseas part of a split tax year
60 days after date of completion of sale (30 days for disposals that completed before 27 October 2021).

Withdrawal of self-assessment notice

[T1.130]

(TMA 1970 s 8B)
HMRC may withdraw a notice to file a self-assessment tax return in certain circumstances. Penalties for failure to make a return may be cancelled.

Simple assessment

[T1.131]

(TMA 1970 ss 28H–28J, 31AA)
HMRC may make an assessment of an individual's or trustee's income tax or capital gains tax liability without that person first being required to complete a self-assessment return. HMRC will instead assess their tax liability on the basis of information already held. The assessment notice must include details of the information used and the amount of tax due. The assessment may be appealed or queried without formal appeal. HMRC may withdraw a simple assessment notice.

Penalties

Penalties — modernised penalty regime

[T1.132]

The penalty regime in force in respect of various defaults is set out below.

Inaccuracy in return or other document

[T1.133]

(FA 2007 Sch 24 para 1)

Applies to	Commencement date	Penalty details
IT, CGT, CT, VAT, CIS, NIC Classes 1 and 4[1]	Return periods starting 1 April 2008 where the return is due to be filed on or after 1 April 2009	Penalty based on potential lost revenue Careless inaccuracy — 30% Deliberate but not concealed — 70% Deliberate and concealed — 100%
IHT, SDLT, SDRT, other taxes, levies and duties (except tax credits)	Return periods starting 1 April 2009 where the return is due to be filed on or after 1 April 2010, or where the liability arises on or after 1 April 2010; for IHT in respect of deaths from 1 April 2009	*Reductions for disclosure*[3] Unprompted disclosure minimum penalties nil, 20% and 30% Prompted disclosure minimum penalties 15%, 35% and 50%
Class 1A NIC	2010–11 returns	
Corporation tax credit, return by registered pension scheme	Return periods starting 1 April 2009 where the return is due to be filed on or after 1 April 2010	
Annual tax on enveloped dwellings	2013–14 returns	
Non-resident CGT[4]	6 April 2015	
Class 2 NIC	6 April 2015	
Apprenticeship levy	6 April 2017	
Disposals of UK land	6 April 2019	
Digital Services Tax	1 April 2020	
IT, CGT but offshore matter Extended to IHT and offshore transfers (see note)[2]	6 April 2011 (see note)[2]	Penalties above are increased by either 0%, 50% or 100% depending on the territory concerned (see table at **T1.139** for a list of territories in each category) Statutory limits for reductions for disclosure apply

[1] From 2013–14 for RTI purposes an inaccuracy in any full payment submission can attract a penalty. HMRC may issue one penalty notice for multiple inaccuracy penalties in a year.

[2] From 1 April 2016 the offshore penalty regime includes IHT. From 1 April 2017 for IHT transfers and from 6 April 2016 otherwise, the regime also applies to domestic offences where the proceeds are hidden offshore. From a date to be appointed the territory classification system will be updated to reflect the jurisdictions that adopt the new global standard of automatic tax information exchange and there will be four levels of penalty instead of three.

[3] In December 2017 HMRC announced a restriction on quality of disclosure penalty reductions where taxpayers take 'a significant period' (normally 3 years) to correct or disclose the inaccuracy. They will restrict the penalty range by 10% above the minimum before working out the reductions. It is not clear when the 3-year period starts.

[4] Applies up to 5 April 2019. Replaced by returns for disposals of UK land.

Inaccuracy in return or other document as a result of third party providing incorrect (or withholding) information

[T1.134]

(FA 2007 Sch 24 para 1A)

Applies to	Commencement date	Penalty details
IT, CGT, CT, VAT, IHT, CIS, NIC Classes 1 and 4, SDLT, SDRT, other taxes, levies and duties (except tax credits)	1 April 2009 where the return is due to be filed on or after 1 April 2010	100% of potential lost revenue Subject to reduction for disclosure as for inaccuracies above
Class 1A NIC	2010–11 returns	
Annual tax on enveloped dwellings	2013–14 returns	

Failure to notify HMRC of an error in an assessment (within 30 days)

[T1.135]

(FA 2007 Sch 24 para 2)

Applies to	Commencement date	Penalty details
IT, CGT, CT, VAT, CIS, NIC Classes 1 and 4	1 April 2008 where the return is due to be filed on or after 1 April 2009	30% of potential lost revenue *Reductions for disclosure*[1] Unprompted disclosure minimum penalty nil Prompted disclosure minimum penalty 15%
IHT, SDLT, SDRT, other taxes, levies and duties (except tax credits)	1 April 2009 where the return is due to be filed on or after 1 April 2010	
Class 1A NIC	2010–11 returns	
Annual tax on enveloped dwellings	2013–14 returns	

[1] HMRC apply a restriction on quality of disclosure penalty reductions where taxpayers take 'a significant period' (normally 3 years) to correct or disclose the inaccuracy. They will restrict the penalty range by 10% above the minimum before working out the reductions. See CH82465.

Failure to notify chargeability

[T1.136]

(FA 2008 Sch 41)

Applies to	Commencement date	Penalty details
IT, CGT, VAT, NIC Class 4	1 April 2010	Penalty based on potential lost revenue Failure to notify — 30% Deliberate but not concealed — 70% Deliberate and concealed — 100%
CT	Accounting periods ending on or after 31 March 2010	*Reductions for disclosure*[2] Unprompted disclosure minimum penalties nil (within 12 months late), 10% (more than 12 months late), 20% and 30% Prompted disclosure minimum penalties 15%, 35%, 50%
Other taxes, levies and duties (not IHT, SDLT, SDRT)	Obligations arising on or after 1 April 2010	
Diverted profits tax	Accounting periods beginning on or after 1 April 2015	
Digital Services Tax	Obligations arising on or after 1 April 2020	

Applies to	Commencement date	Penalty details
IT, CGT but offshore matter Extended to offshore transfers (see note)[1]	6 April 2011 (see note)[1]	Penalties above are increased by either 0%, 50% or 100% depending on the territory concerned (see table at **T1.139** for a list of territories in each category) Statutory limits for reductions for disclosure apply

[1] From 6 April 2016 the offshore penalty regime also applies to domestic offences where the proceeds are hidden offshore.

[2] HMRC apply a restriction on quality of disclosure penalty reductions where taxpayers take 'a significant period' (normally 3 years) to correct the non-compliance. They will restrict the penalty range by 10% above the minimum before working out the reductions. See CH73360.

Failure to make returns on time

[T1.137]

(FA 2009 Sch 55; FA 2010 Sch 1; FA 2021, Schs 24, 25; FA 2024 s 37; SI 2003/2682)

Applies to	Commencement date	Penalty details
IT, CGT, NIC Class 4[5]	6 April 2011	Initial penalty £100[8] Failure continues for more than three months — with notice — £10 per day for up to 90 days[9] Six months late — greater of 5% of the tax due and £300 12 months late — same penalty as for 6 months late unless deliberately withholding the return Deliberate withholding of the return more than 12 months — 70% of tax due (minimum £300) Deliberate and concealed withholding of the return more than 12 months — 100% of tax due (minimum £300)
Return by Registered Pension Scheme	1 April 2011	*Reductions for disclosure*[1] Unprompted disclosure minimum penalty 20% and 30% Prompted disclosure minimum penalties 35% and 50%
Annual tax on enveloped dwellings	2013–14 returns due 1 October 2013	
Stamp duty reserve tax	1 January 2015	
Class 2 NIC	6 April 2015	
Non-resident CGT[6]	26 March 2015	Penalties as above (*except* the £10 daily penalty)[6]
Disposals of UK land[7]	6 April 2019	Penalties as above
CIS returns	6 October 2011	Initial penalty £100 After two months — £200 Six months late — greater of 5% of the tax due and £300 12 months late — same penalty as for 6 months late unless deliberately withholding the return Deliberate withholding of the return more than 12 months — 70% of tax due (minimum £1,500) Deliberate and concealed withholding of the return more than 12 months — 100% of tax due (minimum £3,000) *Reductions for disclosure*[1] Unprompted disclosure minimum penalty 20% and 30% Prompted disclosure minimum penalties 35% and 50% Special rules apply to the first returns made on registration for CIS so that the maximum total penalty that can apply for the initial and second fixed penalties for all such returns is £3,000. Subsequent tax-geared penalties may still be incurred. Where a CIS return only relates to persons registered for 'gross payment' a tax-geared penalty after 6 months or 12 months cannot apply. In these cases the person is liable to the fixed amount penalty.

Applies to	Commencement date	Penalty details
PAYE Real Time Information and Apprenticeship levy. Failure during a tax month to make a return on or before the filing date (normally the date employee is paid)	6 October 2014 in relation to 2014–15 onwards for employers with 50 or more employees 6 March 2015 for employers with fewer than 50 employees	First failure in a tax year — nil Second and subsequent failure in tax year 1–9 employees — £100 10–49 employees — £200 50–249 employees — £300 250 or more employees — £400[2] Failure continues for more than three months — with notice — 5% of tax due New employers only: A failure in the 'initial period'[3] — nil
IT, CGT but offshore matter Extended to offshore transfers (see note)[4]	6 April 2011 (see note)[4]	Penalties above for a return later than 12 months which has been withheld are increased by either 0%, 50% or 100% depending on the territory concerned (see table at **T1.139** for a list of territories in each category) Statutory limits for reductions for disclosure apply
Making Tax Digital for Income Tax[10]	6 April 2024 for voluntary MTD adopters	£200 when maximum number of penalty points have been awarded
Making Tax Digital for Income Tax—deliberate withholding of information[10]	6 April 2024 for voluntary MTD adopters	If return filed late and the withholding of information is deliberate and concealed a further penalty of the greater of 100% of the tax liability and £300; if the withholding is deliberate and not concealed, the greater of 70% of the liability and £300.
		Reductions for disclosure Unprompted disclosure minimum penalty 30% and 40% Prompted disclosure minimum penalties 45% and 60%
		Offshore matter or transfer Penalties are increased by either 0%, 50% or 100% depending on the territory concerned (see table at **T1.139** for a list of territories in each category) Statutory limits for reductions for disclosure apply

[1] HMRC apply a restriction on quality of disclosure penalty reductions where taxpayers take 'a significant period' (normally 3 years) to correct or disclose their non-compliance. They will restrict the penalty range by 10% above the minimum before working out the reductions. See CH63220.

[2] Employers will not normally incur penalties for delays of up to 3 days in filing PAYE information. However, employers who regularly file after the payment date but within three days may be contacted by HMRC or considered for a penalty.

[3] A penalty will not be issued to a new employer if their first FPS is received within 30 days of making the first payment to their employee(s) (known as the 'initial period'). After that, normal penalties rules will apply if there is a failure to file on time.

[4] From 6 April 2016 the offshore penalty regime also applies to domestic offences where the proceeds are hidden offshore.

[5] HMRC will accept reasonable excuses from taxpayers who are generally compliant without further investigation.

[6] Applies up to 5 April 2019. Replaced by returns for disposals of UK land. Does not apply to an elective return made under TMA 1970 s 12ZBA. HMRC confirmed in June 2017 that they no longer issued the £10 daily penalty and such past penalties would be withdrawn.

[7] Penalties were suspended for disposals completed between 6 April 2020 and 30 June 2020, provided return was filed by 31 July 2020. Interest continued to accrue on unpaid tax.

[8] If the 2019–20 return was filed by 28 February 2021 no £100 late filing penalty was issued.

[9] Daily penalties were not charged in respect of late 2018–19 tax returns.

[10] A points-based system of late filing penalties applies to taxpayers within the Making Tax Digital for Income Tax regime. From 6 April 2024, it applies to anyone who adopts MTD voluntarily. It is expected that mandatory MTD will apply from 6 April 2026 for those with business or property turnover over £50,000, from 6 April 2027 for those with business or property turnover of £30,000 or over and from a later, as yet unspecified date, for all others within self-assessment. The system applies for VAT for accounting periods beginning on or after 1 January 2023.

Failure to pay tax on time

(FA 2009 Sch 56; FA 2010 Sch 1; FA 2021, Sch 26; FA 2024 s 37)

Applies to	Commencement date	Penalty details
PAYE[1], NIC Class 1, CIS[2], student loan deductions	2010–11 liabilities (on a risk assessed basis at present)	Penalty based on number of late payments in a year applied to the amounts paid late 1 late payment — nil 2, 3, 4 late payments — 1% 5, 6, 7 late payments — 2% 8, 9, 10 late payments — 3% 11, 12 late payments — 4% Any amount paid 6 months late — 5% Any amount paid 12 months late — 5%
NIC Class 1A and 1B (SI 2001/1004 reg 67B)	2010–11	31 days late — 5% 6 months late — 5% 12 months late — 5%
Tax due by Registered Pension schemes	Payments due 30 September 2010	31 days late — 5% 6 months late — 5% 12 months late — 5%
IT, CGT payable under self-assessment	6 April 2011 for self-assessment for 2010–11 onwards	31 days late — 5%[4] 6 months late — 5% 12 months late — 5%
Annual tax on enveloped dwellings	2013–14 payments due 31 October 2013	31 days late — 5% 6 months late — 5% 12 months late — 5%
Stamp duty reserve tax	1 January 2015	31 days late — 5% 6 months late — 5% 12 months late — 5%
Class 2 NIC	6 April 2015	31 days late — 5% 6 months late — 5% 12 months late — 5%
Apprenticeship levy	15 September 2016	1 day late — 5% 5 months late — 5% 11 months late — 5%
Pension scheme overseas transfer charge	9 March 2017	31 days late — 5% 6 months late — 5% 12 months late — 5%
Disposals of UK land where not included in self-assessment	6 April 2019	31 days late — 5% 6 months late — 5% 12 months late — 5%
CGT exit charge payment plan[3]	6 April 2019	31 days late — 5%[3] 6 months late — 5% 12 months late — 5%
Making Tax Digital for Income Tax[5]	6 April 2024 for voluntary MTD adopters	16 days late — 2% 31 or more days late[6] first penalty — 2% of tax unpaid after 15 days plus 2% of tax unpaid after 30 days second penalty — 4% per annum of tax from time to time unpaid until tax is paid in full

[1] HMRC apply a 'tolerance' of £100 for PAYE in-year late payment penalties. Where the difference between the total of all the amounts that the employer is due to pay to HMRC for a tax period and the amount paid over for that period is no more than £100 the employer will not be liable to a late payment penalty.

[2] HMRC apply a 'tolerance' of £100 for CIS in-year late payment penalties. Where the difference between the amount that the contractor is due to pay to HMRC for a tax period and the amount paid over for that period is no more than £100 the contractor will not be liable to a late payment penalty.

[3] Penalty applies from day after date on which the amount is payable under the plan, if that is later than the date specified in TMA 1970 s 59B.

[4] If the 2019–20 tax due was either paid or a time to pay arrangement was in place by 1 April 2021, the first late payment penalty was not charged.

[5] A new system of late payment penalties based on a percentage of the outstanding amount will come into effect for taxpayers within the Making Tax Digital for Income Tax regime. From 6 April 2024, it applies to anyone who adopts MTD voluntarily. It is expected that mandatory MTD will apply from 6 April 2026 for those with business or property turnover over £50,000, from 6 April 2027 for those with business or property turnover of £30,000 or over and from a later, as yet unspecified date, for all others within self-assessment. The system applies for VAT for accounting periods beginning on or after 1 January 2023.

[6] If a time to pay agreement is made with HMRC as a result of proposals for paying the tax due made by the taxpayer after the end of the 15-day period but before the end of the 30-day period, the first penalty is 2% of the tax unpaid after 15 days. It does not matter whether the agreement itself is made before the end of the 30-day period. If the taxpayer breaks the time to pay agreement, the first penalty is charged as if no agreement had been made.

Offshore penalties — territory categories[8]

[T1.139]

(SI 2011/976)

Category 1

Anguilla	Estonia	Japan	Poland
Aruba	Finland	Korea, South	Portugal[4]
Australia	France[2]	Latvia	Romania
Belgium	Germany	Liechtenstein (from 24 July 2013)[7]	Slovakia
Bulgaria	Greece	Lithuania	Slovenia
Canada	Guernsey[3]	Malta	Spain[5]
Cayman Islands	Hungary	Montserrat	Sweden
Cyprus	Ireland	Netherlands (not including Bonaire, Sint Eustatius and Saba)	Switzerland (from 24 July 2013)[7]
Czech Republic	Isle of Man	New Zealand (not including Tokelau)	USA (not including overseas territories and possessions)[6]
Denmark (not including Faroe Islands or Greenland)[1]	Italy	Norway	

[1] Faroe Islands and Greenland are in Category 2.
[2] Includes overseas Departments of France; the overseas collectivities of France are in Category 2.
[3] Includes Alderney and Sark.
[4] Includes Madeira and the Azores.
[5] Includes the Canary Islands and other overseas territories of Spain.
[6] The overseas territories and possessions of the USA are in Category 2.
[7] SI 2013/1618 changed the level of penalties which may be charged for 14 specified countries from 24 July 2013. This is to reflect the entry into force of tax information exchange and enhanced tax cooperation agreements with those countries. Liechtenstein and Switzerland were previously in Category 2.
[8] From a date to be set by Treasury Order the territory classification system will be updated to reflect the jurisdictions that adopt the new global standard of automatic tax information exchange.

Category 2

[T1.140]

Territories not listed in Categories 1 or 3 (other than the UK) will be in Category 2. Crown Dependencies and Overseas Territories of the UK are, unless listed, in Category 2.

Category 3

[T1.141]

Albania	Costa Rica	Kyrgyzstan	(Before 24 July 2013) Saint Lucia[2]
Algeria	Curaçao	Lebanon	(Before 24 July 2013) Saint Vincent and the Grenadines[2]
Andorra	Cuba	Macau[1]	(Before 24 July 2013) San Marino[2]
(Before 24 July 2013) Antigua and Barbuda[2]	Democratic People's Republic of Korea	Marshall Islands	Seychelles
(Before 24 July 2013) Armenia[2]	(Before 24 July 2013) Dominica[2]	(Before 24 July 2013) Mauritius[2]	Sint Maarten
(Before 24 July 2013) Bahrain[2]	Dominican Republic	Micronesia, Federated States of	Suriname
(Before 24 July 2013) Barbados[2]	Ecuador	Monaco	Syria
(Before 24 July 2013) Belize[2]	El Salvador	Nauru	Tokelau
Bonaire, Sint Eustatius and Saba	Gabon	Nicaragua	Tonga
Brazil	(Before 24 July 2013) Grenada[2]	Niue	Trinidad and Tobago
Cameroon	Guatemala	Palau	United Arab Emirates
continued on next page			

Cape Verde	Honduras	Panama	Uruguay
Colombia	Iran	Paraguay	
Congo, Republic of	Iraq	Peru	
Cook Islands	Jamaica	(Before 24 July 2013) Saint Kitts and Nevis[2]	

[1] China and Hong Kong are in Category 2.
[2] SI 2013/1618 changed the level of penalties which may be charged for 14 specified countries from 24.7.13. This is to reflect the entry into force of tax information exchange and enhanced tax cooperation agreements with those countries. 12 of the countries highlighted in this table are in Category 2 from 24.7.13.

Offshore assets moves

[T1.142]

(FA 2015 Sch 21; SI 2015/866)

Applies to	Commencement date	Penalty details
Offshore assets move from a specified territory to a non-specified territory where IT, CGT or IHT penalty under FA 2007 Sch 24 para 1, FA 2008 Sch 41, or FA 2009 Sch 55 above already applies for a deliberate failure (see table below for a list of specified territories)	27 March 2015	50% of amount of original penalty

Offshore assets move penalties — specified territories

[T1.143]

Andorra	Curaçao	Japan	Qatar
Anguilla	Cyprus	Jersey	Romania
Antigua and Barbuda	Czech Republic	Korea, South	Russia
Argentina	Denmark	Kuwait[1]	Saint Kitts and Nevis
Aruba	Dominica	Latvia	Saint Lucia
Australia	Estonia	Lebanon[1]	Saint Vincent and the Grenadines
Austria	Faroe Islands	Liechtenstein	Samoa
The Bahamas	Finland	Lithuania	San Marino
Bahrain[1]	France	Luxembourg	Saudi Arabia
Barbados	Germany	Macau	Seychelles
Belgium	Ghana[1]	Malaysia	Singapore
Belize	Gibraltar	Malta	Sint Maarten
Bermuda	Greece	Marshall Islands	Slovak Republic
Brazil	Greenland	Mauritius	Slovenia
British Virgin Islands	Grenada	Mexico	South Africa
Brunei Darussalam	Guernsey	Monaco	Spain
Bulgaria	Hong Kong	Montserrat	Sweden
Canada	Hungary	Nauru[1]	Switzerland
Cayman Islands	Iceland	Netherlands (including Bonaire, Sint Eustatius and Saba)	Trinidad and Tobago
Chile	India	New Zealand (not including Tokelau)	Turkey
China	Indonesia	Niue	Turks and Caicos Islands
Colombia	Ireland	Norway	United Arab Emirates
Cook Islands[1]	Isle of Man	Panama[1]	Uruguay
Costa Rica	Israel	Poland	Vanuatu[1]
Croatia	Italy	Portugal	

[1] Added from 3.11.17 when Albania and USA (excluding overseas territories and possessions) removed.

Deliberate enablers of offshore evasion or non-compliance

[T1.144]

Applies to	Commencement date	Penalty details
A person who has enabled another person (Q) to commit a relevant offence in relation to IT, CGT or IHT, or to engage in conduct which makes Q liable to a penalty under FA 2007 Sch 24 para 1, FA 2008 Sch 41, FA 2009 Sch 55, or FA 2015 Sch 21 above, provided certain other conditions are met (FA 2016 Sch 20; SI 2016/1249).	1 January 2017	For penalties other than under FA 2015 Sch 21, the higher of— (a) 100% of potential lost revenue; and (b) £3,000 For penalties under FA 2015 Sch 21, the higher of— (a) 50% of potential lost revenue in respect of the original tax non-compliance; and (b) £3,000 Reductions available for disclosure

Asset-based penalty for offshore inaccuracies and failures

[T1.145]

Applies to	Commencement date	Penalty details
A person to whom a CGT, IHT or asset-based IT penalty under FA 2007 Sch 24 para 1, FA 2008 Sch 41, or FA 2009 Sch 55 above already applies for a deliberate failure in relation to an offshore matter or transfer for a tax year in which the potential lost revenue exceeds £25,000 (FA 2016 Sch 22; SI 2017/277).	2016–17 onwards for CGT and IT Transfers of value on or after 1 April 2017 for IHT	The lower of— (a) 10% of the value of the asset; and (b) 10 times the offshore potential lost revenue (as defined) Reductions available for disclosure

Personal tax and corporation tax

[T1.146]

Offence	Penalty
Failure to render return for corporation tax (FA 1998 Sch 18 paras 17, 18).	(a) £100 if up to three months late (£500 if previous two returns also late); (b) £200 if over three months late (£1,000 if previous two returns also late); (c) if failure continues, on final day for delivery of return or, if later, 18 months after return period, 10% of tax unpaid 18 months after return period (20% of tax unpaid at that date if return not made within two years of return period).
Failure to maintain records supporting personal and trustees' returns of partnership returns (TMA 1970 s 12B).	Up to £3,000.
Fraudulently or negligently making an incorrect statement in connection with a claim to reduce payments on account (TMA 1970 s 59A(6)).	Up to the amount (or additional amount) payable on account if a correct statement had been made.
Deliberately or recklessly failing to pay corporation tax due in respect of total liability of company for accounting period, or fraudulently or negligently making claim for repayment (TMA 1970 s 59E(4); SI 1998/3175 reg 13).	Penalty not exceeding twice amount of interest charged under SI 1998/3175 reg 7.

PAYE

[T1.147]

Offence	Penalty
Failure to submit return P9D or P11D (benefits in kind) by due date (6 July following tax year) (TMA 1970 s 98(1)).	(a) Initial penalty up to £300; and (b) continuing penalty up to £60 for each day on which the failure continues.
Failure to submit information in connection with mandatory e-filing from 2004–05 onwards (SI 2003/2682).	Penalty based on number of employees not exceeding £3,000 for 1,000 or more employees.

Offence	Penalty
Failure to submit returns P11D(b) (Class 1A NIC returns) by due date (6 July following tax year) (SI 2001/1004 reg 81(2)).	(a) First 12 months: penalty of £100 for each 50 employees (or part thereof) for each month the failure continues (but total penalty not to exceed total Class 1A NIC due); (b) failures exceeding 12 months: a penalty not exceeding the amount of Class 1A NIC due and unpaid after 19 July following tax year.

Inheritance tax returns and information
[T1.148]

Offence	Penalty
Failure to deliver an account within 12 months of death (unless tax is less than £100 or there is a reasonable excuse) (IHTA 1984 s 245).	(a) Initial penalty of £100 (or the amount of tax payable if less); (b) further penalty up to £60 (where penalty determined by court or tribunal) for each day on which the failure continues; (c) if failure continues after six months after the date on which account is due, and proceedings not commenced, a further penalty of £100 (or amount of tax payable if less); and (d) if failure continues one year after end of the period in which account is due, and IHT is payable, a penalty not exceeding £3,000.
Failure to submit account or notify HMRC under IHTA 1984 s 218A if a disposition on a death is varied within six months of the variation and additional tax is payable (IHTA 1984 s 245A(1A), (1B)).	(a) Initial penalty up to £100; (b) further penalty up to £60 (if determined by court or tribunal) for each day on which the failure continues; (c) up to £3,000 if failure continues after 12 months from date notification is due.
Failure to provide information etc under IHTA 1984 s 218 concerning a settlement by a UK-domiciled settlor with non-resident trustees (IHTA 1984 s 245A(1)).	(a) Initial penalty up to £300; and (b) further penalty up to £60 (where penalty determined by court or tribunal) for each day on which the failure continues.
Person other than the taxpayer fraudulently or negligently delivering, furnishing or producing incorrect accounts, information or documents (IHTA 1984 s 247(3); FA 2004 s 295(4), (9)).	Up to £3,000.

Special returns of information
[T1.149]

Offence	Penalty
Failure to comply with a notice to deliver a return or other document, furnish particulars or make anything available for inspection under any of the provisions listed in column 1 of the table in TMA 1970 s 98.	(a) Initial penalty up to £300; (b) further penalty up to £60 for each day on which the failure continues.
Failure to furnish information, give certificates or produce documents or records under any of the provisions listed in column 2 of the table in TMA 1970 s 98.	(a) Initial penalty up to £300; and (b) further penalty up to £60 for each day on which the failure continues.
Failure to deduct income tax at source from payments of interest or royalties under ITA 2007 Part 15 where the exemption does not apply and the company did not believe or could not reasonably have believed that it would apply (TMA 1970 s 98(4A)–(4E)).	(a) Initial penalty up to £3,000; and (b) further penalty up to £600 for each day on which the failure continues.
Failure of an employment intermediary to furnish information or produce documents or records (TMA 1970 s 98(4F)).	(a) Initial penalty up to £3,000; and (b) further penalty up to £600 for each day on which the failure continues.
Advance pricing agreements: Fraudulently or negligently making a false or misleading statement in the preparation of, or application to enter into, any advance pricing agreement (TIOPA 2010 s 227).	Penalty up to £10,000.

Other offences by taxpayers, agents etc

[T1.150]

Offence	Penalty
GAAR. Applies to arrangements entered into after 15 September 2016 if a taxpayer (or in some cases another person) submits a return, claim, or other document on the basis that a tax advantage arises from the tax arrangements and all or part of that tax advantage is later counteracted under the GAAR (FA 2013 s 212A). From 10 June 2021 applies equally to partners in partnerships.	60% of the value of the counteracted advantage.
Uncertain tax treatment. Failure by large business to make notification of uncertain tax treatment in corporation tax, income tax, PAYE or VAT return (FA 2022 Sch 17). Applies to returns required to be made on or after 1 April 2022.	£5,000 for first failure, £25,000 for second failure, £50,000 for any further failure. In determining whether a failure is the first, second or a further failure, only the period of three years prior to the period for which the affected return is made and the tax in question are considered.
Serial tax avoiders. Use of any avoidance schemes in the warning period after the defeat of a relevant scheme. Applies to defeats incurred after 15 September 2016 (FA 2016 Sch 18).	(a) 20% of the tax understated or overclaimed for the first defeat of a scheme used during the warning period; (b) 40% for the second such defeat; and (c) 60% for any subsequent defeats.
Falsification of documents. Intentionally falsifying, concealing or destroying documents required under TMA 1970 s 20BA (TMA 1970 s 20BB).	On summary conviction, a fine up to the statutory maximum; on conviction on indictment, imprisonment for a term not exceeding two years or a fine or both.
European or UK Economic Interest Groupings– Offences in connection with the supply of information:	
(i) failure to supply information	Initial penalty up to £300 per member of the Grouping at the time of failure and after direction by the tribunal: continuing penalty up to £60 per member of the Grouping at the end of the day for each day on which the failure continues.
(ii) fraudulent or negligent delivery of an incorrect return, accounts or statement	Up to £3,000 for each member of the Grouping at the time of delivery.
(TMA 1970 s 98B). (The ability to form an EEIG within the UK is removed following Brexit. Existing EEIGs registered in the UK before 31 December 2020 were converted into UKEIGs)	
Certificates of non-liability to income tax: Fraudulently or negligently giving such a certificate for the purposes of receiving interest gross on a bank or building society account, or failing to comply with an undertaking given in such a certificate (TMA 1970 s 99A). Interest is paid gross to all taxpayers with effect from 6 April 2016.	Penalty up to £3,000.
Refusal to allow a deduction of income tax at source (TMA 1970 s 106).	£50.
Construction Industry Scheme: Making false statements etc for the purpose of obtaining a gross payment certificate (FA 2004 s 72).	Up to £3,000.
Fraudulent evasion of income tax (TMA 1970 s 106A).	On summary conviction, imprisonment for up to twelve months or a fine up to the statutory maximum or both; on conviction on indictment, imprisonment for up to 14 years from 22 February 2024 (previously, seven years) or a fine or both.
Enterprise investment scheme relief: Issue by a company of a certificate of approval for such relief fraudulently or negligently or without the authority of HMRC (ITA 2007 s 207).	Not exceeding £3,000.
Failure of a company to maintain records (other than those only required for claims, etc, or dividend vouchers and certificates of income tax deducted where other evidence is available) (FA 1998 Sch 18 para 23).	Penalty not exceeding £3,000.

Offence	Penalty
Failure to notify notifiable proposals or notifiable arrangements, or failure to notify the client of the relevant scheme reference number under the provisions of FA 2004 ss 306–319 (TMA 1970 s 98C).	(a) Up to 31 December 2010 an initial penalty not exceeding £5,000; (i) From 1 January 2011 in the case of provisions under FA 2004 ss 308(1) and (3), 309(1) and 310, and from 10 June 2021 in the case of s 311C, up to £600 per day in 'initial period' (but a tribunal can determine a higher penalty up to £1 million); (ii) From 1 January 2011 in the case of provisions in FA 2004 ss 312(2), 312A(2), 313ZA, 313A, 313B, 313C, from 17 July 2013 in the case of provisions in ss 312B and 313ZB, from 26 March 2015 in the case of ss 310C, 312A(2A), 313ZC, and 316A, and from 10 June 2021 in the case of s 312ZA, an initial penalty up to £5,000. Where a disclosure order is made the amount in (i) above is increased up to £5,000 per day that failure continues from ten days after the order is made. (b) a continuing penalty not exceeding £600 for each day on which the failure continues after imposition of initial penalty. Where a disclosure order is made the amount is increased up to £5,000 per day that failure continues from ten days after the order is made.
Failure to notify scheme reference number etc under FA 2004 s 313(1);	Penalty not exceeding £5,000 in respect of each scheme to which the failure relates;
for second failure, occurring within three years from the date on which the first failure began;	penalty not exceeding £7,500 in respect of each scheme to which the failure relates;
for subsequent failures, occurring within three years from the date on which the previous failure began.	penalty not exceeding £10,000 in respect of each scheme to which the failure relates.
(TMA 1970 s 98C; FA 2004 s 315(1)).	
Failure to comply with HMRC investigatory powers under FA 2008 Sch 36.	(a) an initial penalty of £300;
Failure to comply with an information notice within FA 2008 Sch 36 Pt 1 or deliberately obstructing an HMRC officer in the course of an inspection of business premises under FA 2008 Sch 36 Pt 2 which has been approved by the First-tier Tribunal. Applies to IT (including PAYE and CIS), CT, CGT, VAT and certain foreign taxes with effect from 1 April 2009. Extended to IHT, SDLT and other taxes from 1 April 2010, to ATED from 1 July 2013; to pension scheme registration applications from 17 July 2014; to Diverted Profits Tax from 1 April 2015, and to Digital Services Tax from 1 April 2020.	(b) if failure/obstruction continues, a further penalty up to £60 per day; (c) if failure/obstruction continues after penalty under (a) imposed, daily penalty can be increased to a maximum of £1,000. In addition, a tax-related amount can be determined by the Upper Tribunal.
Carelessly or deliberately providing inaccurate information or an inaccurate document in response to an information notice.	Up to £3,000 per inaccuracy.
Breach of non-disclosure requirement in relation to a third party notice or financial institution notice under FA 2008 Sch 36 para 51A. Applies from 10 June 2021.	£1,000.
Failure of a senior accounting officer to ensure a company maintains appropriate tax accounting arrangements (FA 2009 Sch 46).	£5,000.
Failure of a senior accounting officer to provide a certificate stating whether the company had appropriate tax accounting arrangements (FA 2009 Sch 46).	£5,000.
Failure to notify Commissioners of name of senior accounting officer (FA 2009 Sch 46).	£5,000.
Failure of a third party to notify the contact details of a debtor (FA 2009 Sch 49).	£300.
Failure to comply with data-holder notice (FA 2011 Sch 23).	(a) an initial penalty of £300. (b) if failure continues, a further penalty up to £60 per day. (c) increased daily penalty of up to £1,000 to be set by Tribunal if notice still not complied with within 30 days of a daily penalty being notified.
Tax agent failure to comply with file access notice (FA 2012 Sch 38).	(a) an initial penalty of £300. (b) if failure continues, a further penalty up to £60 per day.
Tax agent engaging in dishonest conduct (FA 2012 Sch 38).	£5,000 minimum to £50,0000 maximum subject to the quality of disclosure and compliance with any access notice, with possible special reduction of £5,000 penalty to nil at HMRC's discretion.

Offence	Penalty
Failure to keep records for the purposes of the annual tax on enveloped dwellings (FA 2013 Sch 33).	Up to £3,000
Corrective action not taken in response to follower notice (FA 2014 s 208).	30% of value of the denied advantage (12% for relevant partners). May be reduced for co-operation. (50% and 20% respectively before 11 June 2021).
Additional penalty for unreasonable tax appeal in response to follower notice. Applies from 10 June 2021.	20% of value of the denied advantage (8% for relevant partners). May be reduced for co-operation.
Failure to pay accelerated payment (FA 2014 s 226).	(a) Initial penalty of 5% of any amount unpaid at end of payment period (or where the accelerated payment relates to an instalment of IHT, 5% of any amount unpaid by the later due date of that instalment if applicable). (b) Further penalty of 5% of any amount unpaid after 5 months. (c) Further penalty of 5% of any amount unpaid after 11 months.
Failure of monitored promoter of a tax avoidance scheme, or their intermediary, to comply with various duties to notify clients, provide information or produce documents (FA 2014 Sch 35 paras 2, 3).	(a) Initial maximum penalty of £300, £5,000, £7,500, £10,000, £25,000, £100,000, £250,000 or £1,000,000 depending on failure. (b) Further daily penalty for each day on which failure continues of up to £10,000 where the maximum penalty could have been £1,000,000, or otherwise, £600.
Failure of monitored promoter of a tax avoidance scheme to comply with a stop notice (FA 2014, ss 277A, 277B; FA 2024 s 34)	On summary conviction, a fine; on conviction on indictment, imprisonment for up to two years or a fine or both.
Provision of inaccurate information or document by a monitored promoter of a tax avoidance scheme when complying with an information duty (FA 2014 Sch 35 para 4).	Maximum penalty of £5,000, £10,000, or £1,000,000 depending on duty being complied with.
Concealing, destroying etc documents required to be produced in connection with a monitored promoter of a tax avoidance scheme (FA 2014 s 280).	On summary conviction, a fine; on conviction on indictment, imprisonment for up to two years or a fine or both.
Facilitating avoidance schemes involving non-resident promoters. Further penalty where a person incurred a specified penalty relating to avoidance schemes due to activities they carried out on or after 24 February 2022 as a member of the same promotion structure as a non-resident promoter (P) and those activities related to a proposal or arrangements for which P was a promoter (FA 2022 Sch 13).	Total value of all consideration received by all members of the promotion structure in connection with the proposal or arrangements or any other proposals or arrangements which are substantially the same. HMRC can reduce the amount of the penalty to an amount they consider just and reasonable.
Failure of a company to provide a return in respect of a SIP, SAYE option, CSOP, EMI or other employee share scheme (ITEPA 2003 Sch 2 para 81C; Sch 3 para 40C; Sch 4 para 28C; Sch 5 para 57B; s 421JC).	(a) Initial penalty of £100. (b) Further penalty of £300 if failure continues for 3 months. (c) Further penalty of £300 if failure continues for 6 months. (d) Further penalty of £10 for each day that failure continues beyond 9 months (with notice).
Inaccurate return provided by a company, or return not filed electronically as required in respect of a SIP, SAYE option, CSOP, EMI or other employee share scheme (ITEPA 2003 Sch 2 para 81E; Sch 3 para 40E; Sch 4 para 28E; Sch 5 para 57C; s 421JD).	Up to £5,000.
Failure of a company to comply with the rules in respect of a SIP, SAYE option, or CSOP scheme (ITEPA 2003 Sch 2 para 81H–81I; Sch 3 para 40H–41I; Sch 4 para 28H–28I).	If scheme does not comply at all, penalty not exceeding twice the tax and NIC HMRC estimate has been 'saved'. Otherwise, up to £5,000.
Failure of a company to provide to HMRC a declaration under ITEPA 2003 Sch 5 para 44(6) by individual to whom an EMI option is granted (ITEPA 2003 Sch 5 para 57A).	£500.
A social enterprise fraudulently or negligently issuing a compliance certificate or statement (ITA 2007 s 257PD).	Up to £3,000.
Failure by a qualifying company or partnership, or by the head of a UK group of companies or by the head of a UK sub-group of a foreign group of companies to publish the company's, partnership's, group's or sub-group's tax strategy or to make it freely available after publication. Applies to financial years beginning on or after 15 September 2016 (FA 2016 Sch 19).	(a) Initial penalty of up to £7,500. (b) further penalty of £7,500 if failure continues for 6 months; and (c) further penalty of £7,500 for every subsequent month that failure continues.
Enablers of defeated tax avoidance. Penalty applies to persons who enable the use of abusive tax avoidance arrangements which are later defeated (F(No 2)A 2017 Sch 16).	The amount of consideration received or receivable by enabler for enabling the tax avoidance arrangements.
Failure to correct on or by 30 September 2018 irregularities in relation to undeclared past UK IT, CGT and IHT liabilities involving offshore interests which exist at 5 April 2017 (F(No 2)A 2017 Sch 18).	200% of the offshore potential lost revenue (PLR). Reductions apply for disclosure but minimum penalty will be 100% of PLR.

Offence	Penalty
Failure to provide loan charge information for income provided through third parties (F(No 2) A 2017 Schs 11 and 12).	(a) an initial penalty of £300. (b) if failure continues, a further penalty up to £60 per day up to a maximum of 90 days.
Inaccuracy in information or document relating to loan charge for income provided through third parties (F(No 2)A 2017 Schs 11 and 12).	Up to £3,000 per inaccuracy.
Failure to amend a company tax return in relation to corporate interest restriction (TIOPA 2010 Sch 7A).	£500.
Failure by the lead trustee to register a trust before the trust deadline, or to tell HMRC about any changes to the registration.	(a) £100 if registered within up to 3 months of deadline[1]. (b) £200 if registered between 3 to 6 months of deadline. (c) higher of £300 or 5% of total tax liability in relevant year if registered more than 6 months after deadline.
Failure by a fund manager to notify a participant of certain deemed disposals of UK land (TCGA 1992 Sch 5AAA).	Up to £3,000
Failure to deliver a Digital Services Tax (DST) return (FA 2020 Sch 8 paras 52, 53).	(a) £100 if delivered within 3 months of the filing date. (b) £200 in any other case. (c) increased to £500 and £1,000 respectively for a third successive failure. (d) if not delivered within 18 months of end of accounting period, tax-geared penalties apply of (i) 10% of the unpaid tax if delivered within 2 years (ii) 20% in any other case.
Failure to preserve records to enable delivery of a DST return (FA 2020 Sch 8 para 55).	Up to £3,000

[1] Failure of lead trustee: Penalties not issued automatically and to be reviewed on a case by case basis. Penalties relating to notification of changes will only apply once facility to notify has been set up.

Mitigation of penalties

[T1.151]

HMRC have discretion to mitigate or entirely remit any penalty or to stay or compound any penalty proceedings (TMA 1970 s 102).

Interest on penalties

[T1.152]

Penalties under TMA 1970 Parts II (ss 7–12B), IV (ss 28A–43B), VA (ss 59A–59D) and X (ss 93–107), and FA 1998 Sch 18 carry interest at the prescribed rate (see **T1.110**): TMA 1970 s 103A. This applies to penalties in relation to promoters of tax avoidance schemes from 17 July 2014. For interest which applies to penalties under the **harmonised interest regime** see **T1.108**.

Publishing details of deliberate tax defaulters

[T1.153]

HMRC have the power to publish the names and details of taxpayers who are penalised for deliberate defaults leading to a loss of tax of more than £25,000. The power extends to certain individuals who control a body corporate or a partnership, or who are trustees of a settlement, which is penalised for such deliberate defaults relating to an offshore matter or transfer, but only where the individual would obtain a tax advantage from the default. Only taxpayers who make full unprompted disclosures are protected (FA 2009 s 94).

Publishing details of deliberate enablers of offshore evasion or non-compliance

[T1.154]

HMRC have the power to publish the names and details of enablers of offshore tax evasion or non-compliance who are found liable for a penalty and the potential lost revenue involved exceeds £25,000. They may also publish information about a person who has been found to have incurred 5 or more penalties in any 5-year period (FA 2016 Sch 20).

Publishing details of serial tax avoiders

[T1.155]

HMRC have the power to publish the names and details of serial tax avoiders if they are given three warning notices in respect of schemes used while in a warning period and which are defeated (FA 2016 Sch 18).

Publishing details of persistently uncooperative large businesses

[T1.156]

HMRC have the power to publish the names and details of a large company, partnership, UK group of companies, or UK sub-group of a foreign group of companies which is subject to a confirmed special measures notice. (FA 2016 Sch 19).

Publishing details of enablers of defeated abusive tax avoidance arrangements

[T1.157]

HMRC have the power to publish the names and details of persons who have been assessed to a penalty which has become final in relation to enabling defeated tax avoidance arrangements, provided they have incurred at least 50 other such penalties, or total penalties incurred including the current one will exceed £25,000 (F(No 2)A 2017 Sch 16).

Criminal offence for offshore matters

[T1.158]

A criminal offence which does not require the need to prove intent applies for failing to accurately declare taxable offshore income and gains. The specific offences are failure to notify, failure to deliver a return and making an inaccurate return. It will apply where the loss of tax exceeds £25,000 (TMA 1970 ss 106B–106H; SI 2017/988).

Corporate offence of failure to prevent criminal facilitation of tax evasion

[T1.159]

An offence will be committed where a body corporate or partnership fails to prevent an associated person (broadly an employee, agent or other person who performs services for them) criminally facilitating the evasion of a tax in the UK or abroad (Criminal Finances Act 2017 ss 44–52).

Tax agent dishonest conduct

[T1.160]

In addition to the penalties listed above, HMRC have the power to publish names and details of tax agents who incur penalties for dishonest conduct over £5,000 (FA 2012 Sch 38).

Failure to provide security

[T1.161]

A person who fails to comply with a requirement imposed under the PAYE regulations to give security or further security is liable on summary conviction to a fine (not exceeding level 5 on the standard scale (£5,000) in Scotland or Northern Ireland). Also applies to construction industry scheme deductions and corporation tax payments from 6 April 2019 (FA 1998 Sch 18 para 88A(5); ITEPA 2003 s 684(4A); FA 2004 s 70A(5)).

Time limits for claims and elections

[T1.162]

Whenever possible, a claim or election must be made on the tax return or by an amendment to the return (TMA 1970 s 42 and FA 1998 Sch 18 paras 9, 10, 67 and 79). Exceptions to this general rule are dealt with in TMA 1970 Sch 1A. Except where another period is expressly prescribed, a claim for relief in respect of income tax and capital gains tax must be made within four years after the end of the tax year. (TMA 1970 s 43(1).) The time limit for claims by companies is four years from the end of the accounting period to which it relates (FA 1998 Sch 18 para 55). The general time limit is extended where it relates to a capital gain or loss arising on a disposal under a contract entered into on or after 6 April 2023 (1 April 2023 for companies) and completion is delayed so that the asset is not conveyed or transferred until a later tax year or accounting period. For capital gains tax purposes, this applies where the asset is not conveyed or transferred until after 5 October following the tax year in which the contract is made. The time limit for making a claim runs from the end of the tax year of the conveyance or transfer. For corporation tax purposes, the extension applies where the asset is not conveyed or transferred until more than twelve months after the end of the accounting period in which the contract is made.

The time limit for making a claim then runs from the end of the accounting period of conveyance or transfer (TCGA 1992 s 28A; F(No 2)A 2023 s 40). The tables below set out some of the main exceptions to the general time limits.

Income tax

[T1.163]

Claim	Time limit
Trading losses: Loss sustained in a trade, profession or vocation to be set against other income of the year or the last preceding year. Extended to certain pre-trading expenditure by ITTOIA 2005 s 57 (ITA 2007 s 64). SEE TOLLEY'S TAX COMPUTATIONS 26.2.	One year after 31 January next following tax year in which loss arose.
Temporary extension of trading loss relief above. Losses to be set against profits of the same trade for the preceding 3 years for losses incurred in 2020–21 and 2021–22 (FA 2021 Sch 2 Part 1)	One year after 31 January next following tax year in which loss arose.
Unrelieved trading losses to be set against capital gains (TCGA 1992 ss 261B, 261C). SEE TOLLEY'S TAX COMPUTATIONS 15.2.	One year after 31 January next following tax year in which loss arose.
Losses of new trade etc: Loss sustained in the first four years of a new trade, profession or vocation to be offset against other income arising in the three years immediately preceding the year of loss. Extended to certain pre-trading expenditure by ITTOIA 2005 s 57 (ITA 2007 s 72). SEE TOLLEY'S TAX COMPUTATIONS 15.3.	One year after 31 January next following tax year in which loss arose.
Property business losses: Claim for relief against total income (ITA 2007 s 124).	One year after 31 January next following tax year specified in claim.
Simplified cash basis for unincorporated property businesses: Cash basis *not* to apply (ITTOIA 2005 s 271A).	One year after 31 January next following tax year specified in claim.
Cash basis for unincorporated trades: Cash basis *not* to apply (for 2024/25 onwards) (ITTOIA 2005 s 25C; FA 2024 Sch 10).	One year after 31 January next following tax year specified in election.
Cash basis for unincorporated trades: Cash basis to apply (for 2023/24 and earlier years) (ITTOIA 2005 s 25A).	One year after 31 January next following tax year specified in election.
Loss on disposal of unlisted shares: Loss on disposal of shares in an EIS company or a qualifying trading company to be offset against other income of the year of loss or the last preceding year (ITA 2007 s 132). SEE TOLLEY'S TAX COMPUTATIONS 15.5.	One year after 31 January next following tax year in which loss arose.
Gift aid: Election to treat donations to charity under gift aid as made in the previous tax year (ITA 2007 s 426).	On or before date on which donor delivers tax return for the previous tax year and not later than 31 January after that year.
Enterprise investment scheme relief: Income tax relief of 30% on amount invested within specified limits (ITA 2007 s 202).	5 years after 31 January next following tax year in which shares are issued.
Seed enterprise investment scheme relief: Income tax relief of 50% on amount invested within specified limits (ITA 2007 s 257EA). SEE TOLLEY'S TAX COMPUTATIONS 227.3.	5 years after 31 January next following tax year in which shares are issued.
Social investment tax relief: Income tax relief of 30% on amount invested before 6 April 2023 within specified limits (ITA 2007 s 257P).	5 years after 31 January next following tax year in which investment is made.
Rent-a-room relief: Relief not to apply; to apply to gross income in excess of limit; withdrawal of claim (ITTOIA 2005 ss 799, 800).	One year after 31 January next following tax year specified in claim.
Trading or property allowance: Full relief not to apply; partial relief to apply (ITTOIA 2005 ss 783AL, 783AM, 783BJ, 783BK).	One year after 31 January next following tax year specified in claim.

Capital gains

[T1.165]

Claim	Time limit
Assets of negligible value: Loss to be allowed where the value of an asset has become negligible (TCGA 1992 s 24(2)). SEE TOLLEY'S TAX COMPUTATIONS 217.1.	Two years after end of chargeable period of deemed sale (and reacquisition).
Assets held on 31 March 1982 for corporation tax purposes only: Events occurring prior to 31 March 1982 to be ignored in computing gains arising after 5 April 1988 (TCGA 1992 s 35(5), (6) as amended). SEE TOLLEY'S TAX COMPUTATIONS 205.2, 214.1 ONWARDS.	Two years after end of accounting period in which first relevant disposal made after 31.3.88; or such further time as HMRC may allow.
Investors' relief: Gain to be taxed at reduced rate of 14% (10% before 6 April 2025) (TCGA 1992 s 169VM).	One year after 31 January next following tax year of qualifying disposal.
Main residence: Determination of main residence for principal private residence exemption (TCGA 1992 s 222(5)(*a*)). SEE TOLLEY'S TAX COMPUTATIONS 223.2.	Two years after acquisition of second residence.

Claim	Time limit
Relief for loans to traders: Losses on certain loans to traders to be allowed as capital losses at the time of claim or 'earlier time' (TCGA 1992 s 253(3A)).	Two years after the end of the tax year or accounting period of loss.
Relief for loans to traders (payments by guarantor): Losses arising from payments by guarantor of certain irrecoverable loans to traders to be allowed as capital losses at time of claim or 'earlier time' (TCGA 1992 s 253(4), (4A)).	Four years after the end of the tax year or accounting period in which payment made.
Election for valuation at 6 April 1965 for corporation tax purposes only: Gain on a disposal of an asset held at 6 April 1965 to be computed as if the asset had been acquired on that date. An election once made is irrevocable (TCGA 1992 Sch 2 para 17).	Two years after end of accounting period in which disposal made; or such further time as HMRC may allow.
Business asset disposal relief / entrepreneurs' relief: Gain to be taxed at reduced rate of 14% (10% before 6 April 2025) (TCGA 1992 s 169M). SEE TOLLEY'S TAX COMPUTATIONS 211.1.	One year after 31 January next following tax year of qualifying business disposal.

Corporation tax

[T1.166]

Claim	Time limit
Trading losses: Loss sustained by a company in a trade in an accounting period to be offset against profits of that accounting period and profits of the preceding year. Extended to certain pre-trading expenditure by CTA 2009 s 61 (CTA 2010 s 37(7)).	Two years after end of loss-making period; or such further period as HMRC may allow.
Temporary extension of trading loss relief above. Losses to be set against profits of that accounting period and profits of preceding 3 years for losses incurred in accounting periods ending between 1 April 2020 and 31 March 2022 (FA 2021 Sch 2 Part 2)	Two years after end of loss-making period; or such further period as HMRC may allow.
Trading losses: Post-1 April 2017 loss to be offset against *total* profits of a later accounting period (CTA 2010 s 45A(7)).	Two years after end of loss-making period; or such further period as HMRC may allow.
Trading losses: Post-1 April 2017 loss *not* to be carried forward against *trade* profits of next accounting period (CTA 2010 s 45B(6)).	Two years after end of loss-making period; or such further period as HMRC may allow.
Property losses: Carry forward of post-1 April 2017 losses (CTA 2010 s 62(5C)).	Two years after end of loss-making period; or such further period as HMRC may allow.
Group relief and Group relief for carried forward losses: Group relief to be given for accounting periods ending after 30 June 1999. The surrendering company must consent to the claim (FA 1998 Sch 18 paras 66–77A).	The last of: (a) one year from filing date of claimant company's return for accounting period for which claim is made; (b) 30 days after end of an enquiry into return; (c) if HMRC amend return after an enquiry, 30 days after issue of notice of amendment; (d) if an appeal is made against amendment, 30 days after determination of appeal; (or such later time as HMRC may allow).
Non-trading deficit on loan relationship: Claim for non-trading deficits on loan relationships (including non-trading debits on derivative contracts) in an accounting period to be: SEE TOLLEY'S TAX COMPUTATIONS 113.1 ONWARDS.	
(a) offset against profits of same period or carried back (CTA 2009 ss 463B–463E);	Two years after end of accounting period in which deficit arose (or such later time as HMRC may allow).
(b) carried forward against *total* profits of succeeding accounting periods (CTA 2009 s 463G).	Two years after end of that subsequent accounting period.
(c) (where claim under (b) not applicable) not treated as non-trading deficit of subsequent accounting period but to be carried forward to succeeding accounting periods (CTA 2009 s 463H).	Two years after end of that subsequent accounting period.
Intangible assets: Election to replace accounts depreciation with fixed writing-down allowance of 4% (CTA 2009 s 730). SEE TOLLEY'S TAX COMPUTATIONS 108.1.	Two years after end of the accounting period in which asset was created or acquired.
Research and development: Claim for tax relief to be made, amended or withdrawn in company tax return (or amended return) (FA 1998 Sch 18 para 83E; FA 2024 Sch 1).	For accounting periods beginning on or after 1 April 2023, 2 years from end of period or, if period of account exceeds 18 months, 42 months from start of period. Previously, one year from filing date for return. In either case, the time limit can be extended if an HMRC officer allows.

Capital allowances

[T1.167]

Claim	Time limit
Corporation tax claims: Claims, amended claims and withdrawals of claims in respect of corporation tax capital allowances (CAA 2001 s 3(2), (3)(*b*); FA 1998 Sch 18 para 82).	The last of: (*a*) one year after filing date of claimant company's return for accounting period for which claim is made; (*b*) 30 days after end of enquiry into return; (*c*) if HMRC amend the return after an enquiry, 30 days after issue of notice of amendment; (*d*) if appeal is made against amendment, 30 days after determination of appeal; (or such later time as HMRC may allow).
Short life assets: Plant or machinery to be treated as a short life asset (CAA 2001 s 85(2)). See Tolley's Tax Computations 4.4.	One year after 31 January after tax year in which chargeable period ends (income tax); two years after end of chargeable period (corporation tax).
Connected persons: Succession to a trade between connected persons to be ignored in computing capital allowances (CAA 2001 s 266). See Tolley's Tax Computations 4.2.	Two years after date of the succession.
Sales between persons under common control treated as made at the lower of open market value and tax written down value (CAA 2001 s 570(5)).	Two years after date of the disposal.

Exchanges

Recognised stock exchanges

[T1.168]

The following is a list of countries with exchanges which have been designated as recognised stock exchanges under ITA 2007 s 1005; CTA 2010 s 1137. Unless otherwise specified, any stock exchange (or options exchange) in a country listed below is a recognised stock exchange provided it is recognised under the law of the country concerned relating to stock exchanges.

HMRC may make an order designating a market in the UK as a recognised stock exchange.

Country	Date of recognition
Astana International Exchange	25 January 2019
Australian Stock Exchange and its stock exchange subsidiaries	22 September 1988
National Stock Exchange of Australia	19 June 2014
Austria[3]	22 October 1970
Bahamas	
Bahamas International Securities Exchange	19 April 2010
Barbados	
Barbados Stock Exchange	2 April 2019
Belgium[3]	22 October 1970
Bermuda	4 December 2007
Botswana	8 October 2018
Brazil	
Rio De Janeiro Stock Exchange	17 August 1995
São Paulo Stock Exchange	11 December 1995
Canada	
Any stock exchange prescribed for the purposes of the Canadian Income Tax Act	22 October 1970
Caribbean	
Dutch Caribbean Securities Exchange	8 December 2014
The Barbados Stock Exchange	2 April 2019
Cayman Islands Stock Exchange	4 March 2004
Cboe Europe Ltd	1 July 2020
Channel Islands Securities Exchange Authority[3]	20 December 2013
China	
Hong Kong – Any stock exchange recognised under Section 2A(1) of the Hong Kong Companies Ordinance[3]	26 February 1971
Cyprus	
Cyprus Stock Exchange	22 June 2009
Denmark	
Copenhagen Stock Exchange	22 October 1970
Estonia	
NASDAQ OMX Tallinn	5 May 2010

Country	Date of recognition
European Wholesale Securities Market	17 January 2013
Finland	
Helsinki Stock Exchange	22 October 1970
France[3]	22 October 1970
Germany[3]	5 August 1971
Gibraltar	16 August 2016
Greece	
Athens Stock Exchange	14 June 1993
Guernsey[3]	10 December 2002
Iceland	31 March 2006
IPSX UK Limited[6]	*25 January 2019*
Irish Republic[3]	22 October 1970
Israel	
The Tel-Aviv Stock Exchange	8 January 2019
Italy[3]	3 May 1972
Japan[3]	22 October 1970
Korea	10 October 1994
Latvia	
NASDAQ Riga	8 January 2019
Lithuania	
NASDAQ OMX Vilnius	12 March 2012
Luxembourg[3]	21 February 1972
Malaysia	
Kuala Lumpur Stock Exchange	10 October 1994
Malta Stock Exchange	29 December 2005
Mauritius Stock Exchange	31 January 2011
MERJ Exchange Limited	28 September 2020
Mexico	10 October 1994
Netherlands[3]	22 October 1970
New Zealand	22 September 1988
Norway[3]	22 October 1970
Poland	
Warsaw Stock Exchange	25 February 2010
Portugal[3]	21 February 1972
Russia	
MICEX Stock Exchange[5]	*5 January 2011–4 May 2022*
Singapore	30 June 1977
Singapore Exchange Securities Trading Limited (SGX-ST)[4]	7 October 2014
Singapore Exchange Derivatives Trading Limited (SGX-DT)[4]	7 October 2014
South Africa	
Bond Exchange of South Africa	16 April 2008
Johannesburg Stock Exchange	22 October 1970
Cape Town Stock Exchange	15 May 2023
Spain[3]	5 August 1971
Sri Lanka	
Colombo Stock Exchange	21 February 1972
Sweden	
Stockholm Stock Exchange	16 July 1985
Swiss Stock Exchange	12 May 1997
Thailand	10 October 1994
United Kingdom	
London Stock Exchange	19 July 2007
PLUS-listed Market	19 July 2007
AQUIS Exchange plc (formerly NEX Exchange Ltd, formerly ICAP Securities & Derivatives Exchange Ltd)	25 April 2013
Mindex Securities Exchange	8 July 2024
United States	
Any stock exchange registered with the SEC as a national securities exchange[1]	22 October 1970
Nasdaq Stock Market[2]	10 March 1992

[1] 'National securities exchange' does not include any local exchanges registered with Securities and Exchange Commission.

[2] As maintained through the facilities of the National Association of Securities Dealers Inc and its subsidiaries.

[3] i.e., a stock exchange according to the law of the country concerned relating to stock exchanges.

[4] The original Singapore Stock Exchange merged with two other exchanges and is now known as SGX. The SGX-ST market was identified as representing the originally designated exchange.
[5] HMRC has revoked the recognised status of the MICEX stock exchange with effect from 5 May 2022.
[6] IPSX UK Limited ceased trading on 1 December 2023.

Recognised futures exchanges

[T1.169]

The following is a list of exchanges which have been designated as recognised futures exchanges under TCGA 1992 s 288(6). By concession, those exchanges were recognised futures exchanges for the tax year of recognition onwards.

Recognised futures exchanges	Year of recognition
International Petroleum Exchange of London	1985–86
London Metal Exchange	1985–86
London Gold Market	1985–86
London Silver Market	1985–86
CME Group (formerly Chicago Mercantile Exchange and Chicago Board of Trade)	1986–87
New York Mercantile Exchange	1986–87
Philadelphia Board of Trade	1986–87
Mid America Commodity Exchange	1987–88
Montreal Exchange	1987–88
Hong Kong Futures Exchange	1987–88
Commodity Exchange (Comex)	1988–89
Sydney Futures Exchange	1988–89
Euronext (London International Financial Futures and Options Exchange)	1991–92
OM Stockholm	1991–92
OMLX (formerly OM London)	1991–92
New York Board of Trade	2004–05
Eurex Deutschland	2014–15

Recognised investment exchanges and clearing houses

[T1.170]

The following is a list of investment exchanges and clearing houses recognised as investment exchanges under the Financial Services and Markets Act 2000 and able to carry out investment business in the UK.

Recognised investment exchanges	Date of recognition
London Stock Exchange plc	22 November 2001
The London Metal Exchange Ltd	22 November 2001
ICE Futures Europe (formerly ICE Futures, formerly The International Petroleum Exchange of London Limited)	22 November 2001
AQUIS Exchange Ltd (formerly NEX Exchange Ltd, formerly ICAP Securities & Derivatives Exchange Ltd, formerly PLUS Stock Exchange Plc)	19 July 2007
Cboe Europe Ltd (formerly BATS Trading Ltd)	11 July 2013
IPSX UK Limited[2]	8 January 2019

[1] List as at 4 November 2024 on Financial Conduct Authority website.
[2] IPSX UK Limited ceased trading on 1 December 2023.

Recognised central counterparties and central securities depositories[2]	Date of recognition
LCH Ltd[1]	22 November 2001
Euroclear UK & International Ltd[2]	23 November 2001
ICE Clear Europe Ltd[1]	15 May 2008
LME Clear Ltd[1]	3 September 2014

[1] These clearing houses are recognised central counterparties. LCH Ltd was recognised as such on 12 June 2014. LME Clear Ltd was recognised as such on 3 September 2014. ICE Clear Europe Ltd was recognised as such on 19 September 2016.
[2] Euroclear UK & International Ltd is recognised as a central securities depository from 8 December 2020.
[3] List as at 5 November 2024 on Bank of England website.

Recognised overseas investment exchanges

[T1.171]

The following is a list of overseas investment exchanges and clearing houses recognised under the Financial Services and Markets Act 2000 and able to conduct investment business in the UK.

Recognised overseas investment exchange	Date of recognition
The Nasdaq Stock Market LLC	23 November 2001
Australian Securities Exchange Ltd	30 January 2002
The Chicago Mercantile Exchange (CME)	23 November 2001
Chicago Board of Trade (CBOT)	23 November 2001
New York Mercantile Exchange Inc (NYMEX Inc)	23 November 2001
SIX Swiss Exchange AG	23 November 2001
ICE Futures US Inc	17 May 2007
European Energy Exchange AG	21 February 2019
ICE Endex Markets B.V.	21 February 2019
Deutsche Börse AG	21 February 2019
Eurex Frankfurt AG	21 February 2019
Singapore Exchange Derivatives Trading Ltd	5 March 2019
Singapore Exchange Securities Trading Ltd	5 March 2019
Commodity Exchange, Inc.	26 March 2019
Euronext Amsterdam N.V.	26 March 2019
Euronext Paris SA	26 March 2019
Cboe Europe B.V.	16 April 2019
BORSA ITALIANA SpA	16 October 2019
Nasdaq Oslo ASA	17 October 2019
MTS S.p.A.	22 January 2020
Bourse de Montréal Inc.	28 April 2020
Nodal Exchange, LLC	19 January 2021
ICE Futures Abu Dhabi Limited	26 March 2021
Nasdaq Stockholm AB	7 October 2021
Nasdaq Helsinki Ltd	7 October 2021
Nasdaq Copenhagen A/S	7 October 2021
Bolsa de Madrid	14 April 2022
MEFF Sociedad Rectora del Mercado de Productos Derivados S.A.U.	14 April 2022
Euronext Brussels SA/NV	24 June 2022
BME Renta Fija, AIAF-MARF-SENAF	13 October 2022
The Stock Exchange of Hong Kong Limited	24 February 2023
Hong Kong Futures Exchange Limited	24 February 2023

[1] List as at 5 November 2024 on Financial Conduct Authority website.

Alternative finance investment bonds

[T1.172]

List of recognised stock exchanges designated solely for the purposes of ITA 2007 s 564G, TCGA 1992 s 151N, CTA 2009 s 507.

Recognised stock exchanges	Date of recognition
Abu Dhabi Securities Market	1 April 2007
Bahrain Stock Exchange	1 April 2007
Dubai Financial Market	1 April 2007
NASDAQ Dubai (formerly Dubai International Financial Exchange)	1 April 2007
Labuan International Financial Exchange	1 April 2007
Saudi Stock Exchange (Tadawul)	1 April 2007
Surabaya Stock Exchange	1 April 2007

Applications for clearances and approvals

[T1.173]

Statutory clearance applications and approvals	Address[3]
Demergers (CTA 2010 s 1091); Company purchase of own shares (CTA 2010 s 1044); Transactions in securities (CTA 2010 s 748; ITA 2007 s 701); Enterprise Investment Scheme – acquisition of shares by new company (ITA 2007 s 247(1)(f)); Share exchanges (TCGA 1992 s 138); Reconstruction regarding transfer of a business (TCGA 1992 s 139); Transfer of a UK trade between EU member states (TCGA 1992 ss 140B, 140D); Intangible fixed assets (CTA 2009 s 831); Loan relationships transfers/mergers (CTA 2009 ss 426, 427, 437); Derivative contracts transfers/mergers (CTA 2009 ss 677, 686); Schemes converting income to capital (TCGA 1992 ss 184G–H); Assignment of lease granted at undervalue (CTA 2009 s 237; ITTOIA 2005 s 300); Collective investment schemes (TCGA 1992 s 103K); Cross-border transfer of a loan relationship, derivative contract or intangible fixed assets (TIOPA 2010 s 117(4)); Continuity of Seed Enterprise Investment Scheme (SEIS) relief (ITA 2007 s 257HB)	HM Revenue & Customs, BAI Clearance, BX9 1JL or email reconstructions@hmrc.gov.uk (Applications should be marked "market sensitive" or "non-market sensitive" as appropriate.)[1]
Employee share schemes (ITEPA 2003 Schs 2, 3, 4)	Self-certification applies and can be made through HMRC Online services; see www.gov.uk/guidance/tell-hmrc-about-your-employment-related-securities
International movements of capital (FA 2009 Sch 17)	The recommendation is that businesses should address the reports directly to the customer relationship manager dealing with their affairs
Pensions	Registration of a pension scheme must be done online, but HMRC can be contacted at Pension Schemes Services, HM Revenue & Customs, BX9 1GH, United Kingdom
Transfers of long-term business (FA 2012 s 133)	HM Revenue & Customs, CS&TD Business, Assets and International, BAI Financial Services Team, Queen Elizabeth House, 1 Sibbald Walk, Edinburgh EH8 8FT

Non-statutory clearance applications	Address[3]
Controlled foreign companies (TIOPA 2010 Part 9A)	HM Revenue & Customs, Business, Assets and International, Base Protection Policy Team, NE98 1ZZ
Company migration (TMA 1970 s 109B–109F)	HM Revenue & Customs, Business, Assets and International, Base Protection Policy Team, NE98 1ZZ
Inward investment (in Statement of Practice 02/07)	Inward Investment Support, HM Revenue & Customs, S1715, Floor 9, Mail Point 3, Central Mail Unit, Newcastle upon Tyne, NE98 1ZZ or email inwardinvestmentsupportmailbox@hmrc.gov.uk
Creative industries (CTA 2009 Pts 15, 15A, 15B)	Creative Industries Unit (Film, Television/Animation and Video Games Tax Reliefs), HM Revenue & Customs - Local Compliance, Manchester Incentives and Reliefs Team S0733, Newcastle upon Tyne, NE98 1ZZ
Enterprise Investment Scheme (EIS), Seed Enterprise Investment Scheme (SEIS) and Venture Capital Trust (VCT) scheme (ITA 2007 Pts 5, 5A, 6)	Venture Capital Relief Team, HM Revenue & Customs, WMBC, BX9 1BN Telephone: 0300 123 3440[3]
Business investment relief (ITA 2007 s 809VC)	Wealthy and Mid-sized Business Compliance, HM Revenue & Customs, BX9 1BN or email businessinvestmentrelief@hmrc.gov.uk
IHT business property relief (IHTA 1984 Pt 5 Ch 1)	HM Revenue & Customs, S1753, B6.07 - Inheritance Tax Technical (Clearances), Central Mail Unit, Newcastle NE98 1ZZ
Social investment tax relief (ITA 2007 Pt 5B)	Venture Capital Reliefs Team, HM Revenue & Customs, WMBC, BX9 1BN Telephone: 0300 123 3440
Other non-statutory clearances including VAT	Large businesses should contact their client relationship manager. All other businesses and their agents should send applications to Wealthy, HM Revenue and Customs BX9 1BN[2] or email nonstatutoryclearanceteam.hmrc@hmrc.gov.uk Regarding emails see[1]

Confirmation or pre-transaction or general advice	Address[3]
General enquiries on IR35	HM Revenue & Customs, IR35 Customer Service Unit, S0733, Newcastle Upon Tyne, NE98 1ZZ Telephone 0300 123 2326
Advance thin capitalisation agreements (Statement of Practice 1/12)	The first contact for information about advance thin capitalisation agreements under the Statement of Practice should be the Customer Relationship Manager (CRM) or Customer Contact (CC) of the business concerned, and they will engage the assistance of a transfer pricing specialist. If there is no known CRM or CC, the application may be sent to the local Transfer Pricing team leader
CGT post-transaction value checks	Completed form CG34 which must be received by HMRC at least two months before the relevant filing deadline
Professional bodies (relief for subscriptions) (ITEPA 2003 s 343)	A list of approved professional bodies and learned societies is available on the HMRC website (at www.gov.uk/government/publications/professional-bodies-approved-for-tax-relief-list-3)
General advice on specialist technical issues	See www.gov.uk/contact-hmrc
SDLT transactions	See www.gov.uk/stamp-duty-land-tax
Post-transaction clearances connected to an offshore disclosure	HM Revenue & Customs, WDF Clearance Team, Individual & Small Business Compliance, Compliance Centres, Digital Disclosure Service Room BP3002, Benton Park View, S1250 Newcastle upon Tyne, NE98 1YX Email isbc.disclosureposttransactionclearance@hmrc.gov.uk

[1] Where clearance is sought under any one or more of the sections handled by the Clearance and Counteraction Team, clearance applications may be sent in a single letter to the above Newcastle address for clearances under those sections. The letter should make clear what clearance(s) is required. HMRC acknowledge only those applications that request acknowledgement. An email acknowledgement may be requested. E-mail applications can be sent to reconstructions@hmrc.gov.uk. Attachments to emails should be no larger than 2MB. Self-extracting zip files should not be sent as HMRC software will block them. Security of emails is not guaranteed. Information about market or price sensitive matters, or well known individuals, should not be sent by email.

[2] Non-statutory clearances: Taxpayers may apply for a non-statutory clearance where they require clarification on guidance or legislation for other circumstances after having checked that the transaction is not covered by a more appropriate clearance or approval route. Taxpayers must provide all the necessary information requested in the relevant checklist. HMRC will not give clearances or advice in respect of the application of the 'settlements legislation' in ITTOIA 2005 Pt 5 Ch 5, the tax consequences of executing non-charitable trust deeds or settlements, or the venture capital schemes. See www.gov.uk/non-statutory-clearance-service-guidance.

[3] Courier deliveries to HMRC PO box and BX postcodes should be made to: HM Revenue & Customs, BP8002, Benton Park View, Newcastle Upon Tyne, NE98 1ZZ.

Capital allowances

Rates of capital allowances

Cars
[T2.101]
SEE TOLLEY'S TAX COMPUTATIONS 4.3.
Cars qualify for plant and machinery capital allowances at a rate based on their CO_2 emissions — see table at **T2.106**.
New low-emission cars qualify for first-year allowances — see note 5 at **T2.106**.
Otherwise for **expenditure on or after 1 April 2009 (corporation tax) or 6 April 2009 (income tax)** cars qualify for writing-down allowances and are allocated to the special rate pool if the car's CO_2 emissions exceed 50g/km for expenditure incurred on or after 1 April 2021 (corporation tax) or 6 April 2021 (income tax) (110g/km for expenditure incurred before 1 April 2021 (corporation tax) or 6 April 2021 (income tax), 130g/km for expenditure incurred before 1 April 2018, 160g/km for expenditure incurred before 1 April 2013 (corporation tax) or 6 April 2013 (income tax)) and otherwise to the general pool. See notes 9 and 12 at **T2.106**. Cars with non-business use are allocated to a single asset pool, but the rate of WDA depends on emissions (CAA 2001 ss 104AA, 104F, 208A, 268A–268D; SI 2021/120.)

Dredging
[T2.102]
SEE TOLLEY'S TAX COMPUTATIONS 3.2.

	Expenditure incurred after	% Rate
Writing-down allowance	5 November 1962	4

Know-how
[T2.103]
Expenditure incurred after 31 March 1986: **annual 25% writing-down allowance** (reducing balance basis).

Mineral extraction
[T2.104]
SEE TOLLEY'S TAX COMPUTATIONS 3.3.
First-year allowance: **100% FYA** is available for certain expenditure incurred after 16 April 2002 wholly for the purposes of a North Sea Oil ring-fence trade or on plant and machinery used in such a trade.
Writing-down allowance: for expenditure incurred after 31 March 1986, **10%** for expenditure on the acquisition of a mineral asset and certain pre-trading expenditure, otherwise **25%** (on reducing balance basis) (CAA 2001 s 418.)

Patent rights
[T2.105]
SEE TOLLEY'S TAX COMPUTATIONS 3.4.
Writing-down allowance
Expenditure incurred after 31 March 1986: **annual 25% writing-down allowance** (reducing balance basis) (CAA 2001 s 472.)

Plant and machinery
[T2.106]

	Expenditure incurred after	Expenditure incurred before	Up to pa
Annual investment allowance[1]			
for income tax purposes	**31 December 2018**		**£1,000,000**
	31 December 2015	1 January 2019	£200,000
	5 April 2014	1 January 2016	£500,000
for corporation tax purposes	**31 December 2018**		**£1,000,000**
	31 December 2015	1 January 2019	£200,000
	31 March 2014	1 January 2016	£500,000
First-year allowance (FYA)[13,14]			
			% Rate
Low-emission cars[3]	**16 April 2002**	**1 April 2026**	**100**
Certain refuelling equipment[3]	16 April 2002	1 April 2025	100
Zero-emission goods vehicles[5]			
for income tax purposes	5 April 2010	6 April 2025	100
for corporation tax purposes	31 March 2010	1 April 2025	100
Enterprise zones[6]	**31 March 2012**		**100**
Electric charge-point equipment[7]			
for income tax purposes	**22 November 2016**	**6 April 2026**	**100**
for corporation tax purposes	**22 November 2016**	**1 April 2026**	**100**
Freeport tax sites[18]			
in respect of English Freeports	**Date of tax designation of site**	**1 October 2031**	**100**
in respect of Scottish Green Freeports and Welsh Freeports	**Date of tax designation of site**	**1 October 2034**	**100**
Investment Zone special tax sites[19]	**Date of tax designation of site**	**1 October 2034**	**100**
Full expensing and special rate FYA[20]			
main rate assets	**31 March 2023**		**100**
special rate assets	**31 March 2023**		**50**
Super-deduction and temporary FYA[8]			
main rate assets	31 March 2021	1 April 2023	130
special rate assets	31 March 2021	1 April 2023	50
Energy-saving plant or machinery[2]			
for income tax purposes	31 March 2001	6 April 2020	100
for corporation tax purposes	31 March 2001	1 April 2020	100
Environmentally beneficial plant or machinery[4]			
for income tax purposes	31 March 2003	6 April 2020	100
for corporation tax purposes	31 March 2003	1 April 2020	100
	Chargeable period beginning on or after	**Chargeable period ending before**	
Writing-down allowance (WDA)			
General pool[9]			
for income tax purposes	**6 April 2012**		**18**
for corporation tax purposes	**1 April 2012**		**18**
Special rate pool[9]			
Long-life assets[9,10]			
for income tax purposes	**6 April 2019**		**6**
for corporation tax purposes	**1 April 2019**		**6**
for income tax purposes	6 April 2012	6 April 2019	8
for corporation tax purposes	1 April 2012	1 April 2019	8
Integral features[9,11]			
for income tax purposes	**6 April 2019**		**6**
for corporation tax purposes	**1 April 2019**		**6**
for income tax purposes	6 April 2012	6 April 2019	8
for corporation tax purposes	1 April 2012	1 April 2019	8
Thermal insulation[9,16]			
for income tax purposes	**6 April 2019**		**6**
for corporation tax purposes	**1 April 2019**		**6**
for income tax purposes	6 April 2012	6 April 2019	8
for corporation tax purposes	1 April 2012	1 April 2019	8
Certain cars[9,12]			
for income tax purposes	**6 April 2019**		**6**
for corporation tax purposes	**1 April 2019**		**6**
for income tax purposes	6 April 2012	6 April 2019	8
for corporation tax purposes	1 April 2012	1 April 2019	8

Solar panels[9,15]			
for income tax purposes	**6 April 2019**		**6**
for corporation tax purposes	**1 April 2019**		**6**
for income tax purposes	6 April 2012	6 April 2019	8
for corporation tax purposes	1 April 2012	1 April 2019	8
Cushion gas[9,17]			
for income tax purposes	**6 April 2019**		**6**
for corporation tax purposes	**1 April 2019**		**6**
for income tax purposes	6 April 2012	6 April 2019	8
for corporation tax purposes	1 April 2012	1 April 2019	8

[1] **Annual investment allowance:** The first £1,000,000 (for expenditure on or after 1 January 2019; see table for earlier amounts) of qualifying expenditure incurred in a chargeable period qualifies for the annual investment allowance at 100%. Where a chargeable period spans the date of an increase or decrease, transitional rules apply. The limit is proportionately increased or decreased where the chargeable period is longer or shorter than a year. A group of companies (defined as for company law purposes) can only receive a single allowance. This restriction also applies to certain related businesses or companies. Expenditure on cars and that qualifying for structures and buildings allowance does not qualify (CAA 2001 ss 38A, 38B, 51A–51N; FA 2019 s 32, Sch 13; FA 2021, s 15; FA 2022 s 12; F(No 2)A 2023 s 8; FA 2024 s 1).
SEE TOLLEY'S TAX COMPUTATIONS 4.3.

[2] **Energy-saving plant or machinery:** The allowance is withdrawn for expenditure on or after 1 April 2020 (corporation tax) and 6 April 2020 (income tax). The allowances were available for investment by *any* business in designated energy-saving plant and machinery in accordance with the Government's Energy Technology Product List. 100% first-year allowances were not available for expenditure incurred on or after 1 April 2012 (corporation tax) or 6 April 2012 (income tax) on plant or machinery to generate renewable electricity or heat where tariff payments are received under either of the renewable energy schemes introduced by the Department of Energy and Climate Change. The restriction applied from April 2014 for combined heat and power equipment (CAA 2001 ss 45A–45C, 46; SI 2018/268; SI 2019/501). The product lists are available at www.gov.uk/energy-technology-list.

[3] **Low-emission cars:** The allowance is given on new cars which are either electrically propelled or emit not more than 0g/km of CO_2 for expenditure incurred on or after 1 April 2021 (50g/m for expenditure incurred before 1 April 2021, 75g/km for expenditure incurred before 1 April 2018, 95g/km for expenditure incurred before 1 April 2015, 110g/km for expenditure incurred before 1 April 2013, 120g/km for expenditure incurred before 1 April 2008), registered after 16 April 2002. **Certain refuelling equipment:** The allowance is withdrawn for expenditure on or after 1 April 2025. The allowance was given on new plant and machinery to refuel vehicles in a gas refuelling station with natural gas, hydrogen fuels, or (for expenditure on or after 1 April 2008) biogas. For expenditure incurred after 31 March 2013 cars provided for leasing do not qualify for the FYA (CAA 2001 ss 45D, 45E, 46; SI 2021/120).
SEE TOLLEY'S TAX COMPUTATIONS 4.3.

[4] **Environmentally beneficial plant or machinery:** The allowance is withdrawn for expenditure on or after 1 April 2020 (corporation tax) and 6 April 2020 (income tax). The allowances were available for expenditure by *any* business on new and unused designated technologies and products which satisfy the relevant environmental criteria in accordance with the Government's technologies or products lists (CAA 2001 ss 45H–45J, 46; SI 2003/2076; SI 2019/499). The product lists are available at www.gov.uk/government/publications/water-efficient-enhanced-capital-allowances.

[5] **Zero-emission goods vehicles:** The allowance is withdrawn for expenditure on or after 1 April 2025 (corporation tax) and 6 April 2025 (income tax). The allowance was given on new (and not second hand) vehicles which cannot under any circumstances produce CO_2 emissions when driven and which are of a design primarily suited to the conveyance of goods or burden. The expenditure is limited to €85 million per undertaking (as defined) over the period for which the provisions apply. The allowance is not available where another State aid has been or will be received towards the qualifying expenditure. Other exclusions apply (CAA 2001 ss 45DA–45DB, 212T; SI 2017/1304).

[6] **Enterprise zones:** For expenditure incurred for the purpose of a qualifying activity in the period ending on the later of 31 March 2021 or eight years from the date the area is (or is treated as) designated, 100% first-year allowances are available for companies which invest in unused (not second hand) plant or machinery for use primarily in designated assisted areas within certain enterprise zones. Expenditure must be incurred for the purposes of broadly a new or expanding business carried on by the company, must not be replacement expenditure and is limited to €125 million per single investment project (as defined) over the eight years. Exclusions apply. See SI 2014/3183, SI 2015/2047, SI 2016/751 and SI 2018/485 for details of the current enterprise zones (CAA 2001 ss 45K–45N, 212U; SI 2020/260).

[7] **Electric charge-point equipment:** 100% first-year allowance is available for expenditure on new (not second hand), unused electric vehicle charging point equipment installed solely for the purpose of charging electric vehicles (CAA 2001 s 45EA; F(No 2)A 2023 s 9).

[8] **Super-deduction and 50% first-year allowances:** For qualifying expenditure incurred from 1 April 2021 up to and including 31 March 2023, companies can claim in the period of investment: *(a)* a super-deduction providing allowances of 130% on unused (not second hand) plant and machinery that ordinarily qualifies for 18% main rate writing down allowances; *(b)* a first year allowance of 50% on unused (not second hand) plant and machinery that ordinarily qualifies for 6% special rate writing down allowances. The rate of the super-deduction requires apportioning where super-deduction expenditure is incurred in an accounting period that straddles 1 April 2023 (FA 2021 ss 9–14).

[9] **WDAs** are calculated either at the general rate or the special rate on a reducing balance basis. For special rate expenditure for chargeable periods beginning before 1 April 2019 (corporation tax) or 6 April 2019 (income tax) and ending on or after that date a hybrid rate applies, calculated by time apportionment of

the 8% and 6% rates. The special rate for ring fence trades is 10%. For chargeable periods beginning on or after 6 April 2008 (income tax) or 1 April 2008 (corporation tax), a WDA of up to £1,000 can be claimed in respect of the main pool and/or the special rate pool where the unrelieved expenditure in the pool concerned is £1,000 or less.

10 **Long-life assets:** Applies to plant or machinery with an expected working life, when new, of 25 years or more where expenditure on long-life assets in a year is more than £100,000 (in the case of companies the de minimis limit is £100,000 divided by one plus the number of associated companies). It does not apply to plant or machinery in a building used wholly or mainly as, or for purposes ancillary to, a dwelling-house, retail shop, showroom, hotel or office; cars; or sea-going ships and railway assets acquired before 1 January 2011. Expenditure qualifies as special rate expenditure, see note 9 above regarding the hybrid rate applying for periods spanning a change of rate (CAA 2001 ss 90–104E, Sch 3 para 20).
SEE TOLLEY'S TAX COMPUTATIONS 4.5.

11 **Integral features** of a building are electrical systems (including lighting systems); cold water systems; space or water heating systems, powered ventilation systems, air cooling or purification and any floor or ceiling comprised in such systems; lifts, escalators and moving walkways and external solar shading. Expenditure qualifies as special rate expenditure, see note 9 above regarding the hybrid rate applying for periods spanning a change of rate (CAA 2001 ss 33A, 104A–104E).
SEE TOLLEY'S TAX COMPUTATIONS 4.5.

12 **Cars:** For expenditure on and after 1 April 2009 (corporation tax), 6 April 2009 (income tax), cars with CO_2 emissions exceeding 50g/km for expenditure incurred on or after 1 April 2021 (corporation tax) or 6 April 2021 (income tax) (110g/km for expenditure incurred before 1 April 2021 (corporation tax) or 6 April 2021 (income tax), 130g/km for expenditure incurred before 1 April 2018, 160g/km for expenditure incurred before 1 April 2013 (corporation tax) or 6 April 2013 (income tax)) are allocated to the special rate pool. All other cars will go into the general pool. See note 9 above regarding the hybrid rate applying for periods spanning a change of rate. From 1 April 2025 (corporation tax) or 6 April 2025 (income tax), double cab pick-up vehicles will be treated as cars for the purposes of capital allowances (CAA 2001 ss 104A–104E; SI 2021/120).
SEE TOLLEY'S TAX COMPUTATIONS 4.3.

13 **First-year tax credits:** For expenditure incurred on or after 1 April 2008 and before 1 April 2020, a company can surrender a tax loss attributable to first-year allowances for energy-saving or environmentally beneficial equipment (see notes 2 and 4 above) in exchange for a cash payment from the Government. The cash payment is equal to a percentage of the loss surrendered, subject to an upper limit of the greater of £250,000 and the company's PAYE and NIC liability for the period concerned. For chargeable periods beginning before 1 April 2018 the percentage was fixed at 19%. For chargeable periods beginning on or after 1 April 2018 the percentage is 2/3 of the corporation tax rate chargeable (CAA 2001 Sch A1; SI 2013/464).

14 **First year allowances**, where applicable, are available on expenditure over the annual investment allowance level or on which annual investment allowance has not been claimed, which would otherwise qualify for writing down allowance at 18% in the general plant and machinery pool.

15 **Solar panels**: Expenditure on solar panels qualifies as special rate expenditure, see note 9 above regarding the hybrid rate applying for periods spanning a change of rate (CAA 2001 s 104A–104E).

16 **Thermal insulation**: Expenditure on thermal insulation qualifies as special rate expenditure, see note 9 above regarding the hybrid rate applying for periods spanning a change of rate (CAA 2001 ss 28, 104A–104E).

17 **Cushion gas**: Expenditure on cushion gas qualifies as special rate expenditure, see note 9 above regarding the hybrid rate applying for periods spanning a change of rate (CAA 2001 ss 70J, 104A–104E).

18 **Freeport tax sites**: Expenditure on unused (not second hand) plant or machinery for use primarily in designated tax sites within Freeports for companies only. See SI 2021/1193, SI 2021/1194, SI 2021/1195, SI 2021/1389, SI 2022/184, SI 2022/185, SI 2022/186, SI 2022/643, SI 2022/972, SI 2022/973, SI 2024/71, SI 2024/380, SI 2024/671, SI 2024/1035 for details of the current freeport tax sites. (CAA 2001 ss 45P–45R; FA 2021 s 113, Sch 22; FA 2022 s 13; F(No 2)A 2023 s 332).

19 **Investment Zone special tax sites**: Expenditure on unused (not second hand) plant or machinery for use primarily in a special tax site for companies only. See SI 2024/383 for details of current investment zone special tax sites. (CAA 2001 ss 45P–45R; FA 2021 s 113, Sch 22; FA 2022 s 13; F(No 2)A 2023 ss 331, 332, Sch 23).

20 **Full expensing and special rate first-year allowances:** For qualifying expenditure incurred from 1 April 2023, companies can claim one of two first-year allowances: *(a)* a 100% first-year allowance for main rate expenditure, known as **full expensing**, on unused (not second hand) plant and machinery that ordinarily qualifies for 18% writing down allowances; *(b)* a 50% first-year allowance for special rate expenditure on unused (not second hand) plant and machinery that ordinarily qualifies for 6% writing down allowances. Originally these FYAs were temporary and applied only to expenditure incurred before 1 April 2026, but they have now been extended indefinitely. The government will consider an extension to include plant and machinery for leasing when fiscal conditions allow. (CAA 2001 ss 45S, 45T, 59A–59C; F(No 2)A 2023 s 7; FA 2024 s 1).

Cars: Car hire, see **T6.121**.

Research and development
[T2.108]

SEE TOLLEY'S TAX COMPUTATIONS 3.5.

	Expenditure incurred after	% Rate
Allowance in year 1	**5 November 1962**	**100**

Note: Land and houses are excluded.

Structures and buildings allowance
[T2.109]

	Annual rate on or after	Annual rate before	% Rate
General			
for income tax purposes	**6 April 2020**		**3**
	28 October 2018	6 April 2020	2
for corporation tax purposes	**1 April 2020**		**3**
	28 October 2018	1 April 2020	2
Freeport tax sites			
for income tax purposes	Date of tax designation of site		10
for corporation tax purposes	Date of tax designation of site		10
Investment Zone special tax sites			
for income tax purposes	Date of tax designation of site		10
for corporation tax purposes	Date of tax designation of site		10

Applies on a straight-line basis to qualifying construction expenditure on new non-residential structures and buildings (but not land) where contract for construction is entered into after 28 October 2018. Relief applies to UK and overseas structures and buildings, including new conversions or renovations, where the business is within the charge to UK tax. Where a chargeable period spans 1 or 6 April 2020 the rate of 2% applies for days before the relevant date and 3% for the days after (CAA 2001 Part 2A; SI 2019/1087; FA 2020 s 29; FA 2021 s 114, Sch 22; FA 2022 s 13; F(No 2)A 2023 ss 331, 332, Sch 23; SI 2024/574).

The annual rate for Freeport tax sites will apply where the first contract for construction is entered into on or after the date the tax site is designated, and the building or structure must be brought into qualifying use before 1 October 2034 (1 October 2031 for freeports in England). See SI 2021/1193, SI 2021/1194, SI 2021/1195, SI 2021/1389, SI 2022/184, SI 2022/185, SI 2022/186, SI 2022/643, SI 2022/972, SI 2022/973, SI 2024/71, SI 2024/380, SI 2024/671, SI 2024/1035 for details of the current freeport tax sites (CAA 2001 ss 270AA(5), 270BNA–270BNC; FA 2021 Sch 22; FA 2022 s 13; F(No 2)A 2023 s 332).

The annual rate for Investment Zone special tax sites will apply where construction begins, expenditure is incurred and the building or structure is brought into non-residential use for the purposes of a qualifying activity between the date the special tax site is designated and 1 October 2034. See SI 2024/383 for details of current investment zone special tax sites. (CAA 2001 ss 270AA(5), 270BNA–270BNC; FA 2021 Sch 22; F(No 2)A 2023 ss 331, 332, Sch 23).

Capital gains

Annual exempt amount

[T3.101]

(TCGA 1992 s 1K, Sch 1C; SI 2020/333; FA 2021 s 40; FA 2023 s 8)

Individuals[a], personal representatives[b] and certain trusts[c]

[T3.102]

SEE TOLLEY'S TAX COMPUTATIONS 201.2.

Exempt amount of net gains	2020–21	2021–22	2022–23	2023–24	2024–25	2025–26
	£12,300	£12,300	£12,300	£6,000	£3,000	£3,000

[a] For 2024–25 and earlier years, an individual who claims to use the remittance basis for a tax year is not entitled to the capital gains tax annual exempt amount for that year. This does not apply if the individual's unremitted foreign income and gains for the year are less than £2,000 (TCGA 1992 s 1K(6); ITA 2007 s 809D). For 2025–26 onwards, a new resident individual who makes a foreign gain claim for a tax year under the foreign income and gains regime is not entitled to the capital gains tax annual exempt amount for that year.
[b] Year of death and following two years (maximum) (TCGA 1992 s 1K(7)).
[c] Trusts for disabled persons as defined. Exemption divided by number of qualifying settlements created (after 9 March 1981) by one settlor, subject to a minimum of one-tenth (TCGA 1992 Sch 1C; FA 2005 Sch 1A).

Trusts generally[a]

[T3.103]

SEE TOLLEY'S TAX COMPUTATIONS 228.1.

Exempt amount of net gains	2020–21	2021–22	2022–23	2023–24	2024–25[b]	2025–26[b]
	£6,150	£6,150	£6,150	£3,000	£1,500	£1,500

[a] Exemption divided by number of qualifying settlements created (after 6 June 1978) by one settlor, subject to a minimum of one-fifth (TCGA 1992 Sch 1C).
[b] The annual exempt amount for trusts generally will remain unchanged at £1,500 for 2026–27 and subsequent years (FA 2023 s 8).

Chattel exemption

[T3.104]

SEE TOLLEY'S TAX COMPUTATIONS 212.1.
(TCGA 1992 s 262)

	Disposals exemption	Marginal relief: Maximum chargeable gain
From 1989–90 onwards	£6,000	5/3 excess over £6,000

Rates of tax

[T3.105]

SEE TOLLEY'S TAX COMPUTATIONS 201.1.
(TCGA 1992 s 1H; F(No 2)A 2024 s 6)

2025–26*	**Gains arising in respect of carried interest**		
	Individuals		**32%**
	Personal representatives		**32%**
	Other gains (including interests in residential properties (where not exempt)		
	Individuals	• to income tax basic rate limit £37,700 (see note)	**18%**
		• above income tax basic rate limit £37,700	**24%**
	Trusts and personal representatives		**24%**
2024–25*	**Gains accruing on the disposal of interests in residential properties (where not exempt)**		
	Individuals	• to income tax basic rate limit £37,700 (see note)	18%
		• above income tax basic rate limit £37,700	24%
	Trusts and personal representatives		24%
	Gains arising in respect of carried interest		
	Individuals	• to income tax basic rate limit £37,700 (see note)	18%
		• above income tax basic rate limit £37,700	28%
	Personal representatives		28%
	Other gains		
	Individuals	• to income tax basic rate limit £37,700 (see note)	
		—disposals before 30 October 2024	10%
		—disposals on or after 30 October 2024	18%
		• above income tax basic rate limit £37,700	
		—disposals before 30 October 2024	20%
		—disposals on or after 30 October 2024	24%
	Trusts and personal representatives		
		—disposals before 30 October 2024	20%
		—disposals on or after 30 October 2024	24%
2023–24*	**Gains accruing on the disposal of interests in residential properties (where not exempt), and gains arising in respect of carried interest**		
	Individuals	• to income tax basic rate limit £37,700 (see note)	18%
		• above income tax basic rate limit £37,700	28%
	Trusts and personal representatives		28%
	Other gains		
	Individuals	• to income tax basic rate limit £37,700 (see note)	10%
		• above income tax basic rate limit £37,700	20%
	Trusts and personal representatives		20%
2022–23*	**Gains accruing on the disposal of interests in residential properties (where not exempt), and gains arising in respect of carried interest**		
	Individuals	• to income tax basic rate limit £37,700 (see note)	18%
		• above income tax basic rate limit £37,700	28%
	Trusts and personal representatives		28%
	Other gains		
	Individuals	• to income tax basic rate limit £37,700 (see note)	10%
		• above income tax basic rate limit £37,700	20%
	Trusts and personal representatives		20%
2021–22*	**Gains accruing on the disposal of interests in residential properties (where not exempt), and gains arising in respect of carried interest**		
	Individuals	• to income tax basic rate limit £37,700 (see note)	18%
		• above income tax basic rate limit £37,700	28%
	Trusts and personal representatives		28%
	Other gains		
	Individuals	• to income tax basic rate limit £37,700 (see note)	10%
		• above income tax basic rate limit £37,700	20%
	Trusts and personal representatives		20%

2020–21*	**Gains accruing on the disposal of interests in residential properties (where not exempt), and gains arising in respect of carried interest**		
	Individuals	• to income tax basic rate limit £37,500 (see note)	18%
		• above income tax basic rate limit £37,500	28%
	Trusts and personal representatives		28%
	Other gains		
	Individuals	• to income tax basic rate limit £37,500 (see note)	10%
		• above income tax basic rate limit £37,500	20%
	Trusts and personal representatives		20%
2019–20*	**Gains accruing on the disposal of interests in residential properties (where not exempt), and gains arising in respect of carried interest**		
	Individuals	• to income tax basic rate limit £37,500 (see note)	18%
		• above income tax basic rate limit £37,500	28%
	Trusts and personal representatives		28%
	Other gains		
	Individuals	• to income tax basic rate limit £37,500 (see note)	10%
		• above income tax basic rate limit £37,500	20%
	Trusts and personal representatives		20%

* A rate of **14% applies where business asset disposal relief (formerly known as entrepreneurs' relief) or investors' relief is claimed** — see **T3.111**. For disposals before 6 April 2025, the rate was 10%. For disposals on or after 6 April 2026, the rate will be increased to 18%. Anti-forestalling measures apply in respect of the increases in the rate.
Anti-forestalling measures also apply in respect of the increase in CGT rates for disposals on or after 30 October 2024.
The rate of tax for an individual is determined by treating gains as the top slice of income. **Scottish taxpayers:** The Scottish basic rate limit (see **T6.102**) does not apply to determine the rate of capital gains tax payable.
Carried interest: For 2026–27 onwards, carried interest gains will be subject to income tax.

Trusts for vulnerable persons: Gains taxed at beneficiary's rates (on beneficiary if UK resident or on trustees if beneficiary not UK-resident) (FA 2005 ss 30–32).
SEE TOLLEY'S TAX COMPUTATIONS **228.2**.

Share identification rules

[T3.106]

SEE TOLLEY'S TAX COMPUTATIONS 230.1, 230.2.

(TCGA 1992 ss 104–106A)

For disposals on or after 6 April 2008 by individuals, trustees or personal representatives, shares and securities of the same class in the same company are identified with acquisitions in the following order[2]:
- acquisitions on the same day as the disposal;
- acquisitions within 30 days after the day of disposal on a first in/first out basis[1];
- shares comprised in a single pool incorporating all other shares of the same class, whenever acquired.

For the purposes of corporation tax on chargeable gains, disposals of shares etc are identified with acquisitions in the following order:
- same day acquisitions;
- acquisitions within the previous nine days on a first in/first out basis;
- the pool of shares acquired after 31 March 1982;
- any shares held at 31 March 1982;
- any shares acquired on or before 6 April 1965 on a last in/first out basis;
- (if shares disposed of still not fully matched) subsequent acquisitions.

[1] The 30-day matching rule does not apply in relation to acquisitions where the individual making the disposal is not (or is not treated as) resident in the UK at the time of the acquisition.
[2] Different rules apply for SIP shares, exempt employee shareholder shares, BES shares, community investment tax relief shares, relevant EMI shares, EIS shares, VCT shares, SEIS shares, EOT exempt shares and social investment tax relief shares.

Business asset disposal relief

[T3.107]

SEE TOLLEY'S TAX COMPUTATIONS 206.1.

(TCGA 1992 ss 169H–169V; FA 2020 s 23, Sch 3)

Business asset disposal relief (formerly known as entrepreneurs' relief) applies to disposals by an individual on or after 6 April 2008 of:
- all or part of a trade carried on alone or in partnership;
- assets of such a trade following cessation; or
- shares or securities in the individual's personal trading company.

Personal trading company is broadly one in which the individual holds at least 5% of ordinary share capital, 5% of voting rights, and, additionally for disposals after 28 October 2018, by virtue of their shareholding, at least 5% of the distributable profits and 5% of assets available for distribution to equity holders on a winding up, and/or is beneficially entitled to at least 5% of the proceeds on the disposal of all the company's ordinary share capital. Where the shareholding is diluted below 5% as a result of a new share issue after 5 April 2019, an election can be made to allow relief for gains up to that time, subject to conditions.

Where a disposal of shares or of an interest in the assets of a partnership qualifies for relief, an associated disposal of assets owned by the individual and used by the company or partnership also qualifies for relief. For disposals on or after 18 March 2015, to qualify the claimant must generally reduce his participation in the business by also disposing of a minimum 5% of the shares of the company carrying on the business, or (where the business is carried on in partnership) of a minimum 5% share in the assets of the partnership carrying on the business. However, the disposal may be of less than a 5% share in the assets of the partnership providing the claimant disposes of the whole of his interest and owned 5% or more of the assets for a continuous period of three years in the eight years preceding the disposal. In addition, for assets acquired on or after 13 June 2016, the asset must have been held for three years before disposal.

Where a qualifying disposal is not of shares or securities in the individual's personal trading company, the relief is given only in respect of 'relevant business assets' comprised in the qualifying business disposal (ie assets used for purpose of the business but excluding shares and securities and other assets held as investments). Relief is not available for disposals of goodwill on or after 3 December 2014 to a close company to which the seller is related unless the business is transferred to a company controlled by 5 or fewer persons or by its directors and the claimant holds less than 5% of the shares, and less than 5% of the voting power, in the acquiring company. Relief will still also be due where the claimant does hold 5% or more of the shares or voting power provided the transfer of the business to the company is part of arrangements for the company to be sold to a new, independent owner.

Trustees can claim relief where a qualifying beneficiary has an interest in the business concerned.

Relief also applies to a disposal by an employee or officer of a trading company (or one or more companies in same trading group) of relevant EMI shares (as defined). Relief applies from 6 April 2013 where the shares were acquired on or after 6 April 2012.

The relief is available where the relevant conditions are met throughout a period of two years (one year for disposals before 6 April 2019, and for cessations of a business or trading company status before 29 October 2018). The relief operates by charging qualifying net gains to CGT at **14%** and is subject to a lifetime limit. The rate was 10% for disposals before 6 April 2025 and will be increased to 18% for disposals on or after 6 April 2026. The **lifetime limit is £1 million of gains** for disposals made on or after 11 March 2020, though anti-forestalling rules may apply for contracts exchanged before 11 March 2020 but not completed until after that date and for certain reorganisations and share exchanges made before 11 March 2020. The lifetime limit was £10 million for disposals before 11 March 2020; £5 million for disposals before 6 April 2011; £2 million for disposals before 23 June 2010; £1 million for disposals before 6 April 2010. Disposals before 6 April 2008 do not count towards the limit. Relief given to trustees counts towards the limit of the qualifying beneficiary.

Transitional rules apply to allow relief to be claimed in certain circumstances where a gain made before 6 April 2008 is deferred and becomes chargeable on or after that date. In addition, gains which would have originally accrued on or after 3 December 2014 but which are deferred into the Enterprise Investment Scheme (see **T3.111**) or Social Investment Tax Relief (see **T3.111**) remain eligible for relief when the deferred gain becomes chargeable.

Investors' relief

[T3.108]

SEE TOLLEY'S TAX COMPUTATIONS 215.1.

(TCGA 1992 ss 169VA–169VY, Sch 7ZB)

Relief is available for gains accruing on the disposal of ordinary shares in an unlisted trading company, held for a period of at least three years starting on or after 6 April 2016, which are newly issued to the claimant and acquired for new consideration on or after 17 March 2016. Generally neither the investor nor a person connected to them can be an employee or officer of the company or a connected company, though some exceptions apply. The relief operates by charging relevant gains to CGT at **14%** and is subject to a lifetime limit. The rate was 10% for disposals before 6 April 2025 and will be increased to 18% for disposals on or after 6 April 2026. The **lifetime limit is £1 million of gains** for disposals on or after 30 October 2024. Previously it was £10 million. Anti-forestalling measures may apply in relation both to the increase in rates and the reduction in the lifetime limit.

Relief can be claimed by trustees where an eligible beneficiary has an interest in settled property which includes the qualifying shares.

Other reliefs

[T3.109]

The following is a summary of the other main capital gains tax reliefs and exemptions.

Charities and CASCs

[T3.110]

Gains accruing to charities and Community Amateur Sports Clubs which are both applicable and applied for charitable purposes are exempt.

Individuals

[T3.111]

Business asset disposal relief (formerly known as entrepreneurs' relief) (see **T3.107**) **SEE TOLLEY'S TAX COMPUTATIONS 206.1 ONWARDS.**	Gains on specified assets chargeable at 14% rate up to lifetime limit (10% for disposals before 6 April 2025).
Companies owned by employee-ownership trusts	Relief from capital gains tax is available for disposals by a person other than a company of shares in either a trading company which is not a member of a group, or a parent company of a trading group, where the disposal is to a trust with specified characteristics. The disposal is treated as being made at no gain/no loss if the settlement is for the benefit of all eligible employees of the company or group and the settlement acquires a controlling interest in the company during the tax year in which the disposal is made. For disposals on or after 30 October 2024, the trustees must be UK-resident and must take all reasonable steps to ensure that the consideration does not exceed market value. With effect from the same date, the vendors must not have control of the trust. Further conditions apply.
Compensation (injury to person, profession or vocation)	Exempt.
Decorations for valour (acquired otherwise than for money or money's worth)	Gain exempt.
Employee shareholder shares (see **T6.181**) **SEE TOLLEY'S TAX COMPUTATIONS 218.2.**	Gains on disposals of shares which were worth up to £50,000 on acquisition are exempt, provided the Employee Shareholder Agreement was entered into before 1 December 2016 (or 2 December 2016 where professional advice was given in relation to the share offer on 23 November 2016 before 1.30pm). A lifetime limit of £100,000 applies to exempt gains on disposal of shares acquired under Employee Shareholder Agreements entered into after 16 March 2016.
Enterprise Investment Scheme (see **T6.167**) **SEE TOLLEY'S TAX COMPUTATIONS 211.1 ONWARDS.**	Gain on disposal after relevant three-year period exempt to extent full relief given on shares. Deferral relief is available on gains on assets where the disposal proceeds are reinvested in EIS shares within one year before and three years after the disposal.
Foreign currency acquired for personal expenditure	Gain exempt.
Gifts for public benefit, works of art, historic buildings etc	No chargeable gain/allowable loss.
Gifts of pre-eminent objects	Donors who gift pre-eminent objects to the nation will receive a reduction in their UK tax liability of 30% of the value of the object they are donating. The tax reduction can be against income or capital gains tax and can be spread forward across a period of up to five years starting with the tax year in which the object is offered. The gift must be accepted as pre-eminent by Arts Council England under the Cultural Gifts Scheme. See **T4.105** for relief applying to companies.
Gilt-edged stock	No chargeable gain/allowable loss.
Hold-over relief for gifts **SEE TOLLEY'S TAX COMPUTATIONS 213.1 ONWARDS.**	Restricted to: (1) gifts of business assets (including unquoted shares in trading companies and holding companies of trading groups). Relief is not available on the transfer of shares or securities to a company; (2) gifts of heritage property; (3) gifts to heritage maintenance funds; (4) gifts to political parties; and (5) gifts which are chargeable transfers for inheritance tax. Where available, transferee's acquisition cost treated as reduced by held-over gain.

Investors' relief (see **T3.108**) **SEE TOLLEY'S TAX COMPUTATIONS 215.1 ONWARDS.**	Gains on qualifying ordinary shares in an unlisted trading company chargeable at 14% rate up to lifetime limit (10% for disposals before 6 April 2025).
Married persons or civil partners living together **SEE TOLLEY'S TAX COMPUTATIONS 218.1 ONWARDS.**	No chargeable gain/allowable loss on transfers between spouses or civil partners. For disposals after 5 April 2023, this treatment extends to separating spouses or partners for three tax years after the year in which they cease to live together and to assets transferred as part of a formal divorce agreement. A spouse or partner who retains an interest in the former family home may claim principal private residence relief on a later sale after 5 April 2023. Where an individual transfers their interest in the home after 5 April 2023 to their spouse or civil partner and are entitled to part of the proceeds on a subsequent sale, the same tax treatment applies to the proceeds as applied on the original transfer.
Motor vehicles	Gain exempt.
Principal private residence **SEE TOLLEY'S TAX COMPUTATIONS 223.1 ONWARDS.**	Gain exempt if property is main residence throughout period of ownership, or throughout the period of ownership except for all or any part of the last 9 months of that period (18 months for disposals before 6 April 2020). A 36-month period applies where property is disposed of by an individual who is, or whose spouse or civil partner is, a disabled person or long-term resident of a care home, provided that neither holds an interest in any other dwelling on which private residence relief can be claimed. Property is treated as not being occupied as a residence for tax years when neither the taxpayer nor their spouse or civil partner is tax-resident in the territory in which the property is situated, and they do not stay overnight at the property at least 90 times during the year (pro-rated for part tax years). Period of ownership does not include any period before 31 March 1982. Certain other periods of absence qualify for exemption.
If residence is partly let, exemption for the let part is limited to the smaller of–	(1) exemption on owner-occupied part; and (2) £40,000*. *For disposals after 5 April 2020 the relief is only available if owner is in shared-occupancy with the tenant.
Qualifying corporate bonds **SEE TOLLEY'S TAX COMPUTATIONS 224.1 ONWARDS.**	No chargeable gain (for loans made before 17 March 1998, allowable loss in certain cases if all or part of loss is irrecoverable).
Seed enterprise investment scheme (see **T6.169**) **SEE TOLLEY'S TAX COMPUTATIONS 227.1 ONWARDS.**	Reinvestment relief may be claimed where an individual realises capital gains on disposals of assets in a tax year and in the same year makes investments that qualify for, and he claims, the main seed enterprise investment scheme (SEIS) relief from income tax. For disposals of assets in 2012–13 the relief applies to the full qualifying re-invested amount. From 2013–14 the relief applies to half the qualifying re-invested amount. SEIS shares can be treated as issued in the previous tax year as a result of a SEIS income tax relief carry-back claim. SEIS re-investment relief then also has effect as if those shares had been issued on a day in the previous tax year. The maximum exemption is £100,000 (£50,000 for 2022–23 and earlier years; £100,000 for 2012–13). A disposal of shares on which SEIS income tax relief has been given and not withdrawn is exempt.
Social investment tax relief (see **T6.171**) **SEE TOLLEY'S TAX COMPUTATIONS 231.1 ONWARDS.**	Deferral relief is available for gains arising on assets in the period 6 April 2014 to 5 April 2023 where the disposal proceeds are reinvested in shares or debt investments which qualify for the social investment tax relief (SITR) income tax relief and investor is UK-resident. The qualifying investment must be made in the period from one year before to three years after the disposal. Limit of £1 million of gains which can be relieved in a tax year. A gain on a disposal of shares on which SITR income tax relief has been given and not withdrawn is exempt from capital gains tax where shares held for at least 3 years. The SITR closed to any new investments from 6 April 2023.
Venture capital trusts (see **T6.173**) **SEE TOLLEY'S TAX COMPUTATIONS 32.3.**	Gain on disposal of shares by original investor exempt if company still a venture capital trust. Exemption applies only to shares acquired up to the permitted maximum of £200,000 per year of assessment. Deferral relief was available on gains on assets where the disposal proceeds were reinvested in VCT shares issued before 6 April 2004 and within one year before or after the disposal. This relief is withdrawn for shares issued after that date.

Businesses

[T3.112]

Roll-over relief for replacement of business assets
SEE TOLLEY'S TAX COMPUTATIONS 103.3, 226.1 ONWARDS.
(TCGA 1992 s 155)

Qualifying assets:
Buildings and land both occupied and used for the purposes of the trade.
Fixed plant and machinery.
Ships, aircraft and hovercraft.
Satellites, space stations and spacecraft.
Goodwill[1].
Milk and potato quotas[1].
Ewe and suckler cow premium quotas[1].
Fish quotas[1].
Payment entitlement under farmers' single payment scheme[1].
Payment entitlement under farmers' basic payment scheme[1].
Lloyd's syndicate rights.

[1] From 1 April 2002 onwards, subject to transitional rules, these items are removed from the list for companies only (as they fall within the intangible assets regime from that date).

[2] The 'replacement' assets must be acquired within 12 months before or three years after the disposal of the old asset. Both assets must be within any of the above classes. Holdover relief is available where the new asset is a depreciating asset (having a predictable useful life not exceeding 60 years).

Roll-over relief on the transfer of a business ('incorporation relief')
SEE TOLLEY'S TAX COMPUTATIONS 213.3.
(TCGA 1992 s 162)

On incorporation of a business, the assets of the business are transferred to a company which then carries on the business in succession to the former proprietor. Gains realised on the transfer can be rolled over where the transfer is wholly or partly in consideration for the issue of shares. Relief is automatic (no claim is required).

See **T4.104** for disincorporation relief for companies.

Personal representatives

[T3.113]

Allowable expenses
(SP 2/04)
Expenses allowable for the costs of establishing title in computing chargeable gains on disposal of assets in a deceased person's estate: deaths occurring after 5 April 2004. (HMRC accepts computations based either on the scale or on the actual allowable expenditure incurred.)

Gross value of estate	Allowable expenditure
Up to £50,000	1.8% of the probate value of the assets sold by the personal representatives.
Between £50,001 and £90,000	£900, to be divided between all the assets of the estate in proportion to the probate values and allowed in those proportions on assets sold by the personal representatives.
Between £90,001 and £400,000	1% of the probate value of the assets sold.
Between £400,001 and £500,000	£4,000, to be divided between all the assets of the estate in proportion to the probate values and allowed in those proportions on assets sold by the personal representatives.
Between £500,001 and £1,000,000	0.8% of the probate value of the assets sold.
Between £1,000,001 and £5,000,000	£8,000 to be divided between all the assets of the estate in proportion to the probate values and allowed in those proportions on assets sold by the personal representatives.
Exceeding £5,000,000	0.16% of the probate value of the assets sold subject to a maximum of £10,000.

Trustees

[T3.114]

Allowable expenses
(SP 2/04)

Expenses allowable in computing chargeable gains of corporate trustees in the administration of trusts and estates: acquisition, disposals and deemed disposals after 5 April 2004. (HMRC accepts computations based either on the scale or on the actual allowable expenditure incurred.)

Transfers of assets to beneficiaries etc	
(a) Quoted stocks and shares	
(i) One beneficiary	£25 per holding.
(ii) More than one beneficiary	£25 per holding, divided equally between the beneficiaries.
(b) Unquoted shares	As (a) above, plus any exceptional expenditure.
(c) Other assets	As (a) above, plus any exceptional expenditure.
Actual disposals and acquisitions	
(a) Quoted stocks and shares	Investment fee as charged by the trustees (where a comprehensive annual management fee is charged, the investment fee is taken to be £0.25 per £100 of the sale or purchase moneys).
(b) Unquoted shares	As (a) above, plus actual valuation costs.
(c) Other assets	Investment fee (as (a) above), subject to a maximum of £75, plus actual valuation costs.
Deemed disposals by trustees	
(a) Quoted stocks and shares	£8 per holding.
(b) Unquoted shares	Actual valuation costs.
(c) Other assets	Actual valuation costs.

Indexation allowance – corporation tax on chargeable gains
[T3.115]
SEE TOLLEY'S TAX COMPUTATIONS 214.1.
(TCGA 1992 ss 53–57, 109)

For corporation tax purposes, an indexation allowance is given as a deduction in calculating gains on disposals from the amount realised (or deemed to be realised) on disposal. Indexation allowance is 'frozen' from 1 January 2018, so for disposals on or after this date the allowance is calculated up to December 2017. Indexation allowance is calculated by multiplying each item of allowable expenditure by:

$$\frac{RD - RI}{RI}$$

Where:
  RD is the retail prices index figure for December 2017 (or month of disposal if earlier);
  RI is the retail prices index for month of expenditure (or March 1982 if later).

Indexation allowance can only be used to reduce or extinguish a gain. It cannot be used to create or increase a capital loss. It is not available to individuals, trustees and personal representatives. See **T3.116** for RPI values.

The figure given by the above formula is commonly called the '*indexation factor*'. The consistent calculation of the indexation factor to more than three decimal places is generally accepted. The indexation factors for disposals by companies in December 2017 (used also for disposals after December 2017 — see above) are:

Date of acquisition	Jan	Feb	Mar	Apr	May	Jun
1982	—	—	2.501	2.432	2.407	2.398
1983	2.366	2.352	2.346	2.300	2.286	2.278
1984	2.202	2.189	2.179	2.137	2.126	2.118
1985	2.049	2.025	1.997	1.934	1.921	1.915
1986	1.889	1.879	1.875	1.847	1.842	1.844
1987	1.781	1.770	1.764	1.732	1.729	1.729
1988	1.692	1.682	1.671	1.629	1.619	1.609
1989	1.505	1.487	1.476	1.433	1.418	1.410
1990	1.327	1.314	1.291	1.223	1.204	1.195
1991	1.136	1.125	1.116	1.089	1.083	1.074
1992	1.051	1.040	1.034	1.004	0.996	0.996
1993	1.017	1.004	0.996	0.978	0.971	0.972
1994	0.968	0.957	0.952	0.929	0.922	0.922
1995	0.905	0.893	0.885	0.866	0.859	0.856
1996	0.852	0.843	0.836	0.822	0.819	0.818
1997	0.801	0.794	0.790	0.779	0.772	0.766
1998	0.744	0.735	0.729	0.710	0.701	0.702
1999	0.702	0.699	0.695	0.683	0.679	0.679
2000	0.669	0.660	0.651	0.635	0.629	0.625
2001	0.625	0.617	0.615	0.607	0.596	0.595
2002	0.605	0.600	0.594	0.583	0.578	0.578
2003	0.559	0.551	0.546	0.535	0.532	0.534
2004	0.519	0.513	0.507	0.498	0.491	0.489
2005	0.472	0.467	0.460	0.451	0.448	0.447
2006	0.438	0.432	0.426	0.415	0.407	0.401
2007	0.379	0.369	0.361	0.354	0.349	0.342
2008	0.326	0.316	0.311	0.300	0.293	0.283
2009	0.324	0.316	0.316	0.315	0.307	0.303
2010	0.276	0.269	0.260	0.248	0.244	0.241
2011	0.214	0.202	0.196	0.186	0.182	0.182
2012	0.168	0.159	0.155	0.147	0.147	0.150
2013	0.131	0.123	0.118	0.115	0.112	0.114
2014	0.101	0.094	0.091	0.088	0.087	0.085
2015	0.089	0.083	0.082	0.078	0.076	0.074
2016	0.075	0.070	0.065	0.064	0.061	0.057
2017	0.047	0.036	0.033	0.028	0.024	0.021

Indexation factors, cont.

Date of acquisition	Jul	Aug	Sep	Oct	Nov	Dec
1982	2.397	2.396	2.398	2.381	2.364	2.371
1983	2.260	2.246	2.232	2.220	2.209	2.200
1984	2.121	2.092	2.086	2.067	2.058	2.060
1985	1.920	1.912	1.914	1.909	1.899	1.895
1986	1.852	1.843	1.829	1.825	1.801	1.792
1987	1.732	1.724	1.716	1.703	1.690	1.692
1988	1.606	1.577	1.565	1.540	1.528	1.521
1989	1.408	1.402	1.385	1.367	1.347	1.341
1990	1.193	1.171	1.151	1.134	1.139	1.141
1991	1.078	1.074	1.066	1.058	1.051	1.049
1992	1.004	1.002	0.995	0.988	0.991	0.998
1993	0.977	0.968	0.960	0.961	0.964	0.960
1994	0.931	0.922	0.918	0.915	0.914	0.905
1995	0.865	0.855	0.847	0.856	0.856	0.845
1996	0.825	0.816	0.808	0.808	0.807	0.801
1997	0.766	0.755	0.746	0.744	0.742	0.738
1998	0.706	0.699	0.692	0.691	0.692	0.692
1999	0.684	0.680	0.673	0.670	0.668	0.662
2000	0.631	0.631	0.620	0.621	0.616	0.615
2001	0.605	0.598	0.593	0.596	0.602	0.604
2002	0.581	0.577	0.566	0.563	0.561	0.558
2003	0.534	0.531	0.524	0.523	0.522	0.516
2004	0.489	0.484	0.478	0.475	0.471	0.464
2005	0.447	0.444	0.440	0.439	0.436	0.433
2006	0.401	0.396	0.390	0.388	0.383	0.372
2007	0.349	0.342	0.337	0.331	0.326	0.319
2008	0.285	0.280	0.273	0.277	0.288	0.306
2009	0.303	0.297	0.292	0.288	0.284	0.276
2010	0.244	0.239	0.234	0.232	0.226	0.218
2011	0.185	0.178	0.169	0.168	0.166	0.162
2012	0.149	0.144	0.139	0.132	0.132	0.127
2013	0.114	0.108	0.104	0.104	0.103	0.101
2014	0.086	0.082	0.080	0.079	0.082	0.080
2015	0.075	0.070	0.071	0.072	0.070	0.067
2016	0.056	0.052	0.050	0.050	0.047	0.041
2017	0.019	0.012	0.011	0.010	0.008	–

Retail prices index
[T3.116]

Details provided from 1982 to December 2017 for the purposes of calculating indexation allowance.

	Jan	Feb	Mar	Apr	May	Jun
1982	78.73	78.76	79.44	81.04	81.62	81.85
1983	82.61	82.97	83.12	84.28	84.64	84.84
1984	86.84	87.20	87.48	88.64	88.97	89.20
1985	91.20	91.94	92.80	94.78	95.21	95.41
1986	96.25	96.60	96.73	97.67	97.85	97.79
1987	100.00	100.40	100.60	101.80	101.90	101.90
1988	103.30	103.70	104.10	105.80	106.20	106.60
1989	111.00	111.80	112.30	114.30	115.00	115.40
1990	119.50	120.20	121.40	125.10	126.20	126.70
1991	130.20	130.90	131.40	133.10	133.50	134.10
1992	135.60	136.30	136.70	138.80	139.30	139.30
1993	137.90	138.80	139.30	140.60	141.10	141.00
1994	141.30	142.10	142.50	144.20	144.70	144.70
1995	146.00	146.90	147.50	149.00	149.60	149.80
1996	150.20	150.90	151.50	152.60	152.90	153.00
1997	154.40	155.00	155.40	156.30	156.90	157.50
1998	159.50	160.30	160.80	162.60	163.50	163.40
1999	163.40	163.70	164.10	165.20	165.60	165.60
2000	166.60	167.50	168.40	170.10	170.70	171.10
2001	171.10	172.00	172.20	173.10	174.20	174.40
2002	173.30	173.80	174.50	175.70	176.20	176.20
2003	178.40	179.30	179.90	181.20	181.50	181.30
2004	183.10	183.80	184.60	185.70	186.50	186.80
2005	188.90	189.60	190.50	191.60	192.00	192.20
2006	193.40	194.20	195.00	196.50	197.70	198.50
2007	201.60	203.10	204.40	205.40	206.20	207.30
2008	209.80	211.40	212.10	214.00	215.10	216.80
2009	210.10	211.40	211.30	211.50	212.80	213.40
2010	217.90	219.20	220.70	222.80	223.60	224.10
2011	229.00	231.30	232.50	234.40	235.20	235.20
2012	238.00	239.90	240.80	242.50	242.40	241.80
2013	245.80	247.60	248.70	249.50	250.00	249.70
2014	252.60	254.20	254.80	255.70	255.90	256.30
2015	255.40	256.70	257.10	258.00	258.50	258.90
2016	258.80	260.00	261.10	261.40	262.10	263.10
2017	265.50	268.40	269.30	270.60	271.70	272.30

Retail prices index, cont.

	Jul	Aug	Sep	Oct	Nov	Dec
1982	81.88	81.90	81.85	82.26	82.66	82.51
1983	85.30	85.68	86.06	86.36	86.67	86.89
1984	89.10	89.94	90.11	90.67	90.95	90.87
1985	95.23	95.49	95.44	95.59	95.92	96.05
1986	97.52	97.82	98.30	98.45	99.29	99.62
1987	101.80	102.10	102.40	102.90	103.40	103.30
1988	106.70	107.90	108.40	109.50	110.00	110.30
1989	115.50	115.80	116.60	117.50	118.50	118.80
1990	126.80	128.10	129.30	130.30	130.00	129.90
1991	133.80	134.10	134.60	135.10	135.60	135.70
1992	138.80	138.90	139.40	139.90	139.70	139.20
1993	140.70	141.30	141.90	141.80	141.60	141.90
1994	144.00	144.70	145.00	145.20	145.30	146.00
1995	149.10	149.90	150.60	149.80	149.80	150.70
1996	152.40	153.10	153.80	153.80	153.90	154.40
1997	157.50	158.50	159.30	159.50	159.60	160.00
1998	163.00	163.70	164.40	164.50	164.40	164.40
1999	165.10	165.50	166.20	166.50	166.70	167.30
2000	170.50	170.50	171.70	171.60	172.10	172.20
2001	173.30	174.00	174.60	174.30	173.60	173.40
2002	175.90	176.40	177.60	177.90	178.20	178.50
2003	181.30	181.60	182.50	182.60	182.70	183.50
2004	186.80	187.40	188.10	188.60	189.00	189.90
2005	192.20	192.60	193.10	193.30	193.60	194.10
2006	198.50	199.20	200.10	200.40	201.10	202.70
2007	206.10	207.30	208.00	208.90	209.70	210.90
2008	216.50	217.20	218.40	217.70	216.00	212.90
2009	213.40	214.40	215.30	216.00	216.60	218.00
2010	223.60	224.50	225.30	225.80	226.80	228.40
2011	234.70	236.10	237.90	238.00	238.50	239.40
2012	242.10	243.00	244.20	245.60	245.60	246.80
2013	249.70	251.00	251.90	251.90	252.10	253.40
2014	256.00	257.00	257.60	257.70	257.10	257.50
2015	258.60	259.80	259.60	259.50	259.80	260.60
2016	263.40	264.40	264.90	264.80	265.50	267.10
2017	272.90	274.70	275.10	275.30	275.80	278.10

Leases

[T3.117]

SEE TOLLEY'S TAX COMPUTATIONS 216.3.
Depreciation table (TCGA 1992 Sch 8 para 1)

Yrs	%	Yrs	%	Yrs	%	Yrs	%
50 (or more)	100	37	93.497	24	79.622	11	50.038
49	99.657	36	92.761	23	78.055	10	46.695
48	99.289	35	91.981	22	76.399	9	43.154
47	98.902	34	91.156	21	74.635	8	39.399
46	98.490	33	90.280	20	72.770	7	35.414
45	98.059	32	89.354	19	70.791	6	31.195
44	97.595	31	88.371	18	68.697	5	26.722
43	97.107	30	87.330	17	66.470	4	21.983
42	96.593	29	86.226	16	64.116	3	16.959
41	96.041	28	85.053	15	61.617	2	11.629
40	95.457	27	83.816	14	58.971	1	5.983
39	94.842	26	82.496	13	56.167	0	0
38	94.189	25	81.100	12	53.191		

Formula: Fraction of expenditure disallowed—

$$\frac{AE - D}{AE}$$

Where:
  AE is the percentage for duration of lease at acquisition or expenditure; and
  D is the percentage for duration of lease at disposal.

Fractions of years: Add one-twelfth of the difference between the percentage for the whole year and the next higher percentage for each additional month. Odd days under 14 are not counted; 14 odd days or more count as a month.

Short leases: premiums treated as rent (TCGA 1992 Sch 8 para 5; ITTOIA 2005 ss 277–281A; CTA 2009 s 217–221A) Part of premium for grant of a short lease which is chargeable to income tax as property income:

$$P - (2\% \times (n - 1) \times P)$$

Where:
  P is the amount of premium;
  n is the number of complete years which lease has to run when granted.

Length of lease (complete years)	Amount chargeable to CGT %	Income tax charge %	Length of lease (complete years)	Amount chargeable to CGT %	Income tax charge %	Length of lease (complete years)	Amount chargeable to CGT %	Income tax charge %
Over 50	100	0	34	66	34	17	32	68
50	98	2	33	64	36	16	30	70
49	96	4	32	62	38	15	28	72
48	94	6	31	60	40	14	26	74
47	92	8	30	58	42	13	24	76
46	90	10	29	56	44	12	22	78
45	88	12	28	54	46	11	20	80
44	86	14	27	52	48	10	18	82
43	84	16	26	50	50	9	16	84
42	82	18	25	48	52	8	14	86
41	80	20	24	46	54	7	12	88
40	78	22	23	44	56	6	10	90
39	76	24	22	42	58	5	8	92
38	74	26	21	40	60	4	6	94
37	72	28	20	38	62	3	4	96
36	70	30	19	36	64	2	2	98
35	68	32	18	34	66	1 or less	0	100

Corporation tax

Rates for non-ring fence profits

[T4.101]

SEE TOLLEY'S TAX COMPUTATIONS 101.2.
(CTA 2010 ss 3, 18–34; FA 2021 ss 6, 7, Sch 1; F(No 2)A 2023 ss 5, 6; F(No 2)A 2024 ss 12, 13)

Financial year	2020	2021	2022	2023	2024	2025
Main rate	19%[2]	19%[2]	19%[2]	25%	25%	25%
Small profits rate	N/A	N/A	N/A	19%	19%	19%
lower limit[1]	N/A	N/A	N/A	£50,000	£50,000	£50,000
upper limit[1]	N/A	N/A	N/A	£250,000	£250,000	£250,000
marginal relief fraction	N/A	N/A	N/A	3/200	3/200	3/200

[1] Reduced proportionally for accounting periods of less than 12 months. The limits are divided by the number of associated companies, including the company in question.
[2] For financial years before 2023, there was a single main rate and no small profits rate.
[3] The power to set the rate of corporation tax in Northern Ireland has been devolved to the Northern Ireland Assembly in relation to such financial year as HM Treasury may appoint.

Marginal relief

The small profits rate applies to taxable total profits where augmented profits (see below) do not exceed the lower limit. Where a company's profits exceed the lower limit but do not exceed the upper limit, the charge to corporation tax on the company's taxable total profits is reduced by an amount calculated in accordance with a statutory formula—

$$F \times (U - A) \times \frac{N}{A}$$

where—
F is the marginal relief fraction;
U is the upper limit;
N is the amount of the taxable total profits;
A is the amount of the augmented profits—the company's adjusted taxable total profits plus exempt qualifying distributions (other than from UK companies in the same group or owned by a consortium of which the recipient is a member). A company's adjusted taxable total profits are its profits chargeable to corporation tax.

Bank levy see **T4.111**. **Patent box** see **T4.106**. **Diverted profits tax** see **T4.113**. **Bank corporation tax surcharge** see **T4.110**. **Residential property developer tax** see **T4.117**. **Tax charge on restitution interest** see **T4.118**.

Rates for ring fence profits

[T4.102]

(CTA 2010 ss 279A–279H)

Financial year	2020	2021	2022	2023	2024	2025
Main rate	30%	30%	30%	30%	30%	30%
Small profits rate	19%	19%	19%	19%	19%	19%
lower limit[1]	£300,000	£300,000	£300,000	£50,000	£50,000	£50,000
upper limit[1]	£1.5m	£1.5m	£1.5m	£250,000	£250,000	£250,000
marginal relief fraction	11/400	11/400	11/400	11/400	11/400	11/400

[1] Reduced proportionally for accounting periods of less than 12 months. The limits are divided by the number of associated companies, including the company in question.

Marginal relief for ring fence profits

[T4.103]

Applies to ring fence profits only. The small ring fence profits rate applies to taxable total profits where augmented profits (see below) do not exceed the lower limit. Where a company's ring fence profits exceed the lower limit but do not exceed the upper limit, the charge to corporation tax on the company's taxable total profits is reduced by an amount calculated in accordance with a statutory formula—

$$R \times (U - A) \times \frac{N}{A}$$

where—
R is the marginal relief fraction;
U is the upper limit;
N is the amount of the taxable total profits;
A is the amount of the augmented profits—its adjusted taxable total profits plus exempt qualifying distributions (other than from UK companies in the same group or owned by a consortium of which the recipient is a member). A company's adjusted taxable total profits are its profits chargeable to corporation tax.

Corporation tax reliefs

Disincorporation relief *before 1 April 2018*

[T4.104]

(FA 2013 ss 58–61)
With effect for disincorporations between 1 April 2013 and 31 March 2018 inclusive, joint claims may be made by a company and its shareholders to allow goodwill or interests in land not held as trading stock to be transferred at a reduced value so that no corporation tax will be payable by the company on the transfer. Relief is restricted to cases where the market value of the assets allowed for disincorporation relief does not exceed £100,000. Joint claims must be made to HMRC within two years of the date of the transfer and other eligibility criteria also apply. Shareholders to whom the assets are transferred will inherit the transfer value for the purpose of capital gains tax.

Gifts of pre-eminent objects

[T4.105]

(FA 2012 Sch 14)
Companies which gift pre-eminent objects to the nation will receive a reduction in their UK tax liability of 20% of the value of the object they are donating. The gift must be accepted as pre-eminent by Arts Council England under the Cultural Gifts Scheme.

Patent box

[T4.106]

(CTA 2010 Pt 8A; F(No 2)A 2023 s 11)
The patent box allows companies to elect to apply a 10% corporation tax rate to a proportion of profits attributable to qualifying patents, whether paid separately as royalties or embedded in the sales price of products, and to certain other qualifying intellectual property rights such as regulatory data protection (also called 'data exclusivity'), supplementary protection certificates and plant variety rights.

Real Estate Investment Trusts (REITs)

[T4.107]

(CTA 2010 ss 518–609)
Qualifying rental income from and gains on disposals of investment properties by UK companies within the REIT scheme are exempt from corporation tax.

Research and development

[T4.108]

(CTA 2009 ss 104A–104Y, 1039–1142; FA 2021 s 19; FA 2023 s 4; F(No 2)A 2023 s 10, Sch 1; FA 2024 s 2, Sch 1)

R&D expenditure credit (RDEC) scheme

SEE TOLLEY'S TAX COMPUTATIONS 117.2.
Trading companies can claim R&D relief as a taxable above the line (ATL) credit, known as RDEC. For accounting periods beginning before 1 April 2024, the scheme was aimed principally at large companies but SMEs with sub-contracted or subsidised R&D expenditure or R&D subject to the project limit could also claim. For subsequent accounting periods, the scheme can be used by companies of any size for all qualifying R&D expenditure. The amount of the credit is 20% (13% for expenditure before 1 April 2023, 12% for expenditure before 1 April 2020) of their qualifying R&D expenditure (49% for ring fence trades). The credit is fully payable, net of tax, to companies with no corporation tax liability. Universities and charities are unable to claim the credit.

SME scheme

SEE TOLLEY'S TAX COMPUTATIONS 117.1.

For accounting periods beginning on or after 1 April 2024, loss-making R&D intensive 'SMEs' incurring qualifying R&D expenditure can, as an alternative to RDEC, claim the following reliefs. For accounting periods beginning before 1 April 2024, the reliefs were the default claim for all SMEs. Large companies cannot claim the reliefs.

An eligible SME incurring R&D expenditure can obtain relief for 186% of that expenditure (230% for expenditure before 1 April 2023).

Eligible **SMEs** not in profit or which have not yet started to trade can claim relief upfront as a cash payment of 14.5% (10% for expenditure before 1 April 2024, 14.5% for expenditure before 1 April 2023) of their 'surrenderable loss' (R&D tax credit) subject to a PAYE cap for accounting periods beginning on or after 1 April 2021. The 14.5% tax credit rate continued to be available to R&D intensive SMEs after 1 April 2023.

An '**SME**' is a company with less than 500 employees and either annual turnover of €100m or less or annual balance sheet total of €86m or less.

Annual tax on enveloped dwellings

[T4.109]

(FA 2013 ss 94–174, Schs 33–35; SI 2021/245; FA 2021 s 90; SI 2022/399; SI 2023/107; SI 2024/379)

A charge is imposed on certain non-natural persons (NNPs), ie companies, partnerships with at least one company member, and collective investment schemes which hold UK residential dwellings valued above a £500,000 threshold on specified valuation dates. Returns and payment for each year are due by 30 April in that year. If the payer is not chargeable for the full year, a later repayment claim can be made. Various reliefs from the charge apply and companies may be able to submit relief declaration returns. See also **T11.101** regarding the 17% **stamp duty land tax** which can apply to acquisitions of such properties (15% before 31 October 2024).

Annual tax charge

Property value[1]	Annual tax 2020–21	Annual tax 2021–22	Annual tax 2022–23	Annual tax 2023–24	Annual tax 2024–25	Annual tax 2025–26
More than £500,000 to £1m	£3,700	£3,700	£3,800	£4,150	£4,400	**£4,450**
More than £1m to £2m	£7,500	£7,500	£7,700	£8,450	£9,000	**£9,150**
More than £2m to £5m	£25,200	£25,300	£26,050	£28,650	£30,550	**£31,050**
More than £5m to £10m	£58,850	£59,100	£60,900	£67,050	£71,500	**£72,700**
More than £10m to £20m	£118,050	£118,600	£122,250	£134,550	£143,550	**£145,950**
More than £20m	£236,250	£237,400	£244,750	£269,450	£287,500	**£292,350**

[1] The valuation is the market value on the last previous valuation date. The first valuation date was 1 April 2012 and then every five years thereafter. Other valuation dates can apply in certain circumstances, for example when a new property is purchased. The valuation is applied on the first day of the chargeable period if the chargeable person is within the charge on that day, otherwise the first day in the chargeable period on which they are first within the charge.

Relief codes for relief declaration returns

	Code for type of relief
Property rental business	1
Dwellings open to the public	2
Property developers	3
Property traders	4
Financial institutions acquiring dwellings	5
Regulated home reversion plans	5A
Occupation by certain employees etc	6
Farmhouses	7
Providers of social housing or housing co-operative	8

Bank corporation tax surcharge

[T4.110]

(CTA 2010 ss 269D–269DO; FA 2022 s 6)

A surcharge is levied on profits of banking companies and building societies. From 1 April 2023, the rate is 3% (previously it was 8%).

Bank levy

[T4.111]

(FA 2011 Sch 19 para 6)

A bank levy is charged based on the total chargeable equity and liabilities reported in the relevant balance sheets of affected banks, banking and building society groups at the end of the chargeable period. It is payable through the existing corporation tax self-assessment system. It is not charged on the first £20 billion of chargeable liabilities.

	1.1.16–31.12.16	1.1.17–31.12.17	1.1.18–31.12.18	1.1.19–31.12.19	1.1.20–31.12.20	**1.1.21 onwards**
Short-term chargeable liabilities	0.18%	0.17%	0.16%	0.15%	0.14%	**0.1%**
Long-term chargeable equity and liabilities	0.09%	0.085%	0.08%	0.075%	0.07%	**0.05%**

Cultural sector reliefs

[T4.112]

Tax credits

(CTA 2009 ss 1180–1218ZFA; FA 2022 ss 16–22; F(No 2)A 2023 ss 13, 14; FA 2024 ss 4–7, Schs 3–6; F(No 2)A 2024 ss 14–18)

		% of surrenderable loss	
		Before 27.10.21	**27.10.21 onwards**
Museums and Galleries Exhibition tax relief			
	Non-touring	20%	**45%**[1]
	Touring	25%	**50%**[1]
Theatre tax relief			
	Non-touring	20%	**45%**[1]
	Touring	25%	**50%**[1]
Orchestra tax relief		25%	**50%**[1]
Film tax relief (see note below)		25%	**25%**
High-end TV tax relief (see note below)		25%	**25%**
Video Games tax relief (see note below)		25%	**25%**

[1] For 27 October 2021 onwards the increased rates apply where production activities commence on or after that date.

[2] Museums and galleries exhibition tax credits are subject to a maximum credit of £100,000 for a touring exhibition and £80,000 for a non-touring exhibition. Under State Aid rules, orchestra tax credits and theatre tax credits are capped at Euro 5 million per undertaking per year, and museums and galleries exhibition tax credits at Euro 75 million.

From 1 January 2024 an Audio-Visual Expenditure Credit (AVEC) and a Video Games Expenditure Credit (VGEC) are introduced. They will replace the pre-existing reliefs for films, TV and video games on a phased basis. Companies claiming for productions under the pre-existing reliefs can instead claim under AVEC or VGEC in relation to expenditure incurred from 1 January 2024. New productions must be claimed under AVEC or VGEC from 1 April 2025, and all productions must claim under AVEC or VGEC from 1 April 2027. VGEC has a rate of 34%. Under AVEC, film and high end TV are eligible for a rate of 34% and animation and children's TV are eligible for a rate of 39%. (CTA 2009, ss 1179A–1179FS; FA 2024 s 3, Sch 2).

From 1 April 2024, a new Independent Film Tax Credit (IFTC) is introduced to provide additional support for certain independent films with projected core expenditure of £15 million or less which are otherwise eligible for AVEC. The credit rate is 53% of qualifying expenditure, capped at the amount that would be available for a production with core expenditure of £15 million. The IFTC is available for films that commence principal photography from 1 April 2024 on expenditure incurred on or after that date. Claims may be made from 1 April 2025. (CTA 2009 ss 1179DJA, 1179DV; F(No 2)A 2024 ss 14, 15).

From 1 January 2025, a 39% rate of AVEC applies to qualifying UK visual effects (VFX) expenditure on films or high end TV. The additional relief will be available when the production is completed; for interim periods the company can claim the standard 34% rate, including on VFX costs. Claims may be made from 1 April 2025.

Diverted profits tax

[T4.113]

(FA 2015 ss 77–116; FA 2021 s 8)

A diverted profits tax of 31% (25% before 1 April 2023) applies to counter the use of aggressive tax planning techniques by multinational enterprises to divert profits from the UK. There are two basic rules which apply. The first rule counteracts arrangements by which foreign companies exploit the permanent establishment rules, and comes into effect if a person is carrying on activity in the UK in connection with supplies of goods and services by a non-UK resident company to customers in the UK, provided that the detailed conditions are met. The second rule applies to certain arrangements which lack economic substance involving entities with an existing UK taxable presence.

Digital services tax

[T4.114]

(FA 2020 ss 39–72, Schs 8–10)
From April 2020 a digital services tax (DST) of 2% applies to revenues which are attributable to UK users and are from digital services activities that fall into three categories: a social media service; an internet search engine; or an online marketplace. There is an annual threshold of £500m digital services revenues and £25m UK digital services revenues below which the DST will not apply, and businesses with low margins or losses can make a safe-harbour election which allows a calculation of DST based on operating margins.

Loans and benefits to participators

[T4.115]

SEE TOLLEY'S TAX COMPUTATIONS 104.2.
(CTA 2010 s 455)
A charge of 33.75% of the loan made or benefit conferred applies (32.5% for loans made and benefits conferred before 6 April 2022).

Pillar 2 global minimum tax

[T4.116]

For accounting periods beginning on or after 31 December 2023, groups with consolidated annual revenue of €750 million or more are liable to top-up tax as follows:

Multinational top-up tax. This requires UK headquartered multinational groups to pay a top-up tax where their operations in a foreign jurisdiction have an effective tax rate of less than 15%. The requirement also applies to non-UK headquartered groups with UK members that are partially owned by third parties or where the headquartered jurisdiction does not implement the Pillar 2 framework (F(No 2)A 2023 ss 121–264; FA 2024 s 22, Sch 12).

Domestic top-up tax. This requires large groups, including those operating exclusively in the UK, to pay a top-up tax where their UK operations have an effective tax rate of less than 15% (F(No 2)A 2023 ss 265–278; FA 2024 s 22, Sch 12).

Undertaxed profits rule (UTPR). The Pillar 2 legislation is amended for accounting periods beginning on or after 31 December 2024 to implement the undertaxed profits rule. This ensures that any top-up taxes that are not paid under another jurisdiction's Pillar 2 rules are brought into charge in the UK.

Residential property developer tax

[T4.117]

(FA 2022 ss 32–52, Schs 7–9)
From 1 April 2022 a residential property developer tax of 4% applies to profits of companies arising from UK residential property development. The charge only applies to profits exceeding an annual allowance of £25 million. Groups of companies are entitled only to one £25 million allowance but this can be allocated between group companies.

Tax charge on restitution interest

[T4.118]

(CTA 2010 ss 357YA–357YW)
Where tax has been overpaid by a company as a result of a mistake in law or following unlawful collection of tax by HMRC a restitution award may be made. Where the award is made as a result of a judgment or an agreement between the parties which became final on or after 21 October 2015, the interest element of the award, whether arising before, on or after 21 October 2015, is chargeable to corporation tax at a special rate of 45%.

Environmental taxes and other levies

Aggregates levy

[T5.101]

(FA 2001 ss 16–49, Schs 4–10)

Levy on commercial exploitation of aggregates including rock, gravel or sand together with any other substance incorporated or naturally occurring with it. Applies to all aggregate (not recycled) extracted in the UK or territorial waters unless exempt. Exemptions apply to quarried or mined products such as clay, slate, metal and metal ores, gemstones, semi-precious gemstones and industrial minerals. There is an exempt process for shale which is not used as aggregate for construction purposes. This enables a person who has commercially exploited and accounted for the levy chargeable on such shale to claim a tax credit for it, when it is used in this new exempt process (HMRC Brief 6/2015).

The aggregates levy has been devolved to the Scottish Parliament. From a date to be appointed (expected to be 1 April 2026) a replacement tax will apply in Scotland.

From 1.4.25	£2.08 per tonne
1.4.24–31.3.25	£2.03 per tonne
1.4.09–31.3.24	£2.00 per tonne

Air passenger duty

[T5.102]

(FA 1994 s 30, Sch 5A; FA 2021 s 107; F(No 2)A 2023 ss 322, 323)

The rates for all *direct* long haul and ultra-long haul flights (ie in bands B or C) departing from Northern Ireland are devolved to the Northern Ireland Assembly and set at £0.

Children under the age of 2 years on the date of the flight without their own seat are exempt from charge in all classes of travel. Children under the age of 16 years on the date of the flight are exempt from charge in the lowest class.

Air passenger duty has been devolved to the Scottish Parliament. A replacement tax (air departure tax) is planned to apply in Scotland from a date to be determined.

Reduced rate (lowest class of travel)

Band and distance of capital city of destination country from UK in miles	1.4.20–31.3.21	1.4.21–31.3.22	1.4.22–31.3.23	1.4.23–31.3.24	1.4.24–31.3.25	1.4.25–31.3.26
Domestic band	N/A	N/A	N/A	£6.50	£7	£7
Band A (0–2,000)	£13	£13	£13	£13	£13	£13
Band B (2,001–5,500)[2]	£80	£82	£84	£87	£88	£90
Band C (over 5,500)	N/A	N/A	N/A	£91	£92	£94

Standard rate (all classes other than lowest class)[1]

Band and distance of capital city of destination country from UK in miles	1.4.20–31.3.21	1.4.21–31.3.22	1.4.22–31.3.23	1.4.23–31.3.24	1.4.24–31.3.25	1.4.25–31.3.26
Domestic band	N/A	N/A	N/A	£13	£14	£14
Band A (0–2,000)	£26	£26	£26	£26	£26	£28
Band B (2,001–5,500)[2]	£176	£180	£185	£191	£194	£216
Band C (over 5,500)	N/A	N/A	N/A	£200	£202	£224

Higher rate (flights aboard aircraft of 20 tonnes and above with fewer than 19 seats)

Band and distance of capital city of destination country from UK in miles	1.4.20–31.3.21	1.4.21–31.3.22	1.4.22–31.3.23	1.4.23–31.3.24	1.4.24–31.3.25	1.4.25–31.3.26
Domestic band	N/A	N/A	N/A	£78	£78	£84
Band A (0–2,000)	£78	£78	£78	£78	£78	£84
Band B (2,001–5,500)[2]	£528	£541	£554	£574	£581	£647
Band C (over 5,500)	N/A	N/A	N/A	£601	£607	£673

[1] If a class of travel provides a seat pitch in excess of 1.016 metres (40 inches) the standard rate is the

minimum rate that applies, even if it is the lowest or only class of travel.
2   Before 1 April 2023, band B included all flights over 2,000 miles.

The following specifies which countries are in band A, band B and band C.

Band A territories — 0–2,000 miles from London		
Albania	Greenland	Morocco
Algeria	Guernsey[1]	Netherlands
Andorra	Hungary	Norway (including Svalbard)
Austria	Iceland	Poland
Azores	Republic of Ireland	Portugal (including Madeira)
Belarus	Isle of Man	Romania
Belgium	Italy (including Sicily and Sardinia)	Russian Federation (west of the Urals)
Bosnia and Herzegovina	Jersey[1]	San Marino
Bulgaria	Republic of Kosovo	Serbia
Croatia	Latvia	Slovak Republic
Cyprus	Libya	Slovenia
Czech Republic	Liechtenstein	Spain (including the Balearic Islands and the Canary Islands)
Denmark (including the Faroe Islands)	Lithuania	Sweden
Estonia	Luxembourg	Switzerland
Finland	North Macedonia	Tunisia
France (including Corsica)	Malta	Turkey
Germany	Moldova	Ukraine
Gibraltar	Monaco	Western Sahara
Greece	Montenegro	
Band B territories — 2,001–5,500 miles from London		
Afghanistan	French Guiana	Qatar
Angola	Gabon	Russian Federation (east of the Urals)
Anguilla	Georgia	Rwanda
Antigua and Barbuda	Ghana	Saba
Armenia	Grenada	Saint Barthélemy
Aruba	Guadeloupe	Saint Lucia
Azerbaijan	Guatemala	Saint Martin
Bahrain	Guinea	Saint Pierre and Miquelon
Bangladesh	Guinea-Bissau	Saint Vincent and the Grenadines
Barbados	Guyana	Sao Tome and Principe
Belize	Haiti	Saudi Arabia
Benin	Honduras	Senegal
Bermuda	India	Seychelles
Bhutan	Iran	Sierra Leone
Bonaire	Iraq	Sint Eustatius
Botswana	Israel	Sint Maarten
Brazil	Ivory Coast	Somalia
British Virgin Islands	Jamaica	South Korea
Burkina Faso	Jordan	South Sudan
Burundi	Kazakhstan	Sri Lanka
Cameroon	Kenya	St Helena Ascension and Tristan da Cunha
Canada	Kuwait	St Kitts and Nevis
Cape Verde	Kyrgyzstan	Sudan
Cayman Islands	Lebanon	Suriname
Central African Republic	Liberia	Syria
Chad	Malawi	Tajikistan
China (including Macau)	Maldives	Tanzania
Colombia	Mali	The Bahamas
Comoros	Martinique	The Gambia
Congo	Mauritania	Togo
Congo (Democratic Republic)	Mayotte	Trinidad and Tobago
Costa Rica	Mongolia	Turkmenistan
Cuba	Montserrat	Turks and Caicos Islands
Curaçao	Namibia	Uganda
Djibouti	Nepal	United Arab Emirates
Dominica	Nicaragua	United States (including Puerto Rico and US Virgin Islands)
Dominican Republic	Niger	Uzbekistan
Egypt	Nigeria	Venezuela
El Salvador	North Korea	Yemen
Equatorial Guinea	Oman	Zambia
Eritrea	Pakistan	Zimbabwe
Ethiopia	Panama	

1   HMRC guidance refers to the Channel Islands, rather than Guernsey and Jersey.

Band C — Journey ends in any other place. All of the territories in band C were in band B before 1 April 2023.

Climate change levy

[T5.103]

(FA 2000 s 30, Sch 6; FA 2021 ss 109, 110; F(No 2)A 2023 s 328)

Levy on supply for industrial or commercial purposes of energy in the form of electricity, gas, petroleum and hydrocarbon gas supplied in a liquid state, coal and lignite, coke and semi-coke of coal or lignite and petroleum coke.

Taxable commodity supplied	Rate[1]						
	1.4.20–31.3.21	1.4.21–31.3.22	1.4.22–31.3.23	1.4.23–31.3.24	1.4.24–31.3.25	**1.4.25–31.3.26**	1.4.26–31.3.27
Electricity	0.811p per kWh	0.775p per kWh	0.775p per kWh	0.775p per kWh	0.775p per kWh	**0.775p per kWh**	0.801p per kWh
Gas supplied by a gas utility or any gas supplied in a gaseous state that is of a kind supplied by a gas utility	0.406p per kWh	0.465p per kWh	0.568p per kWh	0.672p per kWh	0.775p per kWh	**0.775p per kWh**	0.801p per kWh
Any petroleum gas, or other gaseous hydrocarbon supplied in a liquid state	2.175p per kg	2.175p per kg	2.175p per kg	2.175p per kg	2.175p per kg	**2.175p per kg**	2.175p per kg
Any other taxable commodity	3.174p per kg	3.640p per kg	4.449p per kg	5.258p per kg	6.064p per kg	**6.064p per kg**	6.264p per kg

[1] Rate at which payable if supply is not a reduced-rate supply. The levy is charged at a reduced rate for facilities covered by a climate change agreement, generally 11% of the full rate (12% from 1 April 2023 to 31 March 2024; 14% from 1 April 2022 to 31 March 2023; 17% from 1 April 2021 to 31 March 2022; 19% from 1 April 2020 to 31 March 2021; 22% from 1 April 2019 to 31 March 2020) but 8% for electricity supplies (7% from 1 April 2019 to 31 March 2020). From 1 April 2020 there is a reduced rate of 23% for liquefied petroleum (previous reduced rate was same as other taxable commodities). Supplies of taxable commodities used in metallurgical and mineralogical processes are exempt.

Carbon price support rates for climate change levy and fuel duty

[T5.104]

Supplies of solid fossil fuels, gas and liquefied petroleum gas used in most forms of electricity generation are liable to the CPS rates of CCL, which differs from the main CCL rates (see above) levied on consumers' use of these commodities (and electricity). Oils and bioblends are not taxable commodities for CCL purposes, and are taxed under the fuel duty regime. There are, however, CPS rates of fuel duty for oils and bioblends used in the generation of electricity. The carbon price floor does not apply to Northern Ireland. The CPS rate is reduced by the carbon capture percentage where there is a supply of fossil fuels to an electricity generator which uses carbon capture and storage (CCS) technology. Small scale Combined Heat and Power (CHP) stations are not subject to the CPS rate. Fossil fuels used in a CHP station to generate good quality electricity consumed on-site are also excluded.

Supplies of commodity	Rate	
	1.4.15–31.3.16	**1.4.16–31.3.27**
Gas supplied by a gas utility or any gas supplied in a gaseous state that is of a kind supplied by a gas utility	0.334p per kWh	**0.331p per kWh**
Any petroleum gas, or other gaseous hydrocarbon supplied in a liquid state	5.307p per kg	**5.280p per kg**
Coal and other taxable solid fossil fuels	156.86p per gross gigajoule	**154.79p per gross gigajoule**
Gas oil; rebated bioblend; kerosene[1]	4.99p per litre	**4.916p per litre**
Fuel oil; other heavy oil; rebated light oil	5.73p per litre	**5.711p per litre**

[1] The CPS rates of fuel duty apply to duty paid kerosene used in electricity generation.

Economic Crime (Anti-Money Laundering) Levy

[T5.105]

(FA 2022 ss 53–66; SI 2022/269; F(No 2)A 2024 s 21)

FA 2022 established an Economic Crime (Anti-Money Laundering) Levy to help fund anti-money laundering and economic crime reforms. Entities subject to the Money Laundering Regulations pay a fixed fee for each financial year based on the 'size' band they belong to. Small entities are fully exempt from the levy. An entity's UK revenue for a financial year is its UK revenue for the accounting period ending in that year. There are rules to determine the UK revenue where there is more than one accounting period ending in the year or where there is no accounting period ending in the year. HMRC, the Financial Conduct Authority, and the Gambling Commission are responsible for the collection and management of the levy. The levy applies for financial year 2022 (beginning on 1 April 2022) onwards.

		Fee[1]			
Entity or payee size	UK revenue threshold	1.4.22–31.3.23	1.4.23–31.3.24	1.4.24–31.3.25	**1.4.25–31.3.26**
Small	Under £10.2 million	N/A	N/A	N/A	**N/A**
Medium	£10.2 million to £36 million	£10,000	£10,000	£10,000	**£10,000**
Large	£36 million to £1 billion	£36,000	£36,000	£36,000	**£36,000**
Very large	Over £1 billion	£250,000	£250,000	£500,000	**£500,000**

[1] Fee rates are intended to remain unchanged until the levy review in 2027. However, if the levy is yielding more or less than the desired £100 million a year, rates may be updated beforehand.

Fuel duty

[T5.106]

(HODA 1979 s 6; SI 2011/2935; SI 2015/550; Rural Duty Relief Scheme (Notice 2001))
A Rural Fuel Duty relief scheme applies for retailers of road fuel in certain postcodes within the UK.

	Petrol/diesel	Biodiesel or bioethanol	LPG used as road fuel	Natural gas used as road fuel	Red diesel	Fuel oil	Aqua-methanol
From 6pm 23 March 2022 to 11.59pm 22 March 2026	**52.95p per litre**	**52.95p per litre**	**28.88p per kg**	**22.57p per kg**	**10.18p per kg**	**9.78p per kg**	**7.22p per kg**
From 14 November 2016 to 5.59pm 23 March 2022	57.95p per litre	57.95p per litre	31.61p per kg	24.70p per kg	11.14p per litre	10.70p per litre	7.90p per litre
From 6pm 23 March 2011 to 13 November 2016	57.95p per litre	57.95p per litre	31.61p per kg	24.70p per kg	11.14p per litre	10.70p per litre	57.95p per litre

Insurance premium tax

[T5.107]

(FA 1994 ss 48–74, Schs 6A, 7, 7A; FA 2022 s 73)
IPT is a tax on premiums received under insurance contracts other than those which are specifically exempt.

	Standard rate	*Higher rate*[1]
From 1.6.17	**12.0%**	**20.0%**
1.10.16–31.5.17[2]	10.0%	20.0%

[1] The higher rate applies to sales of motor cars, light vans and motorcycles, electrical or mechanical domestic appliances, and travel insurance.
[2] 10% rate applies from 1 February 2017 for insurers who use a special accounting scheme rather than the cash receipt method, and where the premium relates to risks covered by the terms of a contract entered into before 1 October 2016.

Landfill tax

[T5.108]

(FA 1996 ss 39–71, 197, Sch 5; FA 2021 s 111; FA 2022 s 83; F(No 2)A 2023 s 327; SI 1996/1527; SI 1996/1528; Notice LFT1)

Tax on disposal of material imposed on operators of landfill sites calculated by reference to the weight and type of material deposited. Exemption applies to mining and quarrying material, dredging material, pet cemeteries, disposals of NATO material, and inert material used to fill working and old quarries. The scope of the tax extends to disposals of material at sites operating without the appropriate licence or permit, and the exemptions above do not apply to these sites. The power to raise landfill tax devolved to the Scottish Parliament from 1 April 2015 (see table below) and to the Welsh Government from 1 April 2018 (see table below).

Period	Active waste per tonne	Inert waste per tonne[2]	Maximum credit[1]
From 1.4.25–31.3.26	**£126.15**	**£4.05**	**5.3%**
1.4.24–31.3.25	£103.70	£3.30	5.3%
1.4.23–31.3.24	£102.10	£3.25	5.3%
1.4.22–31.3.23	£98.60	£3.15	5.3%
1.4.21–31.3.22	£96.70	£3.10	5.3%
1.4.20–31.3.21	£94.15	£3.00	5.3%

[1] Tax credits are available to operators who make donations to environmental trusts of 90% of the donation to the maximum percentage above of the tax payable in a 12-month period (Landfill Communities Fund). Tax credits do not apply to disposals of material at sites operating without the appropriate licence or permit.
[2] For details of waste materials liable at the lower rate see SI 2011/1017 as amended and HMRC Briefs 15/2012 and 18/2012. The lower rate does not apply to disposals of material at sites operating without the appropriate licence or permit.

Scottish landfill tax

[T5.109]

(Landfill Tax (Scotland) Act 2014; SSI 2019/58; SSI 2020/65; SSI 2021/89; SSI 2022/46; SSI 2023/50; SSI 2024/60)

Tax replaces landfill tax in Scotland from 1 April 2015.

Period	Active waste per tonne	Inert waste per tonne[2]	Maximum credit[1]
1.4.24–31.3.25	£103.70	£3.30	5.6%
1.4.23–31.3.24	£102.10	£3.25	5.6%
1.4.22–31.3.23	£98.60	£3.15	5.6%
1.4.21–31.3.22	£96.70	£3.10	5.6%
1.4.20–31.3.21	£94.15	£3.00	5.6%

[1] Tax credits are available to operators who make donations to environmental trusts of 90% of the donation to the maximum % above of the tax payable in a 12-month period (Scottish Landfill Communities Fund).
[2] For details of waste materials liable at the lower rate see SSIs 2015/45 and 2016/93.

Landfill disposals tax (Wales)

[T5.110]

(Landfill Disposals Tax (Wales) Act 2017; SI 2018/131; SI 2018/1209; SI 2020/95; SI 2021/1470; SI 2022/1316)

Tax replaces landfill tax in Wales from 1 April 2018.

Period	Active waste per tonne	Inert waste per tonne	Unauthorised disposals rate
1.4.24–31.3.25	£103.70	£3.30	£155.55
1.4.23–31.3.24	£102.10	£3.25	£153.15
1.4.22–31.3.23	£98.60	£3.15	£147.90
1.4.21–31.3.22	£96.70	£3.10	£145.05
1.4.20–31.3.21	£94.15	£3.00	£141.20

[1] The Landfill Disposals Tax Communities Scheme operates as a grant scheme and is not delivered by means of a tax credit.

Vehicle excise duty

[T5.111]

(VERA 1994 Sch 1; FA 2021 s 104; FA 2022 ss 78, 79; F(No 2)A 2023 s 324)
Vehicle tax, or 'road tax' is charged according to CO_2 emissions, as follows:

Standard rate for cars registered before 1 April 2017

Band	CO_2 (g/km)	2022–23 Standard rate	2023–24 Standard rate	2024–25 Standard rate	2025–26 Standard rate
A	Up to 100	£0	£0	£0	£20
B	101–110	£20	£20	£20	£20
C	111–120	£30	£35	£35	£35
D	121–130	£135	£150	£160	£165
E	131–140	£165	£180	£190	£195
F	141–150	£180	£200	£210	£215
G	151–165	£220	£240	£255	£265
H	166–175	£265	£290	£305	£315
I	176–185	£290	£320	£335	£345
J	186–200	£330	£365	£385	£395
K	201–225	£360	£395	£415	£430
L	226–255	£615	£675	£710	£735
M	Over 255	£630	£695	£735	£760

Standard and first-year rates for cars registered on or after 1 April 2017

CO_2 (g/km)	2022–23 Standard rate	2022–23 first-year rate	2022–23 first-year rate diesel vehicles	2023–24 Standard rate	2023–24 first-year rate	2023–24 first-year rate diesel vehicles
0	£0	£0	N/A	£0	£0	N/A
1–50	£165	£10	£25	£180	£10	£30
51–75	£165	£25	£120	£180	£30	£130
76–90	£165	£120	£150	£180	£130	£165
91–100	£165	£150	£170	£180	£165	£185
101–110	£165	£170	£190	£180	£185	£210
111–130	£165	£190	£230	£180	£210	£255
131–150	£165	£230	£585	£180	£255	£645
151–170	£165	£585	£945	£180	£645	£1,040
171–190	£165	£945	£1,420	£180	£1,040	£1,565
191–225	£165	£1,420	£2,015	£180	£1,565	£2,220
226–255	£165	£2,015	£2,365	£180	£2,220	£2,605
Over 255	£165	£2,365	£2,365	£180	£2,605	£2,605

CO_2 (g/km)	2024–25 Standard rate	2024–25 first-year rate	2024–25 first-year rate diesel vehicles	2025–26 Standard rate	2025–26 first-year rate	2025–26 first-year rate diesel vehicles
0	£0	£0	N/A	£195	£10	N/A
1–50	£190	£10	£30	£195	£110	£130
51–75	£190	£30	£135	£195	£130	£270
76–90	£190	£135	£175	£195	£270	£350
91–100	£190	£175	£195	£195	£350	£390
101–110	£190	£195	£220	£195	£390	£440
111–130	£190	£220	£270	£195	£440	£540
131–150	£190	£270	£680	£195	£540	£1,360
151–170	£190	£680	£1,095	£195	£1,360	£2,190
171–190	£190	£1,095	£1,650	£195	£2,190	£3,300
191–225	£190	£1,650	£2,340	£195	£3,300	£4,680
226–255	£190	£2,340	£2,745	£195	£4,680	£5,490
Over 255	£190	£2,745	£2,745	£195	£5,490	£5,490

[1] There is an alternative fuel discount of £10 for all cars. For cars registered on or after 1 April 2017 the first-year rate of tax applies in the year of purchase of a new vehicle. In later years, the standard rate applies. Cars with a list price above £40,000 when new have an additional rate of £425 per year (£410 before 1 April 2025; £390 before 1 April 2024; £355 before 1 April 2023) for the first 5 years in which the standard rate is paid. From 1 April 2018 there is a separate first-year rate for diesel cars that do not meet the Euro 6d emissions standard.

Light goods vehicle rates

Tax class	2022–23	2023–24	2024–25	2025–26
Light goods vehicle[1]	£290	£320	£335	£345
Euro 4 & 5 LGV	£140	£140	£140	£140

[1] Registered on or after 1 March 2001.

Motorcycle rates

VED band	2022–23	2023–24	2024–25	2025–26
Up to 150 cc	£22	£24	£25	£26
151–400 cc	£47	£52	£55	£57
401–600 cc	£73	£80	£84	£87
Over 600 cc	£101	£111	£117	£121

Income tax

Starting, basic, higher and additional rates
[T6.101]
(ITA 2007 ss 6–21; FA 2021 ss 1–5; FA 2022 ss 1–5; F(No 2)A 2023 ss 1–4; F(No 2)A 2024 ss 1–4)

Band of taxable income	Band	Rate	Tax	Cumulative tax
£	£	%	£	£
2025–26				
0–37,700	37,700	20	7,540	7,540
37,701–125,140	87,440	40	34,976	42,516
Over 125,140	–	45	–	–
2024–25				
0–37,700	37,700	20	7,540	7,540
37,701–125,140	87,440	40	34,976	42,516
Over 125,140	–	45	–	–
2023–24				
0–37,700	37,700	20	7,540	7,540
37,701–125,140	87,440	40	34,976	42,516
Over 125,140	–	45	–	–
2022–23				
0–37,700	37,700	20	7,540	7,540
37,701–150,000	112,300	40	44,920	52,460
Over 150,000	–	45	–	–
2021–22				
0–37,700	37,700	20	7,540	7,540
37,701–150,000	112,300	40	44,920	52,460
Over 150,000	–	45	–	–
2020–21				
0–37,500	37,500	20	7,500	7,500
37,501–150,000	112,500	40	45,000	52,500
Over 150,000	–	45	–	–

Scottish rate of income tax
[T6.102]

SEE TOLLEY'S TAX COMPUTATIONS 1.6.
(Scotland Act 1998 s 80C)

Band of taxable income	Band	Rate	Tax	Cumulative tax
£	£	%	£	£
2024–25				
0–2,306	2,306	19	438	438
2,307–13,990	11,684	20	2,337	2,775
13,991–31,092	17,102	21	3,591	6,366
31,093–62,430	31,338	42	13,162	19,528
62,431–125,140	62,710	45	28,220	47,748
Over 125,140	–	48	–	–
2023–24				
0–2,162	2,162	19	410	410
2,163–13,118	10,956	20	2,191	2,601
13,119–31,092	17,974	21	3,774	6,375
31,093–125,140	94,048	42	39,500	45,875
Over 125,140	–	47	–	–
2022–23				
0–2,162	2,162	19	410	410
2,163–13,118	10,956	20	2,191	2,601
13,119–31,092	17,974	21	3,774	6,375
31,093–150,000	118,908	41	48,752	55,127
Over 150,000	–	46	–	–
2021–22				
0–2,097	2,097	19	398	398
2,098–12,726	10,629	20	2,125	2,523
12,727–31,092	18,366	21	3,856	6,379

Band of taxable income	Band	Rate	Tax	Cumulative tax
£	£	%	£	£
31,093–150,000	118,908	41	48,752	55,131
Over 150,000	–	46	–	–
2020–21				
0–2,085	2,085	19	396	396
2,086–12,658	10,573	20	2,114	2,510
12,659–30,930	18,272	21	3,837	6,347
30,931–150,000	119,070	41	48,818	55,165
Over 150,000	–	46	–	–

The Scottish Parliament sets its own Scottish income tax rates and bands. The rates and bands do not apply to Scottish taxpayers' dividend and savings income, which are subject to the same tax rates and bands as for taxpayers in the rest of the UK. The definition of a Scottish taxpayer is based on the location of an individual's main place of residence.

Welsh rate of income tax

[T6.103]

(Government of Wales Act 2006; Wales Act 2014)

Band of taxable income	Band	Rate	Tax	Cumulative tax
£	£	%	£	£
2024–25				
0–37,700	37,700	20	7,540	7,540
37,701–125,140	87,440	40	34,976	42,516
Over 125,140	–	45	–	–
2023–24				
0–37,700	37,700	20	7,540	7,540
37,701–125,140	87,440	40	34,976	42,516
Over 125,140	–	45	–	–
2022–23				
0–37,700	37,700	20	7,540	7,540
37,701–150,000	112,300	40	44,920	52,460
Over 150,000	–	45	–	–
2021–22				
0–37,700	37,700	20	7,540	7,540
37,701–150,000	112,300	40	44,920	52,460
Over 150,000	–	45	–	–
2020–21				
0–37,500	37,500	20	7,500	7,500
37,501–150,000	112,500	40	45,000	52,500
Over 150,000	–	45	–	–

A Welsh rate of income tax of 10% applies for Welsh taxpayers from 6 April 2019. The Welsh basic, higher and additional rates are calculated by reducing each of the UK basic, higher and additional rates by ten percentage points and then adding the Welsh rate, resulting in the rates being the same as for the rest of the UK. The rate is charged on non-savings, non-dividends income.

Taxation of savings

[T6.104]

SEE TOLLEY'S TAX COMPUTATIONS 1.2, 1.3.

(ITA 2007 ss 6–21)

A starting rate for savings band of **£5,000** for individuals applies. Where an individual's taxable non-savings income is less than this limit, there is a **0% starting rate** for savings up to the limit. Where taxable non-savings income exceeds the limit, the starting rate for savings does not apply. Savings income includes interest from banks and building societies, interest distributions from authorised unit trusts, interest on gilts and other securities including corporate bonds, purchased life annuities and discounts.

A personal savings allowance (PSA) is available to basic and higher rate taxpayers but not to additional rate taxpayers. The allowance is **£1,000 per year for basic rate taxpayers and £500 per year for higher rate taxpayers**. Savings income above the allowance is taxable at the basic or higher rate as appropriate, with savings income generally being treated as the second top slice of income behind dividends. The PSA is not a deduction in arriving at total income or taxable income. **A 0% rate of income tax applies** to savings income covered by the PSA. It operates in conjunction with the 0% starting rate for savings and income taxable at this rate does not fall within the PSA. Savings income within an ISA is tax-free, and does not need to be covered by the PSA.

Taxation of dividends

[T6.105]

SEE TOLLEY'S TAX COMPUTATIONS 1.1.

(ITA 2007 ss 6–21; FA 2023 s 7)

For 2024–25 and 2025–26 a **dividend allowance of £500** is available to all taxpayers (£1,000 for 2023–24, £2,000 for 2018–19 to 2022–23). A **0% rate of income tax applies** to dividends covered by the allowance. The rates of tax on dividend income above the allowance are 8.75% (7.5% for 2021–22 and earlier years) for dividend income falling within the basic rate band, 33.75% (32.5% for 2021–22 and earlier years) for dividend income falling within the higher rate band, and 39.35% (38.1% for 2021–22 and earlier years) for dividend income falling within the additional rate band. The dividend allowance is not a deduction in arriving at total income or taxable income. UK and foreign dividends (except those foreign dividends taxed under the remittance basis) form the top slice of taxable income.

Taxation of trusts

[T6.106]

SEE TOLLEY'S TAX COMPUTATIONS 27.2.

	Trust rate	Dividend trust rate
2022–23 onwards	**45%**	**39.35%**
2016–17 to 2021–22	45%	38.1%

De minimis trusts amount: For 2024–25 onwards, where the net income of a trust does not exceed £500, the income of the trust is taken to be nil for income tax purposes. The £500 limit is reduced (but not below £100) if there is more than one settlement made by the same settlor which remains in existence and has any income within the trusts rates of tax for the tax year.
First slice of income: For 2023–24 and earlier years, the first £1,000 of income arising to a trust chargeable at the trust rate or the dividend trust rate is instead chargeable at the basic, basic savings or ordinary dividend rate.
Vulnerable beneficiaries: Trustees can be taxed (on election) on trust income as if it were income of the vulnerable beneficiary taking into account the beneficiary's personal allowances, starting and basic rate bands (FA 2005 ss 23–45).

Construction industry sub-contractors

[T6.107]

(SI 2007/46)

	Rate of tax deduction at source
Registered sub-contractors	**20%**
Unregistered sub-contractors	**30%**

High income child benefit charge

[T6.108]

SEE TOLLEY'S TAX COMPUTATIONS 29.1.

(ITEPA 2003 ss 681B–H; Social Security Administration Act 1992, s 13A; F(No 2)A 2024 s 5)

Where an individual or their partner is in receipt of child benefit a high income child benefit charge can arise. The charge is applied to the higher earner. Taxpayers with adjusted net income between £60,000 and £80,000 (£50,000 and £60,000 before 6 April 2024) are subject to an income tax charge of 1% of the amount of child benefit for every £200 (£100 before 6 April 2024) of income that exceeds £60,000 (£50,000 before 6 April 2024). For taxpayers with income above £80,000 (£60,000 before 6 April 2024), the amount of the charge will equal the amount of child benefit received. Alternatively, a taxpayer with expected income over £80,000 (£60,000 before 6 April 2024) can elect not to receive any child benefit. The election has effect for weeks beginning after it is made. It can be revoked at any time to restore payment of child benefit, and, where the election was made in the erroneous belief that the charge would arise, it may be revoked up to two years after the end of the tax year to which it relates in order for child benefit to be paid for the period. For new child benefit claims made after 6 April 2024, any backdated payment will be treated for HICBC purposes as if the entitlement fell in the 2024–25 tax year if backdating would otherwise create a HICBC liability in the 2023–24 tax year.

Charities and Community Amateur Sports Clubs (CASCs)

Gift Aid and Gift Aid Small Donations schemes

[T6.109]

SEE TOLLEY'S TAX COMPUTATIONS 5.1.

Under the **Gift Aid scheme** an individual donor can claim higher rate relief and, if applicable, additional rate relief on the grossed up amount of a monetary donation against income tax and capital gains tax. The charity or CASC claims basic rate relief on the grossed up amount of the donation. Donors must make a declaration that they are UK taxpayers to allow the charity to reclaim the repayment. One declaration can cover a series of donations to the same charity and the declaration can be made in writing, including fax, email and text, or orally, although an oral declaration is not effective until a written confirmation is sent to the donor. Template declarations are provided on Gov.uk. A declaration can be backdated for up to four years prior to the declaration. The basic rate tax deemed to have been deducted by the donor at source is clawed back if the donor's tax liability is insufficient to match it. Donors may elect in their self-assessment tax returns for donations to be treated as made in the preceding tax year for higher rate (and if applicable, additional rate) relief purposes.

Relief for payments under charitable covenants is given under the Gift Aid scheme.

The **Gift Aid Small Donations scheme** allows charities and CASCs to claim a gift aid style payment on broadly £8,000 of small cash donations or contactless payments of up to £30 each in circumstances where it is often difficult to obtain a gift aid declaration, such as street collections. The donations must not have been the subject of a gift aid declaration and must not be deductible in calculating the individual's income.

(ITA 2007 ss 413–430; Small Charitable Donations Act 2012; SI 2019/337)

Gifts in kind

[T6.110]

Relief is available for gifts by traders to charities, community amateur sports clubs or educational establishments of goods produced or sold or of plant or machinery used for the purposes of the trade (CAA 2001 s 63(2)–(4); ITTOIA 2005 ss 107–109; CTA 2009 ss 105–107; CTA 2010 ss 658–671).

Gifts of land, shares and securities etc

[T6.111]

Relief is available where a person disposes of listed shares and securities, unit trust units, AIM shares, etc or of freehold or leasehold interests in land to a charity by way of a gift or sale at an undervalue. The amount deductible from total income is the market value of the shares etc on the date of disposal plus incidental disposal costs less any consideration or value of benefits received by the donor or a connected person. This is in addition to any capital gains tax relief (ITA 2007 ss 431–446).

Payroll giving

[T6.112]

Under the payroll giving scheme, employees authorise their employer to deduct charitable donations from their pay and receive tax relief on their donation at their top rate of tax (FA 2000 s 38; ITEPA 2003 ss 713–715; SI 1986/2211 as amended).

Restriction of tax reliefs to UK charities

[T6.112A]

With effect, broadly, from April 2024, tax reliefs for charities are only available to charities in the UK (ie those subject to the control of a UK court) and to UK CASCs (those based in the UK and providing facilities for sport in the UK). The reliefs are not available in respect of non-UK charities or CASCs on or after 15 March 2023 if the charity or CASC had not asserted its status as such before that date.

Inheritance tax relief see **T7.111**. **Capital gains tax** see **T3.110**. **Gifts of pre-eminent objects** see **T6.183**.

Table of income tax allowances
[T6.113]–[T6.114]

	2025–26	2024–25
	£	£
Personal allowance	**12,570**	12,570
Total income limit[4]	**100,000**	100,000
Not beneficial if individual's total income exceeds	**125,140**	125,140
Transferable marriage allowance[5]	**1,260**	1,260
Married couple's allowance[1]		
Either partner born before 6 April 1935		
Minimum amount	**4,360**	4,280
Total income limit[2]	**37,700**	37,000
Maximum amount	**11,270**	11,080
Reduced to minimum if total income over[2]	**51,520**	50,600
Blind person's allowance[3]	**3,130**	3,070
Dividend allowance[6]	**500**	500
Personal savings allowance[6]		
Basic rate taxpayer	**1,000**	1,000
Higher rate taxpayer	**500**	500
Trading allowance[7]	**1,000**	1,000
Property allowance[7]	**1,000**	1,000

[1] The married couple's allowance is only available to a married couple or, from 2005–06, civil partnership where at least one spouse or partner was born before 6 April 1935. The relief is given as a reduction in income tax liability restricted to the lower of 10% of the amount of the allowance or the claimant's total income tax liability.

For marriages before 5 December 2005, married couple's allowance is given to the husband (subject to right of transfer to the wife), the amount being determined by the level of the husband's income. For marriages and civil partnerships entered into on or after that date, the allowance is given to whichever of the two partners has the higher total income for the tax year in question, the amount being determined by the level of that partner's income (subject to the right to transfer half or all of the basic allowance or excess allowances to the partner). Couples married before 5 December 2005 could make a joint election to be brought within the rules for couples marrying on or after that date.
SEE TOLLEY'S TAX COMPUTATIONS 16.2.

[2] The maximum married couple's allowance is available if the claimant's adjusted net income does not exceed the statutory income limit (subject to relief given as a reduction in tax liability as in note 1 above). If the limit is exceeded the maximum allowance is reduced by one-half of the excess but it cannot be reduced to less than the minimum couple's allowance.

Table of income tax allowances (cont.)
[T6.115]

2023–24	2022–23	2021–22	2020–21	2019–20
£	£	£	£	£
12,570	12,570	12,570	12,500	12,500
100,000	100,000	100,000	100,000	100,000
125,140	125,140	125,140	125,000	125,000
1,260	1,260	1,260	1,250	1,250
4,010	3,640	3,530	3,510	3,450
34,600	31,400	30,400	30,200	29,600
10,375	9,415	9,125	9,075	8,915
47,330	42,950	41,590	41,330	40,530
2,870	2,600	2,520	2,500	2,450
1,000	2,000	2,000	2,000	2,000
1,000	1,000	1,000	1,000	1,000
500	500	500	500	500
1,000	1,000	1,000	1,000	1,000
1,000	1,000	1,000	1,000	1,000

[3] The allowance is available for persons registered blind but not for persons registered partially-sighted.

[4] The personal allowance for income tax is gradually reduced to nil for individuals with adjusted net incomes in excess of £100,000. The reduction is £1 for every £2 of income over the limit. **SEE TOLLEY'S TAX COMPUTATIONS 1.5**.

[5] A spouse or civil partner who is not liable to income tax above the basic rate (or Scottish intermediate rate) is able to transfer an amount of their personal allowance to their spouse or civil partner, provided the transferee is also not liable to income tax above the basic rate (or Scottish intermediate rate). Married couples or civil partnerships entitled to claim the married couple's allowance cannot make a transfer. Transfers can be made on behalf of a deceased spouse or partner or from a surviving spouse / partner to a deceased spouse / partner.

[6] See **T6.104, T6.105** for the tax rates applying where allowance is exceeded.

[7] See **T6.180** for details.

Cars, vans and related benefits

Cars

[T6.117]

SEE TOLLEY'S TAX COMPUTATIONS 9.3.

The income tax charge is based on a percentage of the car's price graduated according to the level of the car's carbon dioxide measured in grams per kilometre (g/km). (ITEPA 2003 ss 114–148, 169)

For cars registered on or after 1.3.01, the definitive CO_2 emissions figure is recorded on the vehicle registration document.

CO_2 emissions (g/km)	Electric range (miles)	% of list price 2022–23 Petrol	% of list price 2022–23 Diesel[1]	% of list price 2023–24 and 2024–25 Petrol	% of list price 2023–24 and 2024–25 Diesel[1]	% of list price 2025–26 Petrol	% of list price 2025–26 Diesel[1]
0	N/A	2%	N/A[1]	2%	N/A[1]	3%	N/A[1]
1–50	>130	2%	N/A[1]	2%	N/A[1]	3%	N/A[1]
1–50	70–129	5%	N/A[1]	5%	N/A[1]	6%	N/A[1]
1–50	40–69	8%	N/A[1]	8%	N/A[1]	9%	N/A[1]
1–50	30–39	12%	N/A[1]	12%	N/A[1]	13%	N/A[1]
1–50	<30	14%	18%[1]	14%	18%[1]	15%	19%
51–54		15%	19%	15%	19%	16%	20%
55–59		16%	20%	16%	20%	17%	21%
60–64		17%	21%	17%	21%	18%	22%
65–69		18%	22%	18%	22%	19%	23%
70–74		19%	23%	19%	23%	20%	24%
75–79		20%	24%	20%	24%	21%	25%
80–84		21%	25%	21%	25%	22%	26%
85–89		22%	26%	22%	26%	23%	27%
90–94		23%	27%	23%	27%	24%	28%
95–99		24%	28%	24%	28%	25%	29%
100–104		25%	29%	25%	29%	26%	30%
105–109		26%	30%	26%	30%	27%	31%
110–114		27%	31%	27%	31%	28%	32%
115–119		28%	32%	28%	32%	29%	33%
120–124		29%	33%	29%	33%	30%	34%
125–129		30%	34%	30%	34%	31%	35%
130–134		31%	35%	31%	35%	32%	36%
135–139		32%	36%	32%	36%	33%	37%
140–144		33%	37%	33%	37%	34%	37%
145–149		34%	37%	34%	37%	35%	37%
150–154		35%	37%	35%	37%	36%	37%
155–159		36%	37%	36%	37%	37%	37%
160 or more		37%	37%	37%	37%	37%	37%

Car benefit – Cars first registered before 6 April 2020[2]					Car benefit – Cars first registered on or after 6 April 2020[2]				
CO_2 emissions (g/km)	Electric range (miles)	% of list price		% of list price		CO_2 emissions (g/km)	Electric range (miles)	% of list price		% of list price	
		2020–21		2021–22				2020–21		2021–22	
		Petrol	Diesel[1]	Petrol	Diesel[1]			Petrol	Diesel[1]	Petrol	Diesel[1]
0	N/A	0%	N/A[1]	1%	N/A[1]	0	N/A	0%	N/A[1]	1%	N/A[1]
1–50	>130	2%	N/A[1]	2%	N/A[1]	1–50	>130	0%	N/A[1]	1%	N/A[1]
1–50	70–129	5%	N/A[1]	5%	N/A[1]	1–50	70–129	3%	N/A	4%	N/A[1]
1–50	40–69	8%	N/A[1]	8%	N/A[1]	1–50	40–69	6%	N/A[1]	7%	N/A[1]
1–50	30–39	12%	N/A[1]	12%	N/A[1]	1–50	30–39	10%	N/A[1]	11%	N/A[1]
1–50	<30	14%	18%[1]	14%	18%[1]	1–50	<30	12%	16%[1]	13%	17%[1]
51–54		15%	19%	15%	19%	51–54		13%	17%	14%	18%
55–59		16%	20%	16%	20%	55–59		14%	18%	15%	19%
60–64		17%	21%	17%	21%	60–64		15%	19%	16%	20%
65–69		18%	22%	18%	22%	65–69		16%	20%	17%	21%
70–74		19%	23%	19%	23%	70–74		17%	21%	18%	22%
75–79		20%	24%	20%	24%	75–79		18%	22%	19%	23%
80–84		21%	25%	21%	25%	80–84		19%	23%	20%	24%
85–89		22%	26%	22%	26%	85–89		20%	24%	21%	25%
90–94		23%	27%	23%	27%	90–94		21%	25%	22%	26%
95–99		24%	28%	24%	28%	95–99		22%	26%	23%	27%
100–104		25%	29%	25%	29%	100–104		23%	27%	24%	28%
105–109		26%	30%	26%	30%	105–109		24%	28%	25%	29%
110–114		27%	31%	27%	31%	110–114		25%	29%	26%	30%
115–119		28%	32%	28%	32%	115–119		26%	30%	27%	31%
120–124		29%	33%	29%	33%	120–124		27%	31%	28%	32%
125–129		30%	34%	30%	34%	125–129		28%	32%	29%	33%
130–134		31%	35%	31%	35%	130–134		29%	33%	30%	34%
135–139		32%	36%	32%	36%	135–139		30%	34%	31%	35%
140–144		33%	37%	33%	37%	140–144		31%	35%	32%	36%
145–149		34%	37%	34%	37%	145–149		32%	36%	33%	37%
150–154		35%	37%	35%	37%	150–154		33%	37%	34%	37%
155–159		36%	37%	36%	37%	155–159		34%	37%	35%	37%
160 or more		37%	37%	37%	37%	160–164		35%	37%	36%	37%
						165–169		36%	37%	37%	37%
						170 or more		37%	37%	37%	37%

[1] **Diesel cars:** A 4% supplement applies to diesel cars up to a maximum of 37%. The supplement does not apply to hybrid cars or to cars registered on or after 1 September 2017 which meet the Euro 6d emissions standards.

[2] **For 2020–21 onwards:** For all cars first registered from 6 April 2020, a new regime for calculating a car's CO_2 emissions, known as the Worldwide Harmonised Light Vehicles Test Procedure (WLTP) applies. This replaces emissions testing under the New European Driving Cycle (NEDC). NEDC emissions values still apply to cars first registered between 1 October 1999 and 5 April 2020 inclusive.

[3] **For 2022–23 onwards:** The same rates apply to both pre and post April 2020 cars.

Cars registered on or after 1 January 1998 with no CO_2 emission figures
[T6.118]

Cylinder capacity of car[2]	Appropriate percentage[1]					
	2020–21	2021–22	2022–23	2023–24	2024–25	2025–26
1,400cc or less	24%	24%	24%	24%	24%	24%
Over 1,400cc up to 2,000cc	35%	35%	35%	35%	35%	35%
Over 2,000cc:	37%	37%	37%	37%	37%	37%
Cars incapable of producing CO_2 when driven	0%	1%	2%	2%	2%	2%

[1] **Diesel cars:** A 4% supplement applies to diesel cars up to a maximum of 37%. The supplement does not apply to hybrid cars or to cars registered on or after 1 September 2017 which meet the Euro 6d emissions standards.
[2] **No cylinder capacity:** For a car with no cylinder capacity 37% applies.

Cars registered before 1.1.98: For **2020–21 onwards** Tax is charged on 24% of the list price for engines to 1,400cc, 35% for engines 1,400cc to 2,000cc and 37% for engines above 2,000cc. Cars without a cylinder capacity are taxed on 37% of the list price.

Automatic cars for disabled drivers: CO_2 figure reduced to equivalent for manual car (ITEPA 2003 s 138).

Car unavailable for part of year: Value of the benefit is reduced proportionately (ITEPA 2003 s 143).

National Insurance: Also used to calculate the national insurance contributions payable by employers on the benefit of cars they provide for the private use of their employees, see **T8.109**.

The cash equivalent is reduced proportionately where the car is not available for the whole tax year. The amount (as so reduced) is reduced by any payments made by the employee for private use.

List price of car:
(1) Includes qualifying accessories, excluding accessories provided after car made available if its list price was less than £100. Accessories designed for use only by disabled people also excluded. Accessories do not include certain security enhancements provided to meet the threat to an employee's personal physical security arising from the nature of the employment. Where a car is manufactured so as to be capable of running on road fuel gas, its price is proportionately reduced by so much of that price as is reasonably attributable to it being manufactured in that way. Where a new car is converted to run on road fuel gas, the equipment is not regarded as an accessory. Disabled drivers of automatic cars who hold a disabled person's badge can use the list price of an equivalent manual car.
(2) Reduced by capital contributions made by employee up to £5,000.
(3) Classic cars (aged 15 years or more and with a market value of £15,000 or more at end of tax year): substitute market value at end of tax year if higher than adjusted list price. Reduction for capital contributions applies.

(ITEPA 2003 ss 120–132)

Vans and fuel for vans

[T6.119]

SEE TOLLEY'S TAX COMPUTATIONS 9.3.

(ITEPA 2003 ss 114–119, 154–164, 168, 169A, 170; FA 2021 s 23; SI 2021/248; SI 2022/1288)

Van benefit[1]	Vans which emit CO_2 when driven	Vans which do not emit CO_2 when driven[2]
2025–26	**£4,020**	**£0**
2023–24 and 2024–25	£3,960	£0
2022–23	£3,600	£0
2021–22	£3,500	£0
2020–21	£3,490	£2,792
2019–20	£3,430	£2,058

[1] Vehicle weight up to 3,500kg.
[2] For 2019–20, 60% of the van benefit charge for vans which emit CO_2 applies. 80% of the charge applies in 2020–21. The charge is reduced to nil from 2021–22 onwards.
[3] No charge applies to employees who have to take their van home and private use is restricted other than for ordinary commuting (insignificant use is disregarded).

Van fuel benefit	
2025–26	**£769**
2023–24 and 2024–25	£757
2022–23	£688
2021–22	£669
2020–21	£666
2019–20	£655

The fuel charge applies where the van benefit charge applies (though not where the reduced charge for zero-emission vans applies) and fuel is provided for private use.

Related benefits

[T6.120]

Parking facilities: No taxable benefit for work place provision of car or van parking spaces, or parking for bicycles or motorcycles (ITEPA 2003 s 237).

Vehicle-battery charging: No taxable benefit for work place provision of charging facilities for electric or plug-in hybrid cars or vans used by the employee (ITEPA 2003 s 237A).

Cycles and cyclist's safety equipment: No taxable benefit in respect of the provision to employees of bicycles or cycling safety equipment for travel to and from work (ITEPA 2003 s 244) nor for subsequent transfer to the employee at market value (ITEPA 2003 s 206; FA 2021 s 25). The qualifying journeys condition (ie travel to and from work) is treated as met from 16 March 2020 to 5 April 2022 where equipment was first provided before 21 December 2020.

On-call emergency vehicles: No tax or NIC charge where emergency service workers have private use of their emergency vehicle (ITEPA 2003 s 248A).

Bus services: No taxable benefit in respect of the provision of works buses with a seating capacity of 9 or more provided to employees (or their children) to travel to and from work (ITEPA 2003 s 242).

Car and motorcycle hire: restricted allowances

[T6.121]

SEE TOLLEY'S TAX COMPUTATIONS 116.1.

(ITTOIA 2005 ss 48–50B; CTA 2009 ss 56–58B; SI 2021/120)

Hire period from April 2009 (subject to transitional provisions), the disallowance is a flat rate of 15%. This applies only to cars with CO_2 emissions exceeding 50g/km from 1 April 2021 (corporation tax) or 6 April 2021 (income tax) (110g/km before 1 April 2021 (corporation tax) or 6 April 2021 (income tax), 130g/km before 1 April 2018, 160g/km before 1 April 2013 (corporation tax) or 6 April 2013 (income tax)).

Capital allowances see **T2.101**.

Car fuel: company cars
[T6.122]

SEE TOLLEY'S TAX COMPUTATIONS 9.3.
(ITEPA 2003 ss 149–153; SI 2021/248; SI 2022/1288)

The same percentage figures on **T6.117** used to calculate the car benefit charge for the company car, which are directly linked to the car's CO_2 emissions, are used to calculate the benefit charge for fuel provided for private motoring. The relevant percentage figure is multiplied by **£28,200 for 2025–26** (£24,100 for 2019–20, £24,500 for 2020–21, £24,600 for 2021–22, £25,300 for 2022–23, £27,800 for 2023–24 and 2024–25).

Benefit is reduced to nil if employee is required to, and does, make good all fuel provided for private use. No taxable benefit where employer only provides fuel for business travel. Charge is proportionately reduced where employee stops receiving free fuel part way through tax year, but where free fuel is subsequently provided in same tax year, full year's charge is payable. Benefit is proportionately reduced where a car is not available or is incapable of being used for part of a year (being at least 30 days).

CO_2 emissions (g/km)	Electric range (miles)	£ 2022–23 Petrol	£ 2022–23 Diesel[1]	£ 2023–24 and 2024–25 Petrol	£ 2023–24 and 2024–25 Diesel[1]	£ 2025–26 Petrol	£ 2025–26 Diesel[1]
0	N/A	506	N/A[1]	556	N/A[1]	846	N/A[1]
1–50	>130	506	N/A[1]	556	N/A[1]	846	N/A[1]
1–50	70–129	1,265	N/A[1]	1,390	N/A[1]	1,692	N/A[1]
1–50	40–69	2,024	N/A[1]	2,224	N/A[1]	2,538	N/A[1]
1–50	30–39	3,036	N/A[1]	3,336	N/A[1]	3,666	N/A[1]
1–50	<30	3,542	4,554[1]	3,892	5,004[1]	4,230	5,358[1]
51–54		3,795	4,807	4,170	5,282	4,512	5,640
55–59		4,048	5,060	4,448	5,560	4,794	5,922
60–64		4,301	5,313	4,726	5,838	5,076	6,204
65–69		4,554	5,566	5,004	6,116	5,358	6,486
70–74		4,807	5,819	5,282	6,394	5,640	6,768
75–79		5,060	6,072	5,560	6,672	5,922	7,050
80–84		5,313	6,325	5,838	6,950	6,204	7,332
85–89		5,566	6,578	6,116	7,228	6,486	7,614
90–94		5,819	6,831	6,394	7,506	6,768	7,896
95–99		6,072	7,084	6,672	7,784	7,050	8,178
100–104		6,325	7,337	6,950	8,062	7,332	8,460
105–109		6,578	7,590	7,228	8,340	7,614	8,742
110–114		6,831	7,843	7,506	8,618	7,896	9,024
115–119		7,084	8,096	7,784	8,896	8,178	9,306
120–124		7,337	8,349	8,062	9,174	8,460	9,588
125–129		7,590	8,602	8,340	9,452	8,742	9,870
130–134		7,843	8,855	8,618	9,730	9,024	10,152
135–139		8,096	9,108	8,896	10,008	9,306	10,434
140–144		8,349	9,361	9,174	10,286	9,588	10,434
145–149		8,602	9,361	9,452	10,286	9,870	10,434
150–154		8,855	9,361	9,730	10,286	10,152	10,434
155–159		9,108	9,361	10,008	10,286	10,434	10,434
160 or more		9,361	9,361	10,286	10,286	10,434	10,434

\multicolumn{5}{c	}{Cars first registered before 6 April 2020}	\multicolumn{5}{c}{Cars first registered on or after 6 April 2020}
CO_2 emissions (g/km)	Electric range (miles)	\multicolumn{2}{c}{£}	\multicolumn{2}{c	}{£}	CO_2 emissions (g/km)	Electric range (miles)	\multicolumn{2}{c}{£}	\multicolumn{2}{c}{£}
		\multicolumn{2}{c}{2020–21}	\multicolumn{2}{c	}{2021–22}			\multicolumn{2}{c}{2020–21}	\multicolumn{2}{c}{2021–22}
		Petrol	Diesel[1]	Petrol	Diesel[1]			Petrol	Diesel[1]	Petrol	Diesel[1]
0	N/A	0	0	246	N/A[1]	0	N/A	0	0	246	N/A[1]
1–50	>130	490	1,470	492	N/A[1]	1–50	>130	0	0	246	N/A[1]
1–50	70–129	1,225	2,205	1,230	N/A[1]	1–50	70–129	735	1,715	984	N/A[1]
1–50	40–69	1,960	2,940	1,968	N/A[1]	1–50	40–69	1,470	2,450	1,722	N/A[1]
1–50	30–39	2,940	3,920	2,952	N/A[1]	1–50	30–39	2,450	3,430	2,706	N/A[1]
1–50	<30	3,430	4,410	3,444	4,428[1]	1–50	<30	2,940	3,920	3,198	4,182[1]
51–54		3,675	4,655	3,690	4,674	51–54		3,185	4,165	3,444	4,428
55–59		3,920	4,900	3,936	4,920	55–59		3,430	4,410	3,690	4,674
60–64		4,165	5,145	4,182	5,166	60–64		3,675	4,655	3,936	4,920
65–69		4,410	5,390	4,428	5,412	65–69		3,920	4,900	4,182	5,166
70–74		4,655	5,635	4,674	5,658	70–74		4,165	5,145	4,428	5,412
75–79		4,900	5,880	4,920	5,904	75–79		4,410	5,390	4,674	5,658
80–84		5,145	6,125	5,166	6,150	80–84		4,655	5,635	4,920	5,904
85–89		5,390	6,370	5,412	6,396	85–89		4,900	5,880	5,166	6,150
90–94		5,635	6,615	5,658	6,642	90–94		5,145	6,125	5,412	6,396
95–99		5,880	6,860	5,904	6,888	95–99		5,390	6,370	5,658	6,642
100–104		6,125	7,105	6,150	7,134	100–104		5,635	6,615	5,904	6,888
105–109		6,370	7,350	6,396	7,380	105–109		5,880	6,860	6,150	7,134
110–114		6,615	7,595	6,642	7,626	110–114		6,125	7,105	6,396	7,380
115–119		6,860	7,840	6,888	7,872	115–119		6,370	7,350	6,642	7,626
120–124		7,105	8,085	7,134	8,118	120–124		6,615	7,595	6,888	7,872
125–129		7,350	8,330	7,380	8,364	125–129		6,860	7,840	7,134	8,118
130–134		7,595	8,575	7,626	8,610	130–134		7,105	8,085	7,380	8,364
135–139		7,840	8,820	7,872	8,856	135–139		7,350	8,330	7,626	8,610
140–144		8,085	9,065	8,118	9,102	140–144		7,595	8,575	7,872	8,856
145–149		8,330	9,065	8,364	9,102	145–149		7,840	8,820	8,118	9,102
150–154		8,575	9,065	8,610	9,102	150–154		8,085	9,065	8,364	9,102
155–159		8,820	9,065	8,856	9,102	155–159		8,330	9,065	8,610	9,102
160 or more		9,065	9,065	9,102	9,102	160–164		8,575	9,065	8,856	9,102
						165–169		8,820	9,065	9,102	9,102
						170 or more		9,065	9,065	9,102	9,102

[1] **Diesel cars:** A 4% supplement applies to diesel cars up to a 37% maximum. It doesn't apply to hybrid cars or to cars registered on or after 1.9.17 which meet the Euro 6d emissions standards.

Mileage allowances

Advisory fuel rates for company cars

[T6.123]

Engine size	Cost per mile		
	Petrol	Diesel	LPG
From 1 December 2024			
1,400cc or less	**12p**	**–**	**11p**
1,600cc or less	**–**	**11p**	**–**
1,401–2,000cc	**14p**	**–**	**13p**
1,601–2,000cc	**–**	**13p**	**–**
Over 2,000cc	**23p**	**17p**	**21p**
1 September 2024–30 November 2024			
1,400cc or less	13p	–	11p
1,600cc or less	–	12p	–
1,401–2,000cc	15p	–	13p
1,601–2,000cc	–	14p	–
Over 2,000cc	24p	18p	21p
1 June 2024–31 August 2024			
1,400cc or less	14p	–	11p
1,600cc or less	–	13p	–
1,401–2,000cc	16p	–	13p
1,601–2,000cc	–	15p	–
Over 2,000cc	26p	20p	21p
1 March 2024–31 May 2024			
1,400cc or less	13p	–	11p
1,600cc or less	–	12p	–
1,401–2,000cc	15p	–	13p
1,601–2,000cc	–	14p	–
Over 2,000cc	24p	19p	21p
1 December 2023–29 February 2024			
1,400cc or less	14p	–	10p
1,600cc or less	–	13p	–
1,401–2,000cc	16p	–	12p
1,601–2,000cc	–	15p	–
Over 2,000cc	26p	20p	18p
1 September 2023–30 November 2023			
1,400cc or less	13p	–	10p
1,600cc or less	–	12p	–
1,401–2,000cc	16p	–	12p
1,601–2,000cc	–	14p	–
Over 2,000cc	25p	19p	19p
1 June 2023–31 August 2023			
1,400cc or less	13p	–	10p
1,600cc or less	–	12p	–
1,401–2,000cc	15p	–	12p
1,601–2,000cc	–	14p	–
Over 2,000cc	23p	18p	18p
1 March 2023–31 May 2023			
1,400cc or less	13p	–	10p
1,600cc or less	–	13p	–
1,401–2,000cc	15p	–	11p
1,601–2,000cc	–	15p	–
Over 2,000cc	23p	20p	17p
1 December 2022–28 February 2023			
1,400cc or less	14p	–	10p
1,600cc or less	–	14p	–
1,401–2,000cc	17p	–	12p
1,601–2,000cc	–	17p	–
Over 2,000cc	26p	22p	18p

Engine size	Cost per mile		
	Petrol	Diesel	LPG
1 September 2022–30 November 2022			
1,400cc or less	15p	–	9p
1,600cc or less	–	14p	–
1,401–2,000cc	18p	–	11p
1,601–2,000cc	–	17p	–
Over 2,000cc	27p	22p	17p
1 June 2022–31 August 2022			
1,400cc or less	14p	–	9p
1,600cc or less	–	13p	–
1,401–2,000cc	17p	–	11p
1,601–2,000cc	–	16p	–
Over 2,000cc	25p	19p	16p
1 March 2022–31 May 2022			
1,400cc or less	13p	–	8p
1,600cc or less	–	11p	–
1,401–2,000cc	15p	–	10p
1,601–2,000cc	–	13p	–
Over 2,000cc	22p	16p	15p
1 December 2021–28 February 2022			
1,400cc or less	13p	–	9p
1,600cc or less	–	11p	–
1,401–2,000cc	15p	–	10p
1,601–2,000cc	–	13p	–
Over 2,000cc	22p	16p	15p
1 September 2021–30 November 2021			
1,400cc or less	12p	–	7p
1,600cc or less	–	10p	–
1,401–2,000cc	14p	–	8p
1,601–2,000cc	–	12p	–
Over 2,000cc	20p	15p	12p
1 June 2021–31 August 2021			
1,400cc or less	11p	–	8p
1,600cc or less	–	9p	–
1,401–2,000cc	13p	–	9p
1,601–2,000cc	–	11p	–
Over 2,000cc	19p	13p	14p
1 March 2021–31 May 2021			
1,400cc or less	10p	–	7p
1,600cc or less	–	9p	–
1,401–2,000cc	12p	–	8p
1,601–2,000cc	–	11p	–
Over 2,000cc	18p	12p	12p
1 December 2020–28 February 2021			
1,400cc or less	10p	–	7p
1,600cc or less	–	8p	–
1,401–2,000cc	11p	–	8p
1,601–2,000cc	–	10p	–
Over 2,000cc	17p	12p	12p
1 September 2020–30 November 2020			
1,400cc or less	10p	–	7p
1,600cc or less	–	8p	–
1,401–2,000cc	12p	–	8p
1,601–2,000cc	–	10p	–
Over 2,000cc	17p	12p	12p

[1] Payments at or below these rates are tax and NIC free. The table figures will be accepted for VAT purposes.
[2] Other rates may be used if the employer can demonstrate that they are justified.
[3] Rates are currently reviewed by HMRC quarterly.
[4] Hybrid cars are treated as petrol or diesel cars.

Advisory electricity rate for company cars
[T6.124]

	Cost per mile
From 1 December 2024	**7p**
1 September 2024–30 November 2024	7p
1 June 2024–31 August 2024	8p
1 March 2024–31 May 2024	9p
1 December 2023–29 February 2024	9p
1 September 2023–30 November 2023	10p
1 June 2023–31 August 2023	9p
1 March 2023–31 May 2023	9p
1 December 2022–28 February 2023	8p
1 December 2021–30 November 2022	5p
Before 1 December 2021	4p

[1] HMRC publish an advisory electricity rate, although electricity is not treated as a fuel for car fuel benefit purposes.

Authorised mileage rates
[T6.125]

SEE TOLLEY'S TAX COMPUTATIONS 9.2.

	Rate per business mile	
	First 10,000 miles	*Over 10,000 miles*
Cars or vans		
2011–12 onwards[1]	**45p**	**25p**

[1] Where the employer pays less than the authorised rate the employee can claim tax relief for the difference (ITEPA 2003 ss 229–232, 235, 236).

	Rate per business mile
Car passengers Allowance for each fellow passenger carried	
2002–03 onwards	**5p**
Cycles	
2002–03 onwards[1]	**20p**
Motorcycles	
2002–03 onwards[1]	**24p**

[1] Where the employer pays less than the authorised rate the employee can claim tax relief for the difference (ITEPA 2003 ss 229–232, 235, 236).

Travel expenses of members of local authorities
[T6.126]

(ITEPA 2003 s 235A)

There is an exemption for qualifying payments made by a local authority in respect of travel expenses incurred by a member on a journey between home and permanent workplace provided the member's home is in the area of the authority or within 20 miles of the boundary of the area. The exemption for mileage payments will be limited to the authorised mileage rates above.

Employment benefits and expenses payments

[T6.127]

T6.127 to **T6.155** cover some common benefits and expenses payments not detailed separately elsewhere. Where indicated, different rules apply to lower-paid ministers of religion earning at a rate of less than £8,500 per year.

Accommodation, supplies, etc used in employment duties

[T6.128]

SEE TOLLEY'S TAX COMPUTATIONS 9.4.

(ITEPA 2003 s 316)

The provision of accommodation, supplies or services used by employees in performance of employment duties is not taxable provided:
- (a) if the benefit is provided on premises occupied by the employer, any private use by the employee (or the employee's family or household) is not significant; or
- (b) in any other case, the sole purpose of providing the benefit is to enable the employee to perform those duties, any private use is not significant and the benefit is not an excluded benefit (eg the provision of a motor vehicle, boat or aircraft).

Amounts which would otherwise be deductible

[T6.129]

SEE TOLLEY'S TAX COMPUTATIONS 9.3.

(ITEPA 2003 ss 289A–289E)

An exemption applies to expenses and benefits paid or reimbursed by the employer where the employee would be due a deduction. The exemption does not apply if the payment or reimbursement is offered in conjunction with a relevant salary sacrifice arrangement.

Assets given to employees

[T6.130]

SEE TOLLEY'S TAX COMPUTATIONS 9.3.

(ITEPA 2003 ss 203, 204)

If new, tax chargeable on cost to employer (market value in the case of a 'lower-paid' minister of religion). If used, tax chargeable on greater of:
- (a) market value at the time of transfer; and
- (b) where the asset is first applied for the provision of a benefit after 5 April 1980 and a person has been chargeable to tax on its use, market value when first so applied less amounts charged to tax for use up to and including the year of transfer.

Buses to shops

[T6.131]

(SI 2002/205)

The provision of buses for journeys of ten miles or less from the workplace to shops etc on a working day is not taxable.

Cheap loans

[T6.132]

SEE TOLLEY'S TAX COMPUTATIONS 9.3.

(ITEPA 2003 ss 174–190; SI 2021/249)

A taxable benefit arises on employer-related loans to all employees other than 'lower-paid' ministers of religion, on the difference between the interest paid and interest payable at the 'official rate' below. There is no tax charge where:
- (a) all the employer-related loans (or all loans not qualifying for tax relief) do not exceed £10,000;
- (b) all the interest payable is or would be eligible for tax relief; and
- (c) the loans are ordinary commercial loans.

The provisions can apply to alternative finance arrangements.

The 'official rate' is:

From 6 April 2023	2.25%
6 April 2021 to 5 April 2023	2.00%
6 April 2020 to 5 April 2021	2.25%
6 April 2017 to 5 April 2020	2.50%

The average rate for the tax year is:

2024–25	**2.25%**
2023–24	2.25%
2022–23	2.00%
2021–22	2.00%
2020–21	2.25%
2019–20	2.50%

The official rate is set in advance for the whole of the following tax year, subject to review if the typical mortgage rates were to fall sharply during a tax year. The average for a tax year is provided after the end of the year. It is proposed that from 6 April 2025 in-year increases may take place where appropriate.

Childcare provision

[T6.133]

(ITEPA 2003 ss 318–318D; CPA 2014; SI 2015/537; SI 2018/462)

No liability arises:
- (a) where the premises (which are not wholly or mainly used as a private dwelling) are made available by the employer; or
- (b) where the scheme is provided under arrangements with other persons, by one or more of those persons; or
- (c) where (a) or (b) does not apply, on the first £55 per week of registered or approved childcare, or where the employee joins the scheme after 5 April 2011, the first £55 (basic rate taxpayers), £28 per week (higher rate taxpayers), £25 per week (additional rate taxpayers) of registered or approved childcare.

From April 2017 a 'tax-free childcare' scheme was introduced under which the Government make a top-up payment of 25% of payments into a childcare account up to a maximum of £8,000 per year (£16,000 for a disabled child). Government support is therefore capped at a maximum of £2,000 each year per qualifying child (£4,000 for a disabled child). A child is a qualifying child until the last day of the week containing 1 September after the child's 11th birthday (16th in the case of a disabled child). There is no liability to income tax or NIC under the scheme. The scheme has now been rolled out to all eligible parents and replaces those under (b) and (c) above for new entrants from 4 October 2018, though existing recipients continue to receive tax and NIC relief for as long as they remain eligible, provided that their employer continues to operate the scheme.

Christmas parties and annual functions

[T6.134]

(ITEPA 2003 s 264)

Not taxable if cost does not exceed £150 per head per tax year and open to staff generally. Otherwise, fully taxable. Expenditure may be split between more than one function. (Not taxable on 'lower-paid' ministers of religion.)

Credit tokens

[T6.135]

(ITEPA 2003 ss 90–96A, 363)

Where money goods or services are provided to employees through credit tokens, the cost to the employer, less any employee contribution, is taxable on the employee, except if they were used to buy certain non-taxable benefits.

Disabled employees

[T6.136]

(ITEPA 2003 ss 246, 247; SI 2002/1596)

The provision of, or payment for, transport for disabled employees for ordinary commuting is tax free. This also applies to the provision of equipment, services or facilities to disabled employees to help them carry out their duties of employment.

Employees' liability insurance

[T6.137]

(ITEPA 2003 s 346)
This is non-taxable.

Eye tests and corrective appliances

[T6.138]

(ITEPA 2003 s 320A)

No liability arises where the provision of tests or special corrective appliances are required under health and safety legislation and are available as required to employees generally.

Homeworkers

[T6.139]

(ITEPA 2003 ss 316, 316A; SI 2020/524; SI 2020/525; SI 2021/225)

Equipment provided by the employer solely to enable the employee to carry out their employment duties is exempt provided there is insignificant private use. A temporary exemption applies and has been extended for 2021–22 where an employee purchases equipment enabling them to work from home as a result of the coronavirus (COVID–19) pandemic and claims reimbursement from the employer.

Employer contributions to additional household costs not taxable where employee works at home. Supporting evidence required if contributions exceed £6 per week from 6 April 2020 (previously £4) or £26 per month for monthly paid employees (previously £18). This exemption can apply where an employee is required to work from home as a result of the coronavirus pandemic.

Incidental overnight expenses

[T6.140]

(ITEPA 2003 ss 240, 241)

Not taxable where employee stays away from home on business and payment from employer does not exceed:
- (a) £5 per night in the UK; or
- (b) £10 per night overseas.

Living accommodation

[T6.141]

SEE TOLLEY'S TAX COMPUTATIONS 9.4.

(ITEPA 2003 ss 97–113)

A taxable benefit (the '*basic charge*') arises on the annual rental value (or actual rent if greater) less any sums made good by the employee. There is an *additional charge* (if the basic charge is not calculated on the full open market rental value) where the cost of accommodation (including costs of any capital improvements less amounts made good by the employee) exceeds £75,000. The additional charge is the excess cost over £75,000 multiplied by the official rate for cheap loans (see above) in force at the start of the tax year less any rent paid by the employee in excess of the basic charge.

For leases of ten years or less, a lease premium paid is to be treated as if it were rent and spread over the period of the lease accordingly.

The charges are apportioned in the case of multiple occupation or if the property is provided for only part of the year or part is used exclusively for business purposes.

Exemption: No taxable benefit arises where living accommodation is provided:
- (a) for the proper performance of duties;
- (b) by reason that it is customary to do so; or
- (c) by reason of special threat to the employee's security.

The above exemptions apply to a full-time working director whose interest in the company does not exceed 5%, otherwise only exemption (c) applies to directors.

Living expenses

[T6.142]

SEE TOLLEY'S TAX COMPUTATIONS 9.4.

(ITEPA 2003 ss 313–315)

A taxable charge arises on the cost to the employer of the employee's living expenses. For the provision of assets such as furniture, see 'Use of employer's assets' below.

Where the exemption for living accommodation above applies, the tax charge relating to living expenses (including the provision of furniture and items normal for domestic occupation) is restricted to 10% of the employee's net earnings from the related employment less any sums made good by the employee.

Expenditure on alteration and structural repairs which are normally the landlord's responsibility do not give rise to a taxable benefit.

Long service awards

[T6.143]

(ITEPA 2003 s 323)

Not taxable provided the employee has at least 20 years' service and cost to the employer does not exceed £50 for each year of service. No similar award may be made within ten years of such an award.

Meals

[T6.144]

(ITEPA 2003 s 317)

Subsidised or free meals provided for staff generally at the workplace are not taxable. This relief does not apply if the provision of meals is made under salary sacrifice or flexible remuneration arrangements.

Medical check-ups, insurance and treatment

[T6.145]

(ITEPA 2003 ss 320B, 325; FA 2021 s 26; HMRC Employment Income Manual EIM21765)

Check-ups:
One screening and one check-up each year not taxable.

Insurance: Premiums paid on behalf of employees (other than 'lower-paid' ministers of religion) are taxable unless for treatment outside the UK whilst the employee is performing duties abroad.

Recommended medical treatment: Any benefit in kind or payment of earnings, up to an annual cap of £500 per employee, is not taxable where an employer meets the cost of certain recommended medical treatment in connection with an employee's return to work after a period of absence due to ill-health or injury.

Coronavirus (COVID–19) tests: Coronavirus test kits provided to employees by their employers are not a taxable benefit in 2020–21 and 2021–22.

Pensions advice

[T6.146]

(SI 2002/205; ITEPA 2003 ss 308B, 308C)

Payments provided to employees in respect of advice on pensions (including on general financial and tax issues relating to pensions) are not taxable if the cost is no more than £500.

Payments by employers in respect of independent advice provided to employees in relation to conversions and transfers of pension scheme benefits are exempt.

Personal expenses

[T6.147]

SEE TOLLEY'S TAX COMPUTATIONS 9.2.

(ITEPA 2003 ss 70–72, 336–341)

Unless covered by specific exemptions, payments to an employee by reason of his employment in respect of expenses or allowances are taxable. Deduction is allowed for expenses the employee is obliged to incur which are:

(a) qualifying travelling expenses (broadly those necessarily incurred other than for ordinary commuting or private travel); or
(b) other amounts incurred wholly, exclusively and necessarily in the performance of employment duties.

Relocation expenses

[T6.148]

SEE TOLLEY'S TAX COMPUTATIONS 9.5.

(ITEPA 2003 ss 271–289)

Qualifying removal expenses and benefits up to £8,000 per move in connection with job-related residential moves are not taxable. Included are expenses of disposal, acquisition, abortive acquisition, transport of belongings, travelling and subsistence, bridging loans and duplicate expenses (replacement domestic items).

Salary sacrifice and flexible benefit arrangements

[T6.149]

(ITEPA 2003 ss 69A, 69B)

From 2017–18 the range of benefits that attract income tax and NIC advantages when provided as part of optional remuneration arrangements is limited but savings can still be made on employer pension contributions and advice, employer-provided childcare, cycle to work schemes, and ultra-low emission company cars. Arrangements in place before 6 April 2017 could continue unaffected until 5 April 2018 (with a further extension until 5 April 2021 for existing longer term agreements covering cars, living accommodation and school fees).

Scholarships

[T6.150]

(ITEPA 2003 ss 211–215)

An employee is taxable on the cost of any scholarship from a trust fund which does not satisfy a 25% distribution test or which is paid because of the employee's employment.

Subscriptions and fees

[T6.151]

(ITEPA 2003 ss 343–345)

Not taxable where paid to professional bodies and the employee has a contractual or professional requirement to be a member of the body.

Third party gifts

[T6.152]

(ITEPA 2003 ss 270, 324)

Gifts during the tax year of goods and non-cash vouchers up to £250 not taxable where provided by a party unconnected with the employer and not for services provided in connection with employment.

Trivial benefits

[T6.153]

(ITEPA 2003 ss 323A–323C)

There is an exemption for qualifying trivial benefits in kind costing less than £50, extending to qualifying benefits provided to former employees. An annual cap of £300 applies to office holders of close companies, and employees who are family members of those office holders.

Use of employer's assets

[T6.154]

SEE TOLLEY'S TAX COMPUTATIONS 9.3.

(ITEPA 2003 ss 203–206, 242, 244, 319, 320; HMRC Brief 02/2012)

Tax is chargeable on all employees other than 'lower-paid' ministers of religion on the annual rental value of land and, for other assets, at 20% of the market value when they are first lent or the rental charge to the employer if higher. No taxable benefit arises on:

- (a) the loan of a mobile phone or smartphone for private use. This is restricted to one phone per employee and does not extend to the employee's family or household;
- (b) the use of works buses (see **T6.120**);
- (c) cycles and cycle safety equipment (see **T6.120**);
- (d) the loan of computer equipment for private use where the equipment was first made available before 6 April 2006, provided use is not restricted to directors or senior staff and value of benefit does not exceed £2,500.

No benefit arises on the subsequent purchase by an employee at market value of computer or cycling equipment previously on loan.

The benefit is reduced by periods during which the asset is unavailable for private use by the employee or his family/household, or where the asset is shared by two or more employees.

Vouchers

[T6.155]

(ITEPA 2003 ss 73–89, 95, 96, 268–270, 362)

Vouchers are taxable as follows.

(a)	Cash vouchers	On amount for which voucher can be exchanged.
(b)	Non-cash vouchers	On cost to employer less any contribution from employee (except where used to obtain certain non-taxable benefits).
(c)	Transport vouchers	On cost to employer less any contribution from employee.

Employment exemption

Employee-ownership trusts

[T6.156]

(ITEPA 2003 ss 312A–312I)

An exemption from income tax applies to qualifying bonus payments of up to £3,600 per tax year made to employees, and qualifying former employees, by a company which is owned directly or indirectly by an employee-ownership trust which meets certain qualifying conditions.

For CGT relief relating to such companies see **T3.111**.

Employment income

PAYE and national insurance thresholds
[T6.157]

	2019–20	2020–21	2021–22	2022–23	2023–24 and 2024–25	2025–26
	£	£	£	£	£	£
Weekly NI	166	183/169	184/170	190[2]/175	242/175	**242/96**
Weekly PAYE	240	240	242	242	242	**242**
Monthly NI	719	792/732	797/737	823[3]/758	1,048/758	**1,048/417**
Monthly PAYE	1,042	1,042	1,048	1,048	1,048	**1,048**

[1] For full list of national insurance rates see **T8.101**.
[2] £190 from 6 April 2022 to 5 July 2022. £242 from 6 July 2022 to 5 April 2023.
[3] £823 from 6 April 2022 to 5 July 2022. £1,048 from 6 July 2022 to 5 April 2023.

PAYE settlement agreements
[T6.158]

SEE TOLLEY'S TAX COMPUTATIONS **506.1**.

(SI 2003/2682 Part 6)
These are voluntary agreements between the employer and HMRC under which the employer agrees to meet the tax payable on certain expenses and benefits in kind that are given to his employees. Once an agreement has been signed for a tax year, there is no need to:
- enter the items covered on form P11D;
- operate PAYE on them, or
- calculate a liability for included items which are liable for Class 1 or Class 1A NICs.

The employer pays Class 1B NICs on the items included in PAYE settlement agreements and on the total amount of tax payable. To be effective for a tax year, an agreement must be signed before 6 July following the end of the year and tax must be paid by 22 October following (or 19 October where not paid electronically). They are most suited for payments and benefits provided on an irregular basis, or where benefits are for a group of employees and apportionment is difficult.

Employers can create an enduring agreement with HMRC which will remain in place for subsequent tax years unless varied or cancelled by the employer or HMRC.

Personal service companies
[T6.159]

SEE TOLLEY'S TAX COMPUTATIONS **20.1**.

(ITEPA 2003 ss 48–61)
These provisions are commonly known under the name 'IR35' and apply where personal services are provided to a client through an intermediary – normally the worker's personal service company. The effect of the legislation is to treat the worker as an employee of the client for working out a 'deemed employment payment'.

Small business clients. Where the client is a small business in the private sector, the provisions operate as follows. The computation involves taking into account all payments and benefits, including those paid direct to the worker for a tax year other than by the intermediary for his services. Certain, restricted, allowable expenses, are deducted from 'earnings'. Finally, any payments or benefits received by the worker from the intermediary are deducted. Tax (under PAYE) and NIC is calculated and the amounts due are payable by the worker and his company. The provisions also apply to office holders.

The provisions applied in this way to public sector engagements before April 2017 and to engagements where the client was medium-sized and large businesses in the private sector before April 2021.

Off payroll working rules. For public sector engagements from April 2017 the liability to pay the correct employment taxes applies to the public sector body or agency/third party paying the company, and the amount is deducted from the amount paid to the company.

From April 2021 the public sector rules are extended to engagements between an intermediary and medium-sized and large businesses in the private sector. The liability to pay the correct employment taxes applies to the private sector business, and the amount will be deducted from the amount paid to the company.

Managed service companies
[T6.160]

(ITEPA 2003 ss 61A–61J)
Where an individual provides his services through a managed service company (as defined) all payments made to him by the company are deemed to be employment income and PAYE and NIC have to be applied. These rules do not apply to an engagement within the personal service company rules as they apply to public sector engagements from April 2017 or engagements with medium-sized and large businesses from April 2021.

National living wage and minimum wage

[T6.161]

(SI 2015/621)
Hourly rate

Age of worker	apprentice rate[2]	Under 18[1]	18–20	21 and over[3]	
From 1 April 2025	**£7.55**	**£7.55**	**£10.00**	**£12.21**	
1.4.24–31.3.25	£6.40	£6.40	£8.60	£11.44	

Age of worker	apprentice rate[2]	Under 18[1]	18–20	21–22	23 and over[3]
1.4.23–31.3.24	£5.28	£5.28	£7.49	£10.18	£10.42
1.4.22–31.3.23	£4.81	£4.81	£6.83	£9.18	£9.50
1.4.21–31.3.22	£4.30	£4.62	£6.56	£8.36	£8.91

Age of worker	apprentice rate[2]	Under 18[1]	18–20	21–24	25 or over[3]
1.4.20–31.3.21	£4.15	£4.55	£6.45	£8.20	£8.72

[1] Applies to all workers under 18 who are no longer of compulsory school age.
[2] The apprentice rate applies to apprentices aged under 19 and other apprentices in their first year of apprenticeship.
[3] The national living wage applies for employees aged 21 and over (23 and over before 1 April 2024, 25 or over before 1 April 2021).

Basis of assessment

[T6.162]

(ITEPA 2003 ss 14–41E)
From 6 April 2025 onwards

	Services performed			
	Wholly in UK	Partly in UK	Partly abroad	Wholly abroad
Non-resident[2]	All	That part	None	None
Resident[2]				
Meets the conditions for overseas workday relief[3,4,5].	All	That part	Effectively exempt (may be subject to a limit)	Effectively exempt (may be subject to a limit)
Does not meet the conditions for overseas workday relief[6]	All	All[1]	All[1]	All[1]

[1] Exemption for seafarers if at least half of qualifying period of over 364 days worked abroad (including 183 consecutive days). Also applies to seafarers who are resident for tax purposes in a European Economic Area or European Union State. Extended with effect from 15 March 2018 to employees of the Royal Fleet Auxiliary (ITEPA 2003 ss 378–385, HMRC Brief 10/2012).
[2] The individual's residence is determined using the statutory residence test.
[3] An employee meets conditions for overseas workday relief for their first four tax years of UK residence as long as they were UK non-resident for the 10 consecutive tax years immediately prior to arrival in the UK. They must also have qualifying foreign employment income in relation to their employment or associated employment. Therefore, the employee must spend time physically working outside the UK and receive income in respect of their overseas workdays (although there is no requirement for this to be received offshore). The qualifying foreign employment income relating to the tax year must be reported on the tax return for the year and a claim must be made to deduct the appropriate amount of relief from the employee's taxable income (see (4) below).
[4] An annual limit applies to overseas workday relief, which is the lower of 30% of the relevant qualifying employment income and £300,000. Where the limit is exceeded, the excess is taxable in the UK irrespective of where the duties are performed, where the employer is based and where the earnings for the non-UK workdays are paid. See also (5) below.
[5] Transitional rules apply where the employee benefitted from overseas workday relief at 5 April 2025. The length of time that they can continue to benefit from overseas workday relief depends on their residence history. If they meet the condition of having been UK non-resident for the 10 consecutive tax years immediately prior to arrival in the UK, they can continue to apply overseas workday relief until the end of their fourth tax year of UK residence (which includes tax years prior to 6 April 2025). If they do not meet that condition, they can continue to apply overseas workday relief until the end of their third tax year of UK residence (which includes tax years prior to 6 April 2025). In either situation the limit on relief discussed in (4) above does not apply.
[6] If the employee does not qualify for overseas workday relief or the transitional overseas workday provisions, they are taxable in the UK on their worldwide earnings irrespective of where the duties are performed, where the employer is based and where the earnings for the non-UK workdays are paid.

Up to 5 April 2025

	Services performed			
	Wholly in UK	*Partly in UK*	*Partly abroad*	*Wholly abroad*
Persons domiciled in UK				
Non-resident[2]	All	That part	None	None
Resident[2]	All	All[1]	All[1]	All[1]
Persons domiciled outside the UK				
UK employer				
Non-resident	All	That part	None	None
Resident and meets the conditions for overseas workday relief[3]	All	That part	Remittance	Remittance
Resident and does not meet the conditions for overseas workday relief[4,5]	All	All[1]	All[1]	All[1]
Foreign employer				
Non-resident	All	That part	None	None
Resident and meets the conditions for overseas workday relief[3]	All	That part	Remittance	Remittance
Resident and does not meet the conditions for overseas workday relief[4,5]	All	That part	Remittance	Remittance

[1] Exemption for seafarers if at least half of qualifying period of over 364 days worked abroad (including 183 consecutive days). Also applies to seafarers who are resident for tax purposes in a European Economic Area or European Union State. Extended with effect from 15 March 2018 to employees of the Royal Fleet Auxiliary (ITEPA 2003 ss 378–385, HMRC Brief 10/2012).

[2] The individual's residence is determined using the statutory residence test.

[3] An employee meets conditions for overseas workday relief for the relevant tax year if (1) they have been non-resident for three consecutive tax years and the relevant tax year is any of the three years immediately following that spell of non-residence and (2) they have duties of employment both in the UK and overseas under a single contract of employment. The employee must also spend time physically working outside the UK, be taxable on the remittance basis in the tax year and receive income in respect of their overseas workdays directly outside the UK (the location of the payroll is irrelevant as long as the earnings for the non-UK workdays are paid into a non-UK bank account, which must meet certain conditions for the special mixed fund rules in ITA 2007 ss 809RA–809RD). Where these conditions are met, the earnings in relation to the non-UK workdays are non-taxable in the UK unless they are remitted.

[4] Where the employee does not meet the conditions for overseas workday relief, worldwide general earnings are taxable in the UK, although if they are taxed on the remittance basis any earnings in respect of duties performed wholly overseas for a foreign employer are taxable in the UK only if they are remitted to the UK. See (5) below.

[5] An anti-avoidance measure applies to tax UK resident non-domiciliaries on an arising basis in respect of certain overseas employment income where separate employment contracts have been artificially arranged to separate the UK and overseas employment to obtain a tax advantage. These rules do not affect overseas workday relief because in order to qualify for that relief the employee must have duties of employment both in the UK and overseas under a single contract of employment.

Termination payments

[T6.163]

SEE TOLLEY'S TAX COMPUTATIONS 6.1.

(ITEPA 2003 ss 401–416)

The following lump sum payments are exempt from tax:
- (a) Payments in connection with the cessation of employment on the death, injury or disability of the employee.
- (b) Payments under tax-exempt pension schemes by way of compensation for loss of employment (or of earnings due to ill-health) or which can properly be regarded as a benefit earned by past service.
- (c) Certain payments of terminal grants to members of the armed forces.
- (d) Certain benefits under superannuation schemes for civil servants in Commonwealth overseas territories.
- (e) Payments in respect of foreign service broadly before 14 September 2017 (but see note below) where the period of foreign service comprises:
  - (i) 75% of the whole period of service; or
  - (ii) the whole of the last 10 years of service; or
  - (iii) where the period of service exceeded 20 years, one-half of that period, including any 10 of the last 20 years.

  Otherwise, a proportion of the payment is exempt, as follows:

  $$\frac{\text{length of foreign service}}{\text{length of total service}} \times \text{amount otherwise chargeable}$$

- (f) The first £30,000 of genuine ex gratia payments (where there is no 'arrangement' by the employer to make the payment).
- (g) Statutory redundancy payments (included in computing £30,000 limit in (f) above).

Foreign service relief is abolished for termination payments and benefits to employees who are UK resident in the tax year in which the employment is terminated. This applies where the date of the termination is on or after 6 April 2018 and the termination payment, or other benefit, is received after 13 September 2017. Foreign service relief continues in termination cases where the employee is non-UK resident in the year of termination, and for UK residents where the payment or benefit is in connection with a change of duties or earnings rather than with termination of the employment. Reductions for foreign service are also retained for seafarers and extended to employees of the Royal Fleet Auxiliary.

Fixed rate expenses

[T6.164]

For most classes of industry fixed rate allowances for the upkeep of tools and special clothing have been agreed between HMRC and the trade unions concerned. Alternatively, the individual employee may claim as a deduction his or her actual expenses (ITEPA 2003 s 367). (HMRC Employment Income Manual EIM32712).

Industry	Occupation		Deduction
Agriculture	All workers[1]		100
Airlines	See note 5 below		
Aluminium	(a)	Continual casting operators, process operators, de-dimplers, driers, drill punchers, dross unloaders, firemen[2], furnace operators and their helpers, leaders, mould-men, pourers, remelt department labourers, roll flatteners	140
	(b)	Cable hands, case makers, labourers, mates, truck drivers and measurers, storekeepers	80
	(c)	Apprentices	60
	(d)	All other workers[1]	120
Banks and building societies	Uniformed doormen and messengers		60
Brass and copper	Braziers, coppersmiths, finishers, fitters, moulders, turners and all other workers		120
Building	(a)	Joiners and carpenters	140
	(b)	Cement works, roofing felt and asphalt labourers	80
	(c)	Labourers and navvies	60
	(d)	All other workers	120
Building materials	(a)	Stone masons	120
	(b)	Tilemakers and labourers	60
	(c)	All other workers	80
Clothing	(a)	Lacemakers, hosiery bleachers, dyers, scourers and knitters, knitwear bleachers and dyers	60
	(b)	All other workers	60
Constructional engineering[3]	(a)	Blacksmiths and their strikers, burners, caulkers, chippers, drillers, erectors, fitters, holders up, markers off, platers, riggers, riveters, rivet heaters, scaffolders, sheeters, template workers, turners, welders	140
	(b)	Banksmen, labourers, shop-helpers, slewers, straighteners	80
	(c)	Apprentices and storekeepers	60
	(d)	All other workers	100
Electrical and electricity supply	(a)	Those workers incurring laundry costs only	60
	(b)	All other workers	120
Engineering (trades ancillary to)	(a)	Pattern makers	140
	(b)	Labourers, supervisory and unskilled workers	80
	(c)	Apprentices and storekeepers	60
	(d)	Motor mechanics in garage repair shops	120
	(e)	All other workers	120
Fire service	Uniformed firefighters and fire officers		80
Food	All workers		60
Forces personnel	See note 7 below		
Forestry	All workers		100
Glass	All workers		80
Health and care staff in the NHS, private hospitals, local authorities and independent care providers	(a)	Ambulance staff on active service	185
	(b)	Nurses and midwives, chiropodists, dental nurses, occupational, speech, physiotherapists and other therapists, healthcare assistants, phlebotomists and radiographers. See note 8 below for shoes and stockings/tights/socks allowances	125
	(c)	Plaster room orderlies, hospital porters, ward clerks, sterile supply workers, hospital domestics, hospital catering staff	125
	(d)	Laboratory staff, pharmacists, pharmacy assistants	80
	(e)	Uniformed ancillary staff: maintenance workers, grounds staff, drivers, parking attendants and security guards, receptionists and other uniformed staff	80
Heating	(a)	Pipe fitters and plumbers	120
	(b)	Coverers, laggers, domestic glaziers, heating engineers and their mates	120
	(c)	All gas workers, all other workers	100
Iron mining	(a)	Fillers, miners and underground workers	120
	(b)	All other workers	100
Iron and steel	(a)	Day labourers, general labourers, stockmen, time keepers, warehouse staff and weighmen	80
	(b)	Apprentices	60
	(c)	All other workers	140
Leather	(a)	Curriers (wet workers), fellmongering workers, tanning operatives (wet)	80
	(b)	All other workers	60

Industry	Occupation		Deduction
Particular engineering[4]	(a)	Pattern makers	140
	(b)	Chainmakers, cleaners, galvanisers, tinners and wire drawers in the wire drawing industry, tool-makers in the lock making industry	120
	(c)	Apprentices and storekeepers	60
	(d)	All other workers	80
Police force		Uniformed police officers (ranks up to and including Chief Inspector) Community Support officers and other police service employees — see note 6 below	140
Precious metals		All workers	100
Printing	(a)	Letterpress section — electrical engineers (rotary presses), electro-typers, ink and roller makers, machine minders (rotary), maintenance engineers (rotary presses) and stereotypers	140
	(b)	Bench hands (periodical and bookbinding section), compositors (letterpress section), readers (letterpress section), telecommunications and electronic section wire room operators, warehousemen (paper box making section)	60
	(c)	All other workers	100
Prisons		Uniformed prison officers	80
Public service	(i)	Dock and inland waterways	
		(a) Dockers, dredger drivers, hopper steerers	80
		(b) All other workers	60
	(ii)	Public transport	
		(a) Garage hands (including cleaners)	80
		(b) Conductors and drivers	60
Quarrying		All workers	100
Railways		(See the appropriate category for craftsmen, eg engineers, vehicles etc.) All other workers	100
Seamen		Carpenters	
	(a)	Passenger liners	165
	(b)	Cargo vessels, tankers, coasters and ferries	140
Shipyards	(a)	Blacksmiths and their strikers, boilermakers, burners, carpenters, caulkers, drillers, furnacemen (platers), holders up, fitters, platers, plumbers, riveters, sheet iron workers, shipwrights, tubers, welders	140
	(b)	Labourers	80
	(c)	Apprentices and storekeepers	60
	(d)	All other workers	100
Textiles and textile printing	(a)	Carders, carding engineers, overlookers and technicians in spinning mills	120
	(b)	All other workers	80
Vehicles	(a)	Builders, railway vehicle repairers, and railway wagon lifters	140
	(b)	Railway vehicle painters and letterers, and builders' and repairers' assistants	80
	(c)	All other workers	60
Wood & furniture	(a)	Carpenters, cabinet makers, joiners, wood carvers and woodcutting machinists	140
	(b)	Artificial limb makers (other than in wood), organ builders and packaging case makers	120
	(c)	Coopers not providing own tools, labourers, polishers and upholsterers	60
	(d)	All other workers	100

[1] 'All workers' and 'all other workers' refer only to manual workers who have to bear the cost of upkeep of tools and special clothing. They do not extend to other employees such as office staff.

[2] 'Firemen' means persons engaged to light and maintain furnaces.

[3] 'Constructional engineering' means engineering undertaken on a construction site, including buildings, shipyards, bridges, roads and other similar operations.

[4] 'Particular engineering' means engineering undertaken on a commercial basis in a factory or workshop for the purposes of producing components such as wire, springs, nails and locks.

[5] A basic flat rate expenses allowance of £1,022 applies to all uniformed commercial pilots, co-pilots and other flight deck crew working in the UK (but not stewards/stewardesses). A further £110 allowance is allowed for the cost of travel to certain regular specified activities. Stewards/stewardesses may claim basic flat rate expenses of £720.

[6] The allowance for police officers applies to community support officers. Other police service employees who must clean their own uniform can claim a deduction of £60.

[7] A flat-rate expenses allowance applies in relation to the laundering of uniforms for naval ratings and other ranks. The annual amount is £80 for the Royal Navy and £100 for the Army, RAF and Royal Marines.

[8] A flat-rate expenses allowance applies of £12 per year for the renewal or repair of shoes, and £6 per year for stockings/tights/socks where the wearing of a prescribed style or colour (style only for shoes) is obligatory for nurses, midwives, auxiliaries, students, dental nurses, nursing assistants and healthcare assistants or workers.

[9] Correct as at 1 November 2024.

Apprenticeship levy

[T6.165]

(FA 2016 ss 98–121)

An apprenticeship levy applies to UK employers in both the private and public sectors. It is set at a rate of 0.5% of an employer's pay bill and paid through PAYE. Each employer receives an allowance of £15,000 to offset against their levy payment. This means that the levy will only be paid on any pay bill in excess of £3 million. The pay bill is the total of employee earnings subject to Class 1 secondary National Insurance Contributions, as if disregarding the secondary and upper secondary thresholds.

Investment reliefs

Community investment tax relief

[T6.166]

(ITA 2007 ss 333–382; CTA 2010 ss 218–269)

Investments made by an individual or company in an accredited community development finance institution (CDFI) are eligible for tax relief up to 25%. The investment may be a loan or a subscription for shares or securities. Tax relief may be claimed for the tax year or accounting period in which the investment is made and each of the four subsequent years. Relief for each year is broadly 5% of the invested amount, but any unused balance of the 5% annual relief can be carried forward, although not beyond the 5-year investment period, and only as long as some part of the investment remains within the CDFI. In addition, to comply with European State aid rules, there is a limit on the amounts of relief a company can obtain in any 3-year period — the amount of CITR relief and any de minimis aid from other sources must not exceed €200,000.

Enterprise investment scheme

[T6.167]

(ITA 2007 ss 156–257; FA 2024 s 11; SI 2018/931)

The EIS applies to investments in qualifying unquoted companies trading in the UK. Eligible shares must be held for at least three years from the issue date or commencement of trade if later. The following reliefs apply subject to this and other conditions.

Relief on investment

[T6.168]

SEE TOLLEY'S TAX COMPUTATIONS 10.1 ONWARDS.

Maximum investment: if amount over £1,000,000 invested in Knowledge Intensive Companies	From 2018–19	£2,000,000
Maximum investment: otherwise	From 2012–13	£1,000,000
Maximum carry-back to preceding year	From 2009–10	No restriction (subject to annual maximum)
Rate of relief	From 2011–12	30%[1]

[1] Given as a deduction against income tax liability.

Other reliefs (TCGA 1992 ss 150A–150C, Sch 5B)
SEE TOLLEY'S TAX COMPUTATIONS 211.1, 211.2, 211.3.
(a) A gain on a disposal of shares on which EIS relief has been given and not withdrawn is exempt from capital gains tax (see **T3.111**).
(b) Deferral relief is available for gains on assets where the disposal proceeds are reinvested in eligible shares in a qualifying company within one year before and three years after the disposal.
(c) A loss on a disposal of shares on which EIS relief has been given may be relieved against income tax or capital gains tax.

Seed enterprise investment scheme

[T6.169]

(ITA 2007 ss 257A–257HG; F(No 2)A 2023 s 15)

SEIS applies to investments in companies with fewer than 25 employees and assets up to £350,000 (£200,000 before 6 April 2023) carrying on or preparing to carry on new business. Eligible shares must be held for at least three years from the issue date. The following reliefs apply subject to this and other conditions.

Relief on investment

[T6.170]

SEE TOLLEY'S TAX COMPUTATIONS 25.1, 25.2.

Maximum investment:	From 2023–24	£200,000
	2012–13 to 2022–23	£100,000
Maximum carry-back to preceding year	From 2013–14	No restriction (subject to annual maximum)
Rate of relief	From 2012–13	50%[1]

[1] Given as a deduction against income tax liability.

Other reliefs (TCGA 1992 ss 150E, 150G, Sch 5BB)
SEE TOLLEY'S TAX COMPUTATIONS 227.1, 227.2, 227.3.
  (a) A gain on a disposal of shares on which SEIS relief has been given and not withdrawn is exempt from capital gains tax.
  (b) Reinvestment relief is available for certain gains on assets where the disposal proceeds are reinvested in SEIS and SEIS relief is claimed (see **T36.111**).

Social investment tax relief

[T6.171]

(ITA 2007 ss 257J–257TE; FA 2021 s 20)
Between 6 April 2014 and 5 April 2023 income tax relief is available to both resident and non-UK resident individuals who subscribe for qualifying shares or make qualifying debt investments in a social enterprise which meets the requirements, and who have a UK tax liability against which to set the relief. The investment must be held for a period of three years. The following reliefs apply subject to conditions. The scheme is abolished with effect from 6 April 2023.

Relief on investment

[T6.172]

Maximum investment:	From 2014–15 to 2022–23	£1,000,000
Maximum carry-back to preceding year	From 2015–16 to 2022–23	No restriction (subject to annual maximum)
Rate of relief	From 2014–15 to 2022–23	30%[1]

[1] Given as a deduction against income tax liability.

Other reliefs
SEE TOLLEY'S TAX COMPUTATIONS 231.1, 231.2, 231.3.
  (a) A gain on a disposal of shares on which SITR income tax relief has been given and not withdrawn is exempt from capital gains tax where shares held for at least 3 years.
  (b) Deferral relief is available for gains arising on assets in the period 6 April 2014 to 5 April 2023 where the disposal proceeds are reinvested in shares or debt investments which also qualify for the SITR income tax relief (see **T3.111**).

Venture capital trusts

[T6.173]

SEE TOLLEY'S TAX COMPUTATIONS 32.1, 32.2, 32.3.
(ITA 2007 ss 258–332; FA 2024 s 11)
An individual who subscribes for ordinary shares in a VCT obtains income tax reliefs at the rates in the table below subject to conditions. The shares must be held for at least five years.

Relief on investment

[T6.174]

| Maximum annual investment: | From 2004–05 | £200,000 |
| Rate of relief: | From 2006–07 | 30% |

Other reliefs
  (a) Dividends on shares within investment limit exempt from income tax (unless the investor's main purpose is tax avoidance) (ITTOIA 2005 s 709).
  (b) Capital gains reliefs (see **T3.111**).

Urban Regeneration Companies

[T6.175]

Relief is available for expenditure incurred by businesses in making contributions to designated Urban Regeneration Companies (ITTOIA 2005 ss 82, 86; CTA 2009 ss 82, 86).

Individual savings accounts ('ISAs')

[T6.176]

(ITTOIA 2005 ss 694–701; SI 1998/1870)

Savers can subscribe to an ISA up to the following limits per tax year.

	2020–21	2021–22	2022–23	2023–24	2024–25	**2025–26**
Overall annual subscription limit	£20,000	£20,000	£20,000	£20,000	£20,000	**£20,000**
Cash limit	£20,000	£20,000	£20,000	£20,000	£20,000	**£20,000**

1. ISA savers are able to subscribe the full subscription amount to a cash account.
2. The subscription limit applies to each spouse or civil partner. An additional ISA allowance is available for spouses or civil partners following the death of an ISA saver, equal to the value of that deceased saver's ISAs.
3. ISA providers can offer a flexible account, whereby withdrawals during the year may be replaced without the replacement counting towards the subscription limit.
4. Shares acquired under a tax-favoured share incentive plan or SAYE option scheme may be transferred to an ISA within 90 days without tax consequences.
5. Subject to certain time limits, investments retained in an ISA during the administration of a deceased saver's estate will retain their tax-advantaged status.
6. From 6 April 2024, multiple subscriptions are allowed in each tax year to ISAs of the same type.

Reliefs

(a) Investments under the scheme are free from income tax and capital gains tax. When an investment is transferred to an investor they are deemed to have made a disposal and reacquisition at market value and any notional gain is exempt from capital gains tax.

(b) Withdrawals may be made at any time without loss of tax relief.

Lifetime ISA

[T6.177]

Individuals aged between 18 and 40 are able to save up to £4,000 per year into one Lifetime ISA and receive a 25% bonus from the Government at the end of the year. Contributions can continue to be made with the bonus paid up to the age of 50. Funds, including the Government bonus, can be used to buy a first home up to the value of £450,000 at any time from 12 months after opening the account, and can be withdrawn tax-free from age 60 for use in retirement. Withdrawals prior to that, other than by the terminally ill, will attract a penalty. If an individual had a Help to Buy: ISA they could transfer those savings into the Lifetime ISA in 2017–18, or continue saving into both, or open a Help to Buy: ISA after opening a Lifetime ISA, but they will only be able to use the bonus from one of the ISAs to buy a house.

Help to Buy: ISAs

[T6.178]

Help to Buy: ISAs could be opened from 1 December 2015 to 30 November 2019 for first-time house buyers. Once opened contributions can continue until 30 November 2029. The maximum monthly savings amount is £200, and provided the balance reaches at least £1,600, the Government will provide a bonus of 25% of savings, up to a maximum bonus of £3,000 on £12,000 of savings. It is possible to deposit an additional £1,000 when the account is first opened. The interest on the account and the bonus will be tax-free. The bonus must be claimed by 1 December 2030 at the latest, and will be paid at the time of completion of the purchase of the property provided the property is worth a maximum of £450,000 in London and £250,000 elsewhere in the UK. Accounts are limited to one per person rather than one per property. See above regarding Lifetime ISAs held at the same time as Help to Buy: ISAs.

Junior individual savings accounts (Junior ISAs)

[T6.179]

(ITTOIA 2005 s 695A; SI 1998/1870)

The Junior ISA scheme is available to all UK resident children under 18 who do not have a Child Trust Fund account and to those who wish to transfer a Child Trust Fund account to a Junior ISA.

	2020–21	2021–22	2022–23	2023–24	2024–25	**2025–26**
Overall annual subscription limit	£9,000	£9,000	£9,000	£9,000	£9,000	**£9,000**

Miscellaneous income tax reliefs

Trading allowance and property allowance

[T6.180]

(ITTOIA 2005 ss 783A–783AR, 783B–783BQ)

A trading allowance and a property allowance of £1,000 each per year are available to certain individuals. They are not available on income of partners or close company participators, or where rent-a-room relief could be claimed. Where total receipts are no more than £1,000, the allowance is given automatically, no tax is payable and the income need not be declared. An election can be made for relief not to apply at all, or for partial relief to apply where receipts exceed £1,000 so that the allowance rather than expenses is deducted from gross receipts.

Employee shareholder shares

[T6.181]

(ITEPA 2003 ss 226A–226D; SI 2013/1755)

The first £2,000 of the value of shares acquired through the adoption of the 'employee shareholder' employment status is not subject to income tax or national insurance, provided the Employee Shareholder Agreement was entered into before 1 December 2016 (or 2 December 2016 where professional advice was given in relation to the share offer on 23 November 2016 before 1.30pm). For the capital gains tax rules see **T3.111**.

Foster carers and shared lives carers (Qualifying care)

[T6.182]

SEE TOLLEY'S TAX COMPUTATIONS 30.12.

(ITTOIA 2005 ss 803–828; SI 2011/712; SI 2024/423)

Generally, local authority payments to foster carers are not taxable to the extent they do no more than meet the actual costs of caring. In other cases, and for shared lives carers (see below):
- where gross receipts do not exceed the 'individual limit' and shared lives care is not being provided to more than three people, the carer is treated as having a nil profit and nil loss for the tax year concerned;
- where gross receipts exceed the 'individual limit' and shared lives care is not being provided to more than three people, the carer can choose to either be taxed on the excess or compute profit or loss using the normal business rules.

The relief also applies to shared lives schemes that are self-funded by the person receiving care.

For 2025–26, the 'individual limit' is made up of a fixed amount of £19,690 (£19,360 for 2024–25; £18,140 for 2023–24; previously £10,000) per residence for a full tax year plus an amount per adult or child for each week or part week that the individual provides qualifying care. The 2025–26 weekly amounts are £415 (£405 for 2024–25; £375 for 2023–24; previously £200) for a child under 11 years and £495 (£485 for 2024–25; £450 for 2023–24; previously £250) for a child of 11 or over and an adult. The fixed amount and weekly amounts are increased by Consumer Price Index (CPI) inflation each tax year, starting from 2024–25.

Gift of pre-eminent objects

[T6.183]

(FA 2012 Sch 14)

Individuals who gift pre-eminent objects to the nation will receive a reduction in their UK tax liability of 30% of the value of the object they are donating. The tax reduction can be against income or capital gains tax and can be spread forward across a period of up to five years starting with the tax year in which the object is offered. The gift must be accepted as pre-eminent by the Arts Council under the Cultural Gifts Scheme.

Maintenance payments

[T6.184]

SEE TOLLEY'S TAX COMPUTATIONS 16.2.

(ITTOIA 2005 ss 727, 729; ITA 2007 ss 453–456)

Where either party to the marriage or civil partnership was born before 6 April 1935 tax relief may be claimed by the payer in respect of the lower of:
- the amount of the payments in the year concerned and
- the minimum amount of the married couple's allowance for the year concerned (see **T6.113**).

The relief is restricted to 10% of the relevant amount. The payment must be made to the former/separated spouse or civil partner. It is made gross and is not taxable in the hands of the recipient.

Rent-a-room relief

[T6.185]

SEE TOLLEY'S TAX COMPUTATIONS 22.3.

(ITTOIA 2005 ss 784–802)

Gross annual receipts from letting furnished accommodation in the only or main home are exempt from tax up to a maximum of £7,500 (provided no other taxable income is derived from a trade, letting or arrangement from which the rent-a-room receipts are derived).

If the gross receipts exceed £7,500, the taxpayer can pay tax on the net receipts after deduction of expenses. Alternatively, the taxpayer can elect to pay tax on the amount by which the gross receipts exceed £7,500, without relief for the actual expenses.

An individual's maximum is halved to £3,750 if during the 'relevant period' for the year (normally the tax year) some other person received income from letting accommodation in that property.

An election can be made to disapply the relief for a particular tax year (for example, if the individual would otherwise make an allowable loss).

Simplified fixed rate deductions

[T6.186]

SEE TOLLEY'S TAX COMPUTATIONS 31.1.

(ITTOIA 2005 ss 94B–94I)

Individuals carrying on a trade, profession or vocation as self-employed sole traders or in partnership with other individuals can choose certain simplified expenses when calculating their profits for income tax purposes. Deductions for vehicle expenditure are also available to those carrying on a property business. Conditions apply.

Vehicle expenditure

Kind of vehicle	Rate per business mile
Car or goods vehicle	45p for the first 10,000 miles
	25p after that
Motor cycle	24p

Use of home for business purposes

Hours worked per month	Amount per month
25 or more	£10
51 or more	£18
101 or more	£26

Premises used both as a home and for business

Note: Amount below is the non-business use amount to be deducted from the total expenses claimed. The flat rate includes all household goods and services, food and non-alcoholic drinks and utilities. It does not include mortgage interest, rent of the premises, council tax or rates. A reasonable apportionment of these expenses should be made based on the extent of the private occupation of the premises — HMRC Brief 14/2013.

Number of occupants	Disallowance amount per month
1	£350
2	£500
3 or more	£650

Capped income tax reliefs

[T6.187]

(ITA 2007 s 24A)

The following income tax reliefs are capped. The limit is set at the greater of £50,000 or 25% of the individual's adjusted total income for the tax year. The specified reliefs which, taken together, will be limited to the extent that they can be relieved by individuals against general income are:

- Trade loss relief against general income (ITA 2007 s 64)
- Early trade losses relief (ITA 2007 s 72)
- Post-cessation trade relief (ITA 2007 s 96)
- Property loss relief against general income (ITA 2007 s 120)
- Post-cessation property relief (ITA 2007 s 125)
- Employment loss relief against general income (ITA 2007 s 128)
- Former employees deduction for liabilities (ITEPA 2003 s 555)
- Share loss relief on non-Enterprise Investment Scheme / Seed Enterprise Investment Scheme shares (ITA 2007 Pt 4 Ch 6)
- Losses on deeply discounted securities (ITTOIA 2005 ss 446, 454)
- Qualifying loan interest (ITA 2007 Pt 8 Ch 1)

Pension provision

[T6.188]

(FA 2004 ss 149–284, Schs 28–36; FA 2021 s 28; F(No 2)A 2023 ss 18–25; FA 2024 s 14, Sch 9)

Tax relief on contributions

[T6.189]

SEE TOLLEY'S TAX COMPUTATIONS 19.1.

Individual contributions: An individual may make unlimited contributions and tax relief is available on contributions up to the higher of:
- the full amount of relevant earnings; or
- £3,600 provided the scheme operates tax relief at source,

and subject to the annual allowance.

Employer contributions: Employer contributions to registered schemes are deductible for tax purposes, with statutory provision for spreading abnormally large contributions over a period of up to four years. The contributions are not treated as taxable income of the employee, although this relief does not extend to payments for the benefit of family members.

Annual allowance

[T6.190]

SEE TOLLEY'S TAX COMPUTATIONS 19.2.

Each individual has an annual allowance as set out in the table below. If the annual increase in an individual's rights under all registered schemes exceeds the annual allowance, the excess is chargeable at the individual's marginal rate. The individual is liable for the tax, unless he makes an election for the scheme to pay the charge if it exceeds £2,000. In such cases a consequential adjustment is made to the individual's entitlement to benefits.

Annual allowance	2014–15 to 2015–16	2016–17 to 2019–20	2020–21 to 2022–23	**2023–24 to 2025–26**
Maximum	£40,000[1, 2]	£40,000[1, 2]	£40,000[1, 2]	**£60,000** [1, 2]
Minimum[3]	N/A	£10,000[3]	£4,000[3]	**£10,000**[3]

[1] Unused allowance can be carried forward three years.
[2] Where members make use of flexible access to their money purchase funds from 6 April 2015 the annual allowance is effectively divided between money purchase inputs and defined benefit inputs, resulting in a 'money purchase annual allowance' of £10,000 (£4,000 before 6 April 2023, £10,000 before 6 April 2017) and an 'alternative annual allowance' that applies to any defined benefit inputs of £50,000 (£36,000 before 6 April 2023, £30,000 before 6 April 2017). The money purchase annual allowance cannot be increased by amounts brought forward.
[3] A tapered reduction in the annual allowance applies for those with an 'adjusted income' (i.e. including pension contributions) over £260,000 (£240,000 from 6 April 2020 to 5 April 2023, £150,000 from 6 April 2016 to 5 April 2020). The reduction is £1 for every £2 of income over the limit and the minimum allowance is £10,000 (£4,000 before 6 April 2023, £10,000 before 6 April 2020).

Taxable benefits

[T6.191]

'Tax-free' lump sum: The maximum 'tax-free' lump sum that can be paid to a member under a registered scheme is broadly the lower of:
- 25% of the value of the pension rights; and
- £268,275 (or, before, 6 April 2023, 25% of the member's lifetime allowance).

Lifetime allowance: Before 6 April 2023, each individual has a lifetime allowance for contributions as set out in the table below. The excess over the lifetime allowance of the benefits crystallising (usually when a pension begins to be paid) is taxable at the following rates:
- 55% if taken as a lump sum;
- 25% in other cases.

Any tax due may be deducted from the individual's benefits. The lifetime allowance tax charges are abolished with effect from 6 April 2023. The lifetime allowance itself is abolished with effect from 6 April 2024. For 2024–25 onwards, the allowance is replaced by two new allowances to retain the previous limits on tax-free lump sums and overseas transfers. A lump sum and death benefit allowance of £1,073,100 is introduced. Authorised lump sums and lump sum death benefits received up to the allowance are tax free. Any such sums paid above that level are taxed at the individual's marginal rate of income tax. Also for 2024–25 onwards, an overseas transfer allowance of £1,073,100 applies. Where the total value of an individual's transfers from registered pension schemes or relieved non-UK schemes to a qualifying recognised overseas pension scheme (QROPS) exceeds their available allowance, the excess is subject to the overseas transfer charge. A transitional calculation applies to determine the available allowances at 6 April 2024.

Lifetime allowance	2016–17 to 2017–18	2018–19	2019–20	**2020–21 to 2022–23**
	£1,000,000	£1,030,000	£1,055,000	**£1,073,100**

Transitional. There are transitional provisions for the protection of lump sum and other pension rights accrued before 6 April 2006. Various protections apply to protect pension rights when the lifetime allowance is decreased.

Age restrictions

[T6.192]

Minimum pension age: The minimum pension age is 55. A pension cannot be paid before the minimum age except on grounds of ill health. Protection applies to those with existing contractual rights to draw a pension earlier and for members of pre-6 April 2006 approved schemes with early retirement ages. A reduced lifetime allowance will apply in the case of early retirement before minimum pension age except in the case of certain professions such as the police and the armed forces (SI 2005/3451). From 6 April 2028, the minimum pension age will increase to 57.

Retired members of the police, fire service and other uniformed services did not lose their protected pension age if they returned to work with the same employer or an employer connected to that employer, in the same field from which they retired, whether or not there is a break between the date they retired and the date they were re-employed, if they did so as part of the Government's response to the coronavirus (COVID–19) pandemic.

Share schemes

Share incentive plans ('SIPs')

[T6.193]

SEE TOLLEY'S TAX COMPUTATIONS 28.4.
(TCGA 1992 ss 236A, 238A, Schs 7C, 7D Pt 1; ITEPA 2003 ss 488–515, Sch 2)

Free share plan

2014–15 onwards	annual maximum	£3,600

Partnership share plan

[T6.194]

2014–15 onwards	annual maximum	£1,800 or 10% of annual salary if lower

Matching shares

[T6.195]

2000–01 onwards	Maximum number of shares given by employer to employee for each partnership share bought	2

Shares are free of tax and NICs if held in the plan for five years. Dividends are tax-free if reinvested in shares. Shares withdrawn from the plan at any time are exempt from capital gains tax and treated as acquired by the employee at their market value at that time.

If shares are withdrawn within between three and five years (with exceptions such as on death, injury, disability, retirement, redundancy, or certain cash takeovers), liability to income tax and NICs arises on the lower of their value on entering and on leaving the plan. If shares are withdrawn within three years (with similar exceptions), liability is on their value on leaving the plan.

Enterprise management incentives

[T6.196]

SEE TOLLEY'S TAX COMPUTATIONS 28.5.
(TCGA 1992 s 238A, Sch 7D Pt 4; ITEPA 2003 ss 527–541, Sch 5; FA 2024 s 13)

Certain independent trading companies with gross assets not exceeding £30 million may grant share options then worth up to £250,000 to an eligible employee. The total value of shares in respect of which unexercised qualifying options exist must not exceed £3 million. Limited to companies with fewer than 250 full-time equivalent employees.

Where the conditions of the scheme are complied with:
  (a) There is no charge to tax or NICs when the option is granted provided the option to acquire the shares is not at less than their market values at that date, and there is no charge on exercise providing the option is exercised within ten years.
  (b) Capital gains tax will be payable when the shares are sold, though shares acquired through exercising EMI options on or after 6 April 2012 are eligible for capital gains tax business asset disposal relief if certain conditions are met.

Save as you earn (SAYE) share option schemes

[T6.197]

(TCGA 1992 s 238A, Sch 7D Pt 2; ITEPA 2003 ss 516–519, Sch 3)

The scheme is linked to a savings arrangement, on which bonuses are exempt from tax, to provide funds for the acquisition of shares when the option is exercised at the end of a three or five-year contract.

Employees are able to take a pause of up to 12 months from saving into their SAYE scheme. HMRC will allow contributions to be postponed for a longer period where the additional months are missed due to coronavirus (COVID–19).

Monthly contributions to SAYE scheme

[T6.198]

	From 6 April 2014
Minimum	£5–£10[1]
Maximum	£500

[1] The company may choose a minimum savings contribution between £5 and £10.

See GOV.UK website (www.gov.uk/government/publications/change-in-bonus-rates-for-save-as-you-earn-saye-share-option-schemes) for the latest bonus rates.

Where the conditions of the scheme are complied with, no income tax charge arises on the employee in respect of:
- (a) the grant of an option to acquire shares at a discount of up to 20% of the share price at time of the grant;
- (b) the exercise of the option (options must not be exercised before the bonus date subject to exceptions such as on injury, disability, redundancy, retirement, death or certain cash takeovers); or
- (c) any increase in the value of the shares.

Capital gains tax is chargeable on disposal of the shares: the CGT base cost is the consideration given by the employee for both the shares and the option.

Company share option plans ('CSOPs')

[T6.199]

(TCGA 1992 s 238A, Sch 7D Pt 3; ITEPA 2003 ss 521–526, Sch 4; F(No 2)A 2023 s 16)

Limit on value of shares under option held by employee at any one time

[T6.200]

From 6 April 2023	**£60,000**
29 April 1996–5 April 2023	£30,000

Scheme shares must be fully paid up and not redeemable. Only full-time directors or qualifying employees may participate in the scheme.

Where the conditions of the scheme are complied with, no tax charge arises on the employee in respect of:
- (a) the grant of an option to acquire shares[1];
- (b) the exercise of the option[2]; or
- (c) any increase in the value of the shares.

Capital gains tax is chargeable on disposal of the shares: the CGT base cost is the consideration given by the employee for both the shares and the option.

[1] At the time the option is granted the price at which shares can be acquired must not be less than the market value of shares of the same class at that time.
[2] The option must be exercised between three and ten years after the grant (or may be exercised less than three years after the grant where the individual ceases to be an employee due to injury, disability, redundancy or retirement, or where there are certain cash takeovers of constituent companies).

Tax credits

[T6.201]

(TCA 2002)

Tax credits are administered and paid by HMRC, and are non-taxable. Claims must be made after the commencement of the tax year and can be backdated for a maximum of one month. Universal credit will replace tax credits. New claimants and those reporting changed circumstances are being directed to universal credit. It is intended that most existing claimants will be transferred by the end of 2024–25 (see **T10.102**).

Child tax credit and working tax credit

[T6.202]

	2024–25	*2025–26*
	Annual amount	*Annual amount*
Child tax credit	£	£
Family element[1]	545	N/A
Child element (for each child or young person)[2]	3,455	N/A
Addition for disabled child or young person	4,170	N/A
Enhancement for severe disabled child or young person	1,680	N/A
Working tax credit	£	£
Basic element	2,435	N/A
Lone parent and couple element	2,500	N/A
30-hour element	1,015	N/A
Disability element	3,935	N/A
Severe disability element	1,705	N/A

	2024–25	2025–26
	Annual amount	*Annual amount*
	Weekly	**Weekly**
Childcare element – up to 70% of eligible costs		
– maximum eligible cost for one child	175	N/A
– maximum eligible cost for two or more children	300	N/A

1   Only one family element per family. It is not payable to those starting a family after 5 April 2017.
2   No child element is payable for third and subsequent children born after 5 April 2017. Does not apply to disabled child element or severely disabled child element and multiple births are protected.

Income thresholds and withdrawal rates	2024–25	2025–26
Income threshold for those entitled to CTC and WTC	£7,955	N/A
Withdrawal rate	41%	N/A
Income threshold for those entitled to CTC only	£19,995	N/A
Income rise disregard	£2,500	N/A
Income fall disregard	£2,500	N/A

Calculation of award. Tax credits are awarded on an annual basis. They are initially based on the income of the claimant or joint claimants for the preceding tax year and adjusted based on actual income in the tax year in which the credit is claimed. Income broadly includes all taxable income excluding the first £300 of income from pensions, savings, property or foreign assets. If current year's income is greater than the previous year's income by less than £2,500, the award is not adjusted. If current year's income is greater than the previous year's income by £2,500 or more, the award is adjusted to reflect current year's income less £2,500. An income fall disregard of £2,500 applies so where previous year's income exceeds the current year's income by not more than £2,500, the previous year's income will be used, but where the previous year's income exceeds the current year's income by more than £2,500, the current year's income plus £2,500 will be used. In any other case current year's income is used. Where circumstances change during a tax year and different rates apply, the award is recalculated on a proportional, daily basis. Such changes must be notified to HMRC within one month if tax credit entitlement will be reduced as a result.

Eligibility. CTC is payable to UK resident single parents and couples responsible for a child or young person. WTC is payable to UK residents who are at least 16 years old and, in the case of single persons, who work at least 16 hours a week. In the case of a couple they must jointly work at least 24 hours a week and one must work at least 16 hours a week, or where only one of the couple works that person must work for at least 24 hours a week. Additionally, the claimant (or one of them if a couple) must either:
- be at least 25 years old and work at least 30 hours a week; or
- have a dependent child or children; or
- have a mental or physical disability which puts them at a disadvantage in getting a job and have previously been in receipt of some form of disability benefit; or
- be over 60 and work at least 16 hours a week, regardless of whether they have dependent children.

Renewal claim. Claims for tax credit must be renewed by 31 July.

Inheritance tax

Rates of inheritance tax

[T7.101]

(IHTA 1984 s 7, Schs 1, 1A; HMRC Inheritance Tax Manual IHTM14593)

From 15 March 1988 onwards

[T7.102]

SEE TOLLEY'S TAX COMPUTATIONS 305.1, 305.2.

	Rate
Cumulative gross transfer rate:	
for gross transfers on death over the cumulative chargeable transfer limit	**40%**
reduced rate on death	**36%**[1]
for gross lifetime transfers over the cumulative chargeable transfer limit	**20%**
Grossing-up net transfer rate for each £1 over the chargeable transfer limit:	
for net transfers on death not bearing own tax	**2/3**
for net lifetime transfers	**1/4**

[1] For deaths occurring on or after 6 April 2012 a reduced rate of 36% applies where at least 10% of the net estate is left to charity or registered community amateur sports clubs.

Nil rate band

[T7.103]

SEE TOLLEY'S TAX COMPUTATIONS 310.3, 310.5.
(IHTA 1984 ss 8–8C; FA 2021 s 86)

Period	Limit £	Period	Limit £
2009–10 to 2029–30[2]	**325,000**[1]	1998–99	223,000
2008–09	312,000[1]	1997–98	215,000
2007–08	300,000[1]	1996–97	200,000
2006–07	285,000	1995–96	154,000
2005–06	275,000	10.3.92–5.4.95	150,000
2004–05	263,000	6.4.91–9.3.92	140,000
2003–04	255,000	1990–91	128,000
2002–03	250,000	1989–90	118,000
2001–02	242,000	15.3.88–5.4.89	110,000
2000–01	234,000	17.3.87–14.3.88	90,000
1999–2000	231,000	18.3.86–16.3.87	71,000

[1] Any nil rate band which is unused on a person's death can be transferred to their surviving spouse or civil partner for the purposes of the charge to tax on the death of the survivor on or after 9 October 2007.
[2] The nil rate band is frozen at £325,000 until 5 April 2030.

Residence nil rate band
(IHTA 1984 s 8D; FA 2021 s 86)

Period	Limit £
2020–21 to 2029–30	**175,000**
2019–20	150,000
2018–19	125,000
2017–18	100,000

[1] The **residence nil rate band** applies when a home is passed on death to direct descendants of the deceased on or after 6 April 2017. Any unused band is transferable to a spouse or civil partner. There is a tapered withdrawal of the band for estates valued at more than £2 million. It also applies where an individual downsizes from a higher value residence to a lower value one or ceases to own a home on or after 8 July 2015 and assets of equivalent value are passed on death to direct descendants.

Capital transfer tax nil rate bands
[T7.104]

Period	Limit £	Period	Limit £
6.4.85–17.3.86	67,000	26.3.80–8.3.82	50,000
13.3.84–5.4.85	64,000	27.10.77–25.3.80	25,000
15.3.83–12.3.84	60,000	13.3.75–26.10.77	15,000
9.3.82–14.3.83	55,000		

Estate duty nil rate bands (England, Scotland and Wales)
[T7.105]

Period	Limit £	Period	Limit £
22.3.72–12.3.75	15,000	9.4.62–3.4.63	4,000
31.3.71–21.3.72	12,500	30.7.54–8.4.62	3,000
16.4.69–30.3.71	10,000	10.4.46–29.7.54	2,000
4.4.63–15.4.69	5,000	16.8.14–9.4.46	100

Delivery of accounts: due dates
[T7.106]

(IHTA 1984 s 216)

Type of transfer	Due date
Chargeable lifetime transfers	Later of: (a) 12 months after the end of the month in which the transfer took place; and (b) three months after the date on which the person delivering the account became liable
Relevant property settlements periodic and exit charges	6 months after end of the month in which the chargeable event occurred.
PETs which become chargeable	12 months after the end of the month in which the transferor died
Gifts with reservation chargeable on death	12 months after the end of the month in which the death occurred
Transfers on death	Later of: (a) 12 months after the end of the month in which the death occurred; and (b) three months after the date on which the personal representatives first act or the person liable first has reason to believe that he is liable to deliver an account
National heritage property	6 months after the end of the month in which the chargeable event occurred

Delivery of accounts: excepted transfers and estates
[T7.107]

(SI 2004/2543; SI 2008/605; SI 2008/606; SI 2021/1167)

Excepted transfers
[T7.108]

No account need be delivered where:
  (i) the transfer is of cash or quoted shares or securities and the value of the transfer and other chargeable transfers made in the preceding seven years does not exceed the IHT threshold; or
  (ii) the value of the transfer and other chargeable transfers made in the preceding seven years does not exceed 80% of the IHT threshold and the value of the transfer does not exceed the net amount of the threshold available to the transferor at the time of the transfer.

Excepted estates

Deaths after 31 December 2021

[T7.109]

No account need be delivered where the deceased died domiciled in the UK provided conditions (i)–(iii) below are met.

(i) the aggregate of the gross value of the estate, and of any 'specified transfers'[1] or 'specified exempt transfers'[2] does not exceed the appropriate IHT threshold[3];

(ii) the gross value of settled property and foreign assets do not exceed £250,000 and £100,000 respectively; and

(iii) there were no chargeable lifetime transfers in the seven years before death other than specified transfers not exceeding £250,000[4].

No account need be delivered where the deceased died domiciled in the UK provided conditions (a)–(d) below are met.

(a) the aggregate of the gross value of the estate, and of any 'specified transfers'[1] or 'specified exempt transfers'[2] does not exceed £3,000,000; at least part of the estate passes to the person's spouse, civil partner or to a charity; and after deducting from that aggregate figure any exempt spouse, civil partner and charity transfers and total estate liabilities[5], it does not exceed the appropriate IHT threshold[3];

(b) the gross value of settled property does not exceed £1,000,000, of which not more than £250,000 does not pass to the person's spouse, civil partner or to a charity;

(c) the gross value of foreign assets does not exceed £100,000; and

(d) there were no chargeable lifetime transfers in the seven years before death other than specified transfers not exceeding £250,000[4].

Where the deceased was never domiciled in the UK, no account need be delivered provided that the value of the estate in the UK is wholly attributable to cash and quoted shares and securities not exceeding £150,000. The deceased must have made no lifetime gifts in the seven years prior to death and must not own overseas property attributable to UK residential property.

Deaths before 1 January 2022

No account need be delivered where the deceased died domiciled in the UK provided either conditions (a) or (b) below are met, and both conditions (c) and (d) below are met.

(a) the aggregate of the gross value of the estate, and of any 'specified transfers'[1] or 'specified exempt transfers'[2] does not exceed the appropriate IHT threshold[3];

(b) the aggregate of the gross value of the estate, and of any 'specified transfers'[1] or 'specified exempt transfers'[2] does not exceed £1,000,000; at least part of the estate passes to the person's spouse, civil partner or to a charity; and after deducting from that aggregate figure any exempt spouse, civil partner and charity transfers and total estate liabilities[5], it does not exceed the appropriate IHT threshold[3];

(c) the gross value of settled property and foreign assets do not exceed £150,000 and £100,000 respectively; and

(d) there were no chargeable lifetime transfers in the seven years before death other than specified transfers not exceeding £150,000[4].

Where the deceased was never domiciled in the UK, no account need be delivered provided that the value of the estate in the UK is wholly attributable to cash and quoted shares and securities not exceeding £150,000.

[1] 'Specified transfers' are chargeable transfers of cash, quoted shares and securities, interests in or over land and personal chattels or corporeal moveable property. Transfers treated as normal expenditure out of income made within 7 years before death and totalling more than £3,000 in any tax year are treated as chargeable transfers for these purposes.

[2] 'Specified exempt transfers' are transfers in the seven years before death between spouses or civil partners, gifts to charity, political parties or housing associations, transfers to maintenance funds for historical buildings, etc or to employee trusts.

[3] For deaths after 31 December 2021, where the deceased was predeceased by a spouse or civil partner, the IHT threshold for these purposes is increased by the percentage of the spouse or civil partner's IHT threshold which was unused on the first death, provided that a claim has been made for the transfer of the unused nil-rate band and the first deceased met certain other criteria similar to those listed above for excepted estates. For deaths before 1 January 2022, the IHT threshold was increased only if all of the first deceased spouse's or civil partner's nil-rate band was unused (so that the increase was by 100%).

[4] Transfers treated as normal expenditure out of income made within 7 years before death and totalling more than £3,000 in any tax year will be treated as chargeable transfers for these purposes.

[5] Total estate liabilities do not include those which are not discharged on or after death out of the estate in money or money's worth, or those which are prevented by any other provision in IHTA 1984 from being taken into account, or those attributable to financing the acquisition of, or maintenance or enhancement of the value of, excluded property.

Excepted settlements

[T7.110]

No account need be delivered of property comprised in an excepted settlement (i.e. one with no qualifying interest in possession) where a chargeable event occurs and cash not exceeding £1,000 is the only property comprised in the settlement. Other conditions to be fulfilled are that, the settlor has not provided further property, the trustees are UK resident throughout the settlement's existence and there are no related settlements.

Inheritance tax reliefs

[T7.111]

The following is a summary of the main reliefs and exemptions under the Inheritance Tax Act 1984 (Parts II and V). The legislation should be referred to for conditions and exceptions.

Agricultural property
SEE TOLLEY'S TAX COMPUTATIONS 302.1, 302.2.

Transfer with vacant possession (or right to obtain it within 12 months); transfer on or after 1 September 1995, of land let (or treated as let) on or after that date.	100% of agricultural value
Any other case.	50% of agricultural value

1. The 100% relief is extended in limited circumstances by Concession F17.
2. From 6 April 2024, relief applies only to land in the UK. Previously it also applied to land in the EEA and Channel Islands.
3. From 6 April 2025, relief is extended to land managed under an environmental agreement with, or on behalf of, the UK Government, Devolved Administrations, public bodies, local authorities or approved responsible bodies.
4. From 6 April 2026, the combined value of agricultural property relief and business property relief available at 100% will be capped at £1m. The relief given on the balance of any property qualifying for APR or BPR will be at 50%. Anti-forestalling measures apply from 30 October 2024.

Annual gifts £3,000
SEE TOLLEY'S TAX COMPUTATIONS 310.1.

Business property
SEE TOLLEY'S TAX COMPUTATIONS 304.1.

Unincorporated business.	100%	Controlling holding in fully quoted companies.	50%
Unquoted shares (including shares in AIM companies) (held for 2 years or more).	100%	Land, buildings, machinery or plant used in business of company or partnership.	50%
Unquoted securities which alone, or together with other such securities and unquoted shares, give the transferor control of the company (held for 2 years or more).	100%		
Settled property used in life tenant's business.	100%		

1. From 6 April 2026, the combined value of business property relief and agricultural property relief available at 100% will be capped at £1m. The relief given on the balance of any property qualifying for BPR or APR will be at 50%. Anti-forestalling measures apply from 30 October 2024.
2. From 6 April 2026, the rate of business property relief available on shares traded on a recognised stock exchange which is designated as 'not listed' will be reduced to 50%. This provision is targeted at AIM shares. Anti-forestalling measures apply from 30 October 2024.

Charities, gifts to	Exempt
Community Amateur Sports Clubs are treated as charities.	
Marriage/civil partnership gifts	
Made by: parent	£5,000
remoter ancestor	£2,500
party to marriage/civil partnership	£2,500
other person	£1,000
National purposes	
SEE TOLLEY'S TAX COMPUTATIONS 315.1.	
Property given or bequeathed to bodies listed in IHTA 1984 Sch 3.	Exempt
Political parties, gifts to	Exempt
Potentially exempt transfers	
SEE TOLLEY'S TAX COMPUTATIONS 305.1.	

Exempt if made 7 or more years before the date of death. Except for gifts with reservation etc, they include:
- (a) transfers by individuals to other individuals or certain trusts for the disabled;
- (b) transfers after 21 March 2006 by individuals to a bereaved minor's trust on the coming to an end of an immediate post-death interest;
- (c) transfers before 22 March 2006 by individuals to accumulation and maintenance trusts;
- (d) transfers by individuals into interest in possession trusts in which, for transfers after 21 March 2006, the beneficiary has a disabled person's interest; and
- (e) certain transfers on the termination or disposal of an individual's beneficial interest in possession in settled property (in restricted circumstances following FA 2006).

Quick succession relief
SEE TOLLEY'S TAX COMPUTATIONS 318.1.

Estate increased by chargeable transfer followed by death within 5 years.

Death within 1st year.	100%
Each additional year: decreased by	20%
Small gifts to same person	£250

Spouses/civil partners with separate long-term residence statuses (one not being in the UK)
SEE TOLLEY'S TAX COMPUTATIONS 310.4.

Total exemption. £325,000[1]

[1] For periods from 6 April 2025, individuals can elect to be treated as long-term resident in the UK if, at any time on or after 6 April 2025 and during the period of 7 years ending with the date on which the election is made, they have a long-term UK resident spouse or civil partner. The election may be made in some cases where the long-term UK resident individual has died. Personal representatives may make an election on behalf of a deceased person in certain circumstances. Other conditions apply. For periods between 6 April 2013 and 5 April 2025 individuals can elect to be treated as domiciled in the UK on broadly the same basis. Transitional rules apply for elections made under the domicile regime.

Tapering relief

The value of the estate on death is taxed as the top slice of cumulative transfers in the 7 years before death. Transfers on or within 7 years of death are taxed on their value at the date of the gift on the death rate scale, but using the scale in force at the date of death, subject to the following taper:

Years between gift and death	Percentage of full charge at death rates
0–3	100
3–4	80
4–5	60
5–6	40
6–7	20

Penalties see **T1.148**.

National insurance contributions

(SI 2001/1004)

From 6 April 2025

[T8.101]

SEE TOLLEY'S TAX COMPUTATIONS 504.1, 505.1, 506.1 ONWARDS.

Class 1 contributions[1]			
Earnings limits and threshold	Weekly £	Monthly £	Yearly £
Lower earnings limit	125	TBA	6,500
Primary threshold	242	1,048	12,570
Secondary threshold	96	417	5,000
Upper secondary threshold[3]	967	4,189	50,270
Upper earnings limit	967	4,189	50,270
Freeport upper secondary threshold	481	2,083	25,000
Investment zone upper secondary threshold	481	2,083	25,000
Veterans' upper secondary threshold	967	4,189	50,270
Rates			
Employees' contributions			
Weekly earnings			
	£242.01–£967	8%	
	Over £967	2%	
Employers' contributions[3,4]			
Weekly earnings:	Over £96[3,4,5]	15%	
Women at reduced rate			
Employees' contributions			
Weekly earnings			
	£242.01–£967	1.85%	
	Over £967	2%	
Employers' contributions			
Weekly earnings:	Over £96	15%	
Employment allowance[2]		**£10,500**	
Class 1A and Class 1B contributions		15%	

[1] Employees' rates are nil for children under 16 and those over state pensionable age but employers' contributions are still payable. Employees' NICs are not payable on earnings up to the primary threshold, employers' NICs are not payable on earnings up to the secondary threshold or, where applicable, one of the upper secondary thresholds.

[2] An employment allowance of £10,500 per year (£5,000 before 6 April 2024; £4,000 before 6 April 2022; £3,000 before 6 April 2020) applies for businesses, charities and CASCs to be offset against their employer Class 1 secondary NICs. The allowance is claimed as part of the normal payroll process through RTI. Only one company in a group may claim. There are some excluded employers such as certain employers of domestic staff, public authorities and those which carry out functions wholly or mainly of a public nature. The allowance is extended to employers of care and support workers where the duties of employment relate to the employer's personal, family or household affairs. It is not available to companies whose only employee is the director. Between 6 April 2020 and 5 April 2025, the allowance is only available to employers with a secondary Class 1 NICs liability below £100,000 in the preceding tax year. This £100,000 threshold applies cumulatively in the case of connected employers.

[3] Employers with employees under the age of 21 or apprentices under the age of 25 are not required to pay Class 1 secondary NICs on earnings up to the upper secondary threshold for those employees.

[4] From 6 April 2021 until 5 April 2026, employers of qualifying veterans are not required to pay Class 1 secondary NICs on earnings up to the veterans upper secondary threshold during the first year of their civilian employment. For 2021–22, employers were required to pay the NIC as normal and claim it back retrospectively from April 2022 onwards.

[5] From 6 April 2022, employers in designated special tax sites in Freeports are not required to pay Class 1 secondary NICs on earnings up to the freeport upper secondary threshold for eligible new employees in the first 3 years of employment. The employer must elect to apply the relief in circumstances where they may also qualify for NIC relief for under 21s, under 25 apprentices or armed forces veterans.

[6] From the date of tax designation of site, employers in special tax sites in investment zones are not required to pay Class 1 secondary NICs on earnings up to the investment zone upper secondary threshold for eligible employees in the first 3 years of employment. The employer must elect to apply the relief in circumstances where they may also qualify for NIC relief for under 21s, under 25 apprentices or armed forces veterans.

[7] Where an earner has more than one employment (including any self-employment), their liability for Class 1 or Class 1 and Class 2 contributions cannot exceed a maximum amount. See **T8.107**.

6 April 2024–5 April 2025

[T8.102]

SEE TOLLEY'S TAX COMPUTATIONS 504.1, 505.1, 506.1 ONWARDS.

Class 1 contributions[1]			
Earnings limits and threshold	Weekly £	Monthly £	Yearly £
Lower earnings limit	123	533	6,396
Primary threshold	242	1,048	12,570
Secondary threshold	175	758	9,100
Upper secondary threshold[3]	967	4,189	50,270
Upper earnings limit	967	4,189	50,270
Freeport upper secondary threshold	481	2,083	25,000
Investment zone upper secondary threshold	481	2,083	25,000
Veterans' upper secondary threshold	967	4,189	50,270
Rates			
Employees' contributions			
Weekly earnings			
	£242.01–£967	8%	
	Over £967	2%	
Employers' contributions[3,4]			
Weekly earnings:	Over £175[3,4,5]	13.8%	
Women at reduced rate			
Employees' contributions			
Weekly earnings			
	£242.01–£967	1.85%	
	Over £967	2%	
Employers' contributions			
Weekly earnings:	Over £175	13.8%	
Employment allowance[2]		**£5,000**	
Class 1A and Class 1B contributions		13.8%	

[1] Employees' rates are nil for children under 16 and those over state pensionable age but employers' contributions are still payable. Employees' NICs are not payable on earnings up to the primary threshold, employers' NICs are not payable on earnings up to the secondary threshold or, where applicable, one of the upper secondary thresholds.

[2] An employment allowance of £5,000 per year (£4,000 before 6 April 2022; £3,000 before 6 April 2020) applies for businesses, charities and CASCs to be offset against their employer Class 1 secondary NICs. The allowance is claimed as part of the normal payroll process through RTI. Only one company in a group may claim. There are some excluded employers such as certain employers of domestic staff, public authorities and those which carry out functions wholly or mainly of a public nature. The allowance is extended to employers of care and support workers where the duties of employment relate to the employer's personal, family or household affairs. It is not available to companies whose only employee is the director. From 6 April 2020 to 5 April 2025 the allowance is only available to employers with a secondary Class 1 NICs liability below £100,000 in the preceding tax year. This £100,000 threshold applies cumulatively in the case of connected employers.

[3] Employers with employees under the age of 21 or apprentices under the age of 25 are not required to pay Class 1 secondary NICs on earnings up to the upper secondary threshold for those employees.

[4] From 6 April 2021 until 5 April 2026 employers of qualifying veterans are not required to pay Class 1 secondary NICs on earnings up to the veterans upper secondary threshold during the first year of their civilian employment. For 2021–22 employers were required to pay the NIC as normal and claim it back retrospectively from April 2022 onwards.

[5] From 6 April 2022 employers in designated special tax sites in Freeports are not required to pay Class 1 secondary NICs on earnings up to the freeport upper secondary threshold for eligible new employees in the first 3 years of employment. The employer must elect to apply the relief in circumstances where they may also qualify for NIC relief for under 21s, under 25 apprentices or armed forces veterans.

[6] From the date of tax designation of site, employers in special tax sites in investment zones are not required to pay Class 1 secondary NICs on earnings up to the investment zone upper secondary threshold for eligible employees in the first 3 years of employment. The employer must elect to apply the relief in circumstances where they may also qualify for NIC relief for under 21s, under 25 apprentices or armed forces veterans.

[7] Where an earner has more than one employment (including any self-employment), their liability for Class 1 or Class 1 and Class 2 contributions cannot exceed a maximum amount. See **T8.107**.

6 April 2023–5 April 2024

[T8.103]

SEE TOLLEY'S TAX COMPUTATIONS 504.1, 505.1, 506.1 ONWARDS.

Class 1 contributions[1]			
Earnings limits and threshold	Weekly £	Monthly £	Yearly £
Lower earnings limit	123	533	6,396
Primary threshold	242	1,048	12,570
Secondary threshold	175	758	9,100
Upper secondary threshold[3]	967	4,189	50,270
Upper earnings limit	967	4,189	50,270
Freeport upper secondary threshold	481	2,083	25,000
Investment zone upper secondary threshold	481	2,083	25,000
Veterans' upper secondary threshold	967	4,189	50,270
Rates			
Employees' contributions			
Weekly earnings			
(6 April 2023–5 January 2024):	£242.01–£967	12%	
(6 January 2024–5 April 2024):	£242.01–£967	10%	
	Over £967	2%	
Employers' contributions[3,4]			
Weekly earnings:	Over £175[3,4,5]	13.8%	
Women at reduced rate			
Employees' contributions			
Weekly earnings			
(6 April 2023–5 January 2024):	£242.01–£967	5.85%	
(6 January 2024–5 April 2024):	£242.01–£967	3.85%	
	Over £967	2%	
Employers' contributions			
Weekly earnings:	Over £175	13.8%	
Employment allowance[2]		**£5,000**	
Class 1A and Class 1B contributions		13.8%	

[1] Employees' rates are nil for children under 16 and those over state pensionable age but employers' contributions are still payable. Employees' NICs are not payable on earnings up to the primary threshold, employers' NICs are not payable on earnings up to the secondary threshold or, where applicable, one of the upper secondary thresholds.

[2] An employment allowance of £5,000 per year (£4,000 before 6 April 2022; £3,000 before 6 April 2020) applies for businesses, charities and CASCs to be offset against their employer Class 1 secondary NICs. The allowance is claimed as part of the normal payroll process through RTI. Only one company in a group may claim. There are some excluded employers such as certain employers of domestic staff, public authorities and those which carry out functions wholly or mainly of a public nature. The allowance is extended to employers of care and support workers where the duties of employment relate to the employer's personal, family or household affairs. It is not available to companies whose only employee is the director. From 6 April 2020 to 5 April 2025 the allowance is only available to employers with a secondary Class 1 NICs liability below £100,000 in the preceding tax year. This £100,000 threshold applies cumulatively in the case of connected employers.

[3] Employers with employees under the age of 21 or apprentices under the age of 25 are not required to pay Class 1 secondary NICs on earnings up to the upper secondary threshold for those employees.

[4] From 6 April 2021 until 5 April 2026 employers of qualifying veterans are not required to pay Class 1 secondary NICs on earnings up to the veterans upper secondary threshold during the first year of their civilian employment. For 2021–22 employers were required to pay the NIC as normal and claim it back retrospectively from April 2022 onwards.

[5] From 6 April 2022 employers in designated special tax sites in Freeports are not required to pay Class 1 secondary NICs on earnings up to the freeport upper secondary threshold for eligible new employees in the first 3 years of employment. The employer must elect to apply the relief in circumstances where they may also qualify for NIC relief for under 21s, under 25 apprentices or armed forces veterans.

[6] From the date of tax designation of site, employers in special tax sites in investment zones are not required to pay Class 1 secondary NICs on earnings up to the investment zone upper secondary threshold for eligible employees in the first 3 years of employment. The employer must elect to apply the relief in circumstances where they may also qualify for NIC relief for under 21s, under 25 apprentices or armed forces veterans.

[7] Where an earner has more than one employment (including any self-employment), their liability for Class 1 or Class 1 and Class 2 contributions cannot exceed a maximum amount. See **T8.107**.

6 April 2022–5 April 2023

[T8.104]

SEE TOLLEY'S TAX COMPUTATIONS 504.1, 505.1, 506.1 ONWARDS.

Class 1 contributions[1]			
Earnings limits and threshold	Weekly £	Monthly £	Yearly £
Lower earnings limit	123	533	6,396
Primary threshold (6 April 2022–5 July 2022)	190	823	9,880
Primary threshold (6 July 2022–5 April 2023)	242	1,048	12,570
Primary threshold (directors)[7]	229	—	11,908
Secondary threshold	175	758	9,100
Upper secondary threshold[3]	967	4,189	50,270
Upper earnings limit	967	4,189	50,270
Veterans' upper secondary threshold	967	4,189	50,270
Freeport upper secondary threshold	481	2,083	25,000
Rates		6 April 2022–5 November 2022	6 November 2022–5 April 2023
Employees' contributions			
Weekly earnings:	Primary threshold–£967	13.25%	12%
	Over £967	3.25%	2%
Employers' contributions[3,4]			
Weekly earnings:	Over £175[3,4,5]	15.05%	13.8%
Women at reduced rate			
Employees' contributions			
Weekly earnings:	Primary threshold–£967	7.1%	5.85%
	Over £967	3.25%	2%
Employers' contributions			
Weekly earnings:	Over £175	15.05%	13.8%
Employment allowance[2]		**£5,000**	
Class 1A and Class 1B contributions[7]		14.53%	

[1] Employees' rates are nil for children under 16 and those over state pensionable age but employers' contributions are still payable. Employees' NICs are not payable on earnings up to the primary threshold, employers' NICs are not payable on earnings up to the secondary threshold or, where applicable, one of the upper secondary thresholds.

[2] An employment allowance of £5,000 per year (£4,000 before 6 April 2022; £3,000 before 6 April 2020) applies for businesses, charities and CASCs to be offset against their employer Class 1 secondary NICs. The allowance is claimed as part of the normal payroll process through RTI. Only one company in a group may claim. There are some excluded employers such as certain employers of domestic staff, public authorities and those which carry out functions wholly or mainly of a public nature. The allowance is extended to employers of care and support workers where the duties of employment relate to the employer's personal, family or household affairs. It is not available to companies whose only employee is the director. From 6 April 2020 to 5 April 2025 the allowance is only available to employers with a secondary Class 1 NICs liability below £100,000 in the preceding tax year. This £100,000 threshold applies cumulatively in the case of connected employers.

[3] Employers with employees under the age of 21 or apprentices under the age of 25 are not required to pay Class 1 secondary NICs on earnings up to the upper secondary threshold for those employees.

[4] From 6 April 2021 until 5 April 2026 employers of qualifying veterans are not required to pay Class 1 secondary NICs on earnings up to the veterans upper secondary threshold during the first year of their civilian employment. For 2021–22 employers must still pay the NIC as normal and claim it back retrospectively from April 2022 onwards.

[5] From 6 April 2022 employers in designated tax sites in Freeports are no longer required to pay Class 1 secondary NICs on earnings up to the freeport upper secondary threshold for eligible new employees in the first 3 years of employment. The employer must elect to apply the relief in circumstances where they may also qualify for NIC relief for under 21s, under 25 apprentices or armed forces veterans.

[6] At the Mini Budget on 23 September 2022, the Chancellor made the following announcements: (a) the increase in the rates of Class 1, Class 1A, Class 1B and Class 4 contributions by 1.25 percentage points that applied from 6 April 2022 is cancelled with effect from 6 November 2022; and (b) the introduction of a separate Health and Social Care Levy of 1.25% in April 2023 is no longer to go ahead.

[7] Primary thresholds for 2022–23 for weekly and annual earnings periods for directors subject to SI 2001/1004, Reg 8. For directors, who are charged to Class 1 NIC on an annual basis, composite rates of 12.73% (main primary percentage) and 2.73% (additional primary percentage) apply for the individual and a composite rate of 14.53% applies for the employer for 2022–23. For Class 1A and Class 1B, a composite rate of 14.53% applies for 2022–23. The Class 1A rate for termination awards and sporting testimonials is

15.05% for payments made in the period 6 April 2022 to 5 November 2022 and 13.8% for payments made in the period 6 November 2022 to 5 April 2023.

[8] Where an earner has more than one employment (including any self-employment), their liability for Class 1 or Class 1 and Class 2 contributions cannot exceed a maximum amount. See **T8.107**.

6 April 2021–5 April 2022

[T8.105]

SEE TOLLEY'S TAX COMPUTATIONS 504.1, 505.1, 506.1 ONWARDS.

Class 1 contributions[1]			
Earnings limits and threshold	Weekly £	Monthly £	Yearly £
Lower earnings limit	120	520	6,240
Primary threshold	184	797	9,568
Secondary threshold	170	737	8,840
Upper secondary threshold[3,4,5]	967	4,189	50,270
Upper earnings limit	967	4,189	50,270
Rates			
Employees' contributions			
Weekly earnings:	£184.01–£967	12%	
	Over £967	2%	
Employers' contributions[3,4,5]			
Weekly earnings:	Over £170[3,4,5]	13.8%	
Women at reduced rate			
Employees' contributions			
Weekly earnings:	£184.01–£967	5.85%	
	Over £967	2%	
Employers' contributions			
Weekly earnings:	Over £170	13.8%	
Employment allowance[2]		£4,000	
Class 1A and Class 1B contributions		13.8%	

[1] Employees' rates are nil for children under 16 and those over state pensionable age but employers' contributions are still payable. Employees' NICs are not payable on earnings up to the primary threshold, employers' NICs are not payable on earnings up to the secondary threshold.

[2] An employment allowance of £4,000 per year (£3,000 from 6 April 2016 to 5 April 2020, £2,000 from 6 April 2014 to 5 April 2016) applies for businesses, charities and CASCs to be offset against their employer Class 1 secondary NICs. The allowance is claimed as part of the normal payroll process through RTI. Only one company in a group may claim. There are some excluded employers such as certain employers of domestic staff, public authorities and those which carry out functions wholly or mainly of a public nature. From 6 April 2015 the allowance was extended to employers of care and support workers where the duties of employment relate to the employer's personal, family or household affairs. From 6 April 2016 the allowance is no longer available to companies whose only employee is the director. From 6 April 2020 to 5 April 2025 the allowance is only available to employers with a secondary Class 1 NICs liability below £100,000 in the preceding tax year. This £100,000 threshold will apply cumulatively in the case of connected employers.

[3] From 6 April 2015 employers with employees under the age of 21 are no longer required to pay Class 1 secondary NICs on earnings up to the upper secondary threshold for those employees.

[4] From 6 April 2016 employers with apprentices under the age of 25 are no longer required to pay Class 1 secondary NICs on earnings up to the upper secondary threshold for those employees.

[5] From 6 April 2021 until 5 April 2026 employers of qualifying veterans are no longer required to pay Class 1 secondary NICs on earnings up to the upper secondary threshold during the first year of their civilian employment. For 2021-22 employers must still pay the NIC as normal and claim it back retrospectively from April 2022 onwards.

[6] From 6 April 2022 employers in designated tax sites in Freeports are no longer required to pay Class 1 secondary NICs on earnings up to an upper secondary threshold (£481 per week) for eligible new employees in the first 3 years of employment. The employer must elect to apply the relief in circumstances where they may also qualify for NIC relief for under 21s, under 25 apprentices or armed forces veterans.

[7] Where an earner has more than one employment (including any self-employment), their liability for Class 1 or Class 1 and Class 2 contributions cannot exceed a maximum amount. See **T8.107**.

6 April 2020–5 April 2021

[T8.106]

See Tolley's Tax Computations 504.1, 506.1, 505.1 onwards.

Class 1 contributions[1]			
Earnings limits and threshold	Weekly £	Monthly £	Yearly £
Lower earnings limit	120	520	6,240
Primary threshold	183	792	9,500
Secondary threshold	169	732	8,788
Upper secondary threshold[3,4]	962	4,167	50,000
Upper earnings limit	962	4,167	50,000
Rates			
Employees' contributions			
Weekly earnings:	£183.01–£962	12%	
	Over £962	2%	
Employers' contributions[3,4]			
Weekly earnings:	Over £169[3,4]	13.8%	
Women at reduced rate			
Employees' contributions			
Weekly earnings:	£183.01–£962	5.85%	
	Over £962	2%	
Employers' contributions			
Weekly earnings:	Over £169	13.8%	
Employment allowance[2]		£4,000	
Class 1A and Class 1B contributions		13.8%	

[1] Employees' rates are nil for children under 16 and those over state pensionable age but employers' contributions are still payable. Employees' NICs are not payable on earnings up to the primary threshold, employers' NICs are not payable on earnings up to the secondary threshold.

[2] An employment allowance of £4,000 per year (£3,000 from 6 April 2016 to 5 April 2020, £2,000 from 6 April 2014 to 5 April 2016) applies for businesses, charities and CASCs to be offset against their employer Class 1 secondary NICs. The allowance is claimed as part of the normal payroll process through RTI. Only one company in a group may claim. There are some excluded employers such as certain employers of domestic staff, public authorities and those which carry out functions wholly or mainly of a public nature. From 6 April 2015 the allowance was extended to employers of care and support workers where the duties of employment relate to the employer's personal, family or household affairs. From 6 April 2016 the allowance is no longer available to companies whose only employee is the director. From 6 April 2020 to 5 April 2025 the allowance is only available to employers with a secondary Class 1 NICs liability below £100,000 in the preceding tax year. This £100,000 threshold will apply cumulatively in the case of connected employers.

[3] From 6 April 2015 employers with employees under the age of 21 are no longer required to pay Class 1 secondary NICs on earnings up to the upper secondary threshold for those employees.

[4] From 6 April 2016 employers with apprentices under the age of 25 are no longer required to pay Class 1 secondary NICs on earnings up to the upper secondary threshold for those employees.

[5] Where an earner has more than one employment (including any self-employment), their liability for Class 1 or Class 1 and Class 2 contributions cannot exceed a maximum amount. See **T8.107**.

Class 2, 3 and 4 contributions

[T8.107]

SEE TOLLEY'S TAX COMPUTATIONS 503.1, 507.1, 513.1 ONWARDS.

	2025–26	2024–25	2023–24
Class 2 (self-employed)[1, 4]			
Flat rate—per week	£3.50	£3.45	£3.45
Share fishermen—per week	£4.15	£4.10	£4.10
Volunteer development workers—per week	£6.25	£6.15	£6.15
Small profits threshold—per year	£6,845	£6,725	£6,725
Lower profits threshold—per year	N/A	N/A	£12,570
Class 3 (voluntary contributions)			
Flat rate—per week	£17.75	£17.45	£17.45
Class 4 (self-employed)[1]			
Lower annual profits limit	£12,570	£12,570	£12,570
Upper annual profits limit	£50,270	£50,270	£50,270
Rate between lower and upper limits	6%	6%	9%
Rate on profits above upper limit	2%	2%	2%
Maximum contributions			
Class 1 or Class 1/Class 2[2]	£3,074.00	£3,074.00	£4,418.88
– plus rate on earnings above upper limit	2%	2%	2%
Class 4 limiting amount[3]	£2,262.00	£2,262.00	£3,575.85
– plus rate on profits above upper limit	2%	2%	2%

[1] Not payable if pensionable age is reached by the beginning of the tax year.
[2] Where an earner has more than one employment (including any self-employment), liability for Class 1 or Class 1 and Class 2 contributions cannot exceed a maximum amount which will vary depending on individual circumstances. For 2021–22 and earlier years, the maximum is equal to 53 employees' Class 1 contributions at the standard rate (12%), plus 2% on earnings over the individual's upper earnings limit. For 2022–23, the maximum is equal to 53 employees' Class 1 contributions at the standard rate (taking the primary threshold to be £229 and the standard rate to be 12.73%) plus 2.73% on earnings over the upper earnings limit. For 2023–24, the maximum is equal to 53 employees' Class 1 contributions (taking the standard rate to be 11.5%), plus 2% on earnings over the upper earnings limit. For 2024–25, the maximum is equal to 53 employees' Class 1 contributions at the standard rate (8%), plus 2% on earnings over the individual's upper earnings limit. For 2025–26, the maximum is equal to 53 employees' Class 1 contributions at the standard rate (8%), plus 2% on earnings over the individual's upper earnings limit.
[3] Where Class 4 contributions are payable in addition to Class 1 and/or Class 2 contributions, liability for Class 4 contributions cannot exceed such an amount as, when added to the Class 1 (and, for 2023–24 and earlier years, Class 2) contributions payable (after applying the maximum if appropriate), equals the limiting amount. The limiting amount is the maximum Class 4 contributions payable (including contributions on earnings over the upper profit limit) plus, for 2023–24 and earlier years, 53 Class 2 contributions.
[4] For 2024–25 onwards, self-employed individuals are not required to pay Class 2 contributions. Those with profits in excess of the small profits threshold continue to qualify for state benefits. Individuals with profits below the small profits threshold can choose to pay Class 2 contributions to get access to benefits. For 2022–23 and 2023–24, Class 2 contributions are not payable where an individual's profits fall between the small profits threshold and the lower profits threshold. The individual is treated as having paid Class 2 contributions for the purposes of benefits entitlement.

	2022–23	2021–22	2020–21
Class 2 (self-employed)[1]			
Flat rate—per week	£3.15	£3.05	£3.05
Share fishermen—per week	£3.80	£3.70	£3.70
Volunteer development workers—per week	£6.15	£6.00	£6.00
Small earnings exception—per year	£6,725	£6,515	£6,475
Lower profits threshold—per year	£11,908	N/A	N/A
Class 3 (voluntary contributions)			
Flat rate—per week	£15.85	£15.40	£15.30
Class 4 (self-employed)[1]			
Lower annual profits limit	£11,908	£9,568	£9,500
Upper annual profits limit	£50,270	£50,270	£50,000
Rate between lower and upper limits	9.73%	9%	9%
Rate on profits above upper limit	2.73%	2%	2%
Maximum contributions			
Class 1 or Class 1/Class 2[2]	£4,979.21	£4,979.88	£4,954.44
– plus rate on earnings above upper limit	2.73%	2%	2%
Class 4 limiting amount[3]	£3,899.57	£3,824.83	£3,806.65
– plus rate on profits above upper limit	2.73%	2%	2%

¹ Not payable if pensionable age is reached by the beginning of the tax year.
² Where an earner has more than one employment (including any self-employment), liability for Class 1 or Class 1 and Class 2 contributions cannot exceed a maximum amount which will vary depending on individual circumstances. For 2021–22 and earlier years, the maximum is equal to 53 employees' Class 1 contributions at the standard rate (12%), plus 2% on earnings over the individual's upper earnings limit. For 2022–23, the maximum is equal to 53 employees' Class 1 contributions at the standard rate (taking the primary threshold to be £229 and the standard rate to be 12.73%) plus 2.73% on earnings over the upper earnings limit. For 2023–24, the maximum is equal to 53 employees' Class 1 contributions (taking the standard rate to be 11.5%), plus 2% on earnings over the upper earnings limit. For 2024–25, the maximum is equal to 53 employees' Class 1 contributions at the standard rate (8%), plus 2% on earnings over the individual's upper earnings limit. For 2025–26, the maximum is equal to 53 employees' Class 1 contributions at the standard rate (8%), plus 2% on earnings over the individual's upper earnings limit.
³ Where Class 4 contributions are payable in addition to Class 1 and/or Class 2 contributions, liability for Class 4 contributions cannot exceed such an amount as, when added to the Class 1 (and, for 2023–24 and earlier years, Class 2) contributions payable (after applying the maximum if appropriate), equals the limiting amount. The limiting amount is the maximum Class 4 contributions payable (including 2% on earnings over the upper profit limit) plus, for 2023–24 and earlier years, 53 Class 2 contributions.

Employers' contributions: benefits in kind

[T8.108]

Class 1A NICs are payable by employers on most taxable benefits in kind, excluding benefits:
(1) included in a PAYE settlement agreement (see **T6.158**);
(2) provided to 'lower-paid' ministers of religion;
(3) otherwise not required to be included on a P11D;
(4) on which Class 1 NICs were due.

Class 1 and Class 1A Benefits provided under optional remuneration arrangements are not covered by existing exemptions except in limited circumstances. Where this is the case Class 1 or Class 1A NICs are due as appropriate.

Class 1B contributions are payable by employers by reference to the value of any items included in a PAYE settlement agreement (PSA) which would otherwise be earnings for Class 1 or Class 1A, including the amount of tax paid. Income tax and Class 1B contributions on a PSA are payable by 22 October after the end of the tax year to which the PSA relates (or 19 October if not paid electronically).

Common benefits subject to Class 1 and Class 1A NICs (CWG5 2024)

[T8.109]

Benefit	NICs Class	PAYE or P11D
Assets transferred to employees but not readily convertible assets	1A	P11D
Assets placed at employee's disposal for mixed business and private use	1A	P11D
Car fuel supplied for private motoring in company car	1A	P11D
Car/van fuel supplied for private motoring in privately owned car/van – supplied using company credit card, garage account, agency card or employer's own fuel pump	1A	P11D
– any other circumstances	1	P11D
Cars available for private use	1A	P11D
Car parking facilities other than at or near place of work or as part of business travel	1A	P11D
Car parking fees paid for or reimbursed to employee other than at or near place of work or as part of business travel	1	P11D
Childcare where employer contracts with provider and either the value exceeds the permitted maximum or the qualifying conditions are not met	1A	P11D
Childcare where employee reimbursed or additional salary provided to meet cost	1	PAYE
Christmas boxes – cash	1	PAYE
– goods	1A	P11D
Clothing and uniforms		
– cash payment to employee for clothing that can be worn at any time	1	PAYE or P11D[1]
– clothing provided by employer that can be worn at any time	1A	P11D
Council tax, unless employee provided with living accommodation which is not a benefit	1	P11D
Credit and charge cards – personal expenses on employer's card	1	P11D
Entertaining staff — expenses/allowances – employer contract with provider	1A	P11D
– employee contract with provider	1	PAYE or P11D[1]
Expenses not covered by an exemption— any profit element in payment	1	P11D[4]

Benefit		NICs Class	PAYE or P11D
Food, groceries, farm produce	– employer contract with provider	1A	P11D
	– employee contract with provider	1	PAYE or P11D[1]
Goods transferred to employee	– employer contract with provider	1A	P11D
	– employee contract with provider	1	PAYE or P11D[1]
Holidays	– employer contract with provider	1A	P11D
	– employee contract with provider, or holiday vouchers	1	PAYE or P11D[1]
Income tax paid but not deducted from employee, or paid on notional payments not borne by employee within 90 days of the end of the tax year		1	P11D
Insurance premiums for pensions etc on employee's death or retirement, employee contract with provider		1	PAYE or P11D[1]
Living accommodation (beneficial)		1A	P11D
Loans	– non-qualifying	1A	P11D
	– written off	1	P11D
Meals vouchers (all values)		1	P11D
Meals provided other than at canteen or at business premises open to all staff on a reasonable scale where all employees may obtain free or subsidised meals not provided in connection with salary sacrifice or flexible remuneration arrangements		1A	P11D
Medical, dental insurance or treatment provided in the UK by employer	– employer contract with provider	1A	P11D
	– employee contract with provider	1	PAYE or P11D[1]
Mobile phone[5] — cost of private calls, employee contract with provider		1	PAYE or P11D[1]
Personal bills		1	PAYE or P11D[1]
Readily convertible assets[2]		1	PAYE
Relocation payments	– qualifying over £8,000	1A	P11D
	– non-qualifying benefits or qualifying expenses paid after relevant day	1A	P11D
	– non-qualifying expenses	1	P11D
Round sum allowances (not identified as business expense)		1	P11D
Scholarships awarded to students because of parent's employment or payment of school fees	– employer contract with provider	1A	P11D
	– employee contract with provider	1	PAYE or P11D[1]
Social functions unless ITEPA 2003 s 264 satisfied		1A	P11D
Sporting or recreational facilities unless ITEPA 2003 s 261 satisfied		1A	P11D
Subscriptions, professional and fees not allowable as tax deduction	– employer contract with provider	1A	P11D
	– employee contract with provider	1	PAYE or P11D[1]
Staff suggestions unless ITEPA 2003 s 321 satisfied	– cash payment or a non-cash voucher	1	PAYE or P11D
	– benefit in kind	1A	P11D
Telephones	– employer contract with provider, unless private use is insignificant or employee reimburses cost of all private calls	1A	P11D
	– employee contract with provider, unless used exclusively for business. If mixed use, not applicable to business calls if supported by evidence	1	PAYE or P11D[1]
Third party benefits or payments	– cash payment	1	PAYE or P11D[1]
	– non-cash voucher	1A	P11D
Training payments	– employer contract with provider, unless work-related or encouraged or required by employer	1A	P11D

Benefit	NICs Class	PAYE or P11D
– employee contract with provider, unless work-related or encouraged or required by employer	1	PAYE or P11D[1]
Vans available for commuting and other private use	1A[3]	P11D
Van fuel provided for use in van available for commuting & other private use	1A[3]	P11D
Vouchers (other than exceptions for childcare, meals, etc)	1	P11D

[1] Payments by employer to provider should be entered on P11D. Reimbursements to the employee are subject to PAYE.
[2] See detailed information in HMRC booklet CWG2(2024) para 5.13.1.
[3] No Class 1A due if van is available mainly for employee's business travel and commuting and other private use is insignificant.
[4] Specific and distinct business expenses within the payments should be recorded in appropriate section of P11D.
[5] No limit to number of mobile phones which employer can contract to provide NIC free solely for business with insignificant private use. Only one mobile per employee NIC free for private use where employer contracts. No mobile phone may be provided NICs free to a member of an employee's family or household.

Overseas

Average rates of exchange

[T9.101]

Note: The rates of exchange in T9.101 and **T9.102** are reproduced from information provided by HMRC and are Crown copyright.
The rates for 31.12.23 were updated by HMRC on 31 March 2024 and are correct at 31 March 2024.

Average for year ending	31.3.22	31.12.22	31.03.23	31.12.23	31.03.24
Abu Dhabi (Dirham)	5.036608	4.587583	4.476675	4.5660	4.6012
Albania (Lek)	143.280958	140.518158	137.496725	125.9306	122.9802
Algeria (Dinar)	186.727808	177.218483	172.102683	169.2453	169.8818
Angola (Readj Kwanza)	840.224358	584.521292	556.979375	834.3142	944.5533
Antigua (EC$)	3.702267	3.372242	3.290717	3.3578	3.3846
Argentina (Peso)	134.622542	155.678025	176.4786	324.8720	528.1742
Armenia (Dram)	679.396625	554.851658	513.773608	485.6374	492.2780
Aruba (Florin)	2.454475	2.235675	2.181633	2.2254	2.2426
Australia (A$)	1.8529	1.786317	1.759892	1.8648	1.8990
Austria (Euro)	1.174183	1.177958	1.166525	1.1495	1.1543
Azerbaijan (New Manat)	2.32985	2.122550	2.071808	2.1150	2.1315
Bahamas ($ pegged to US$)	1.371217	1.249458	1.219267	1.2432	1.2529
Bahrain (Dinar)	0.51695	0.470883	0.459492	0.4683	0.4716
Bangladesh (Taka)	116.877292	114.828175	118.187492	134.1947	136.5890
Barbados (BD$)	2.742417	2.497967	2.437575	2.4864	2.5057
Belarus (Rouble)	3.474067	3.595008	3.502592	3.2762	3.5477
Belgium (Euro)	1.174183	1.177958	1.166525	1.1495	1.1543
Belize (Dollar)	2.742417	2.497967	2.437575	2.4924	2.5162
Benin (CFA Franc)	770.204875	772.533083	765.028242	753.9941	757.1598
Bermuda ($ pegged to US$)	1.371217	1.249458	1.219267	1.2432	1.2529
Bhutan (Ngultrum)	101.97445	97.560208	97.412425	102.6182	103.7034
Bolivia (Boliviano)	9.475058	8.630467	8.421825	8.5888	8.6536
Bosnia-Herzegovina (Marka)	2.296483	2.303408	2.281792	2.2489	2.2576
Botswana (Pula)	15.346392	15.296442	15.332908	16.5098	16.8560
Brazil (Real)	7.383258	6.488892	6.252975	6.2356	6.1877
Brunei ($)	1.849633	1.721442	1.674575	1.6697	1.6844
Bulgaria (Lev)	2.296692	2.303508	2.281125	2.2480	2.2575
Burkina Faso (CFA Franc)	770.204875	772.533083	765.028242	753.9941	757.1598
Burundi (Franc)	2,720.572308	2,532.150683	2,489.052558	3,132.6406	3,401.9690
Cambodia (Riel)	5,377.713067	4,887.786717	4,982.176633	5,108.4976	5,141.6954
Cameroon Republic (CFA Franc)	770.204875	772.533083	765.028242	753.9941	757.1598
Canada (Can$)	1.718633	1.615100	1.599892	1.6765	1.6896
Cape Verde Islands (Escudo)	129.912975	129.823058	128.549225	126.9686	127.3846
Cayman Islands (CI$)	1.124392	1.024167	0.9994	1.0204	1.0291
Central African (CFA Franc)	770.204875	772.533083	765.028242	753.9941	757.1598
Chad (CFA Franc)	770.204875	772.533083	765.028242	753.9941	757.1598
Chile (Peso)	1,061.542942	1,086.696008	1,064.248783	1,043.8887	1,080.7344
China (Renminbi Yuan)	8.822225	8.342033	8.301708	8.7899	8.9547
Colombia (Peso)	5,246.333825	5,215.888425	5,344.492408	5,443.1967	5,218.4105
Comoros (Franc)	577.653042	579.399825	573.771192	565.4956	567.8698
Congo Brazzaville (CFA Franc)	770.204875	772.533083	765.028242	753.9941	757.1598
Congo Dem Rep (Congolese Franc)	2,724.914992	2,513.077133	2,464.980317	2,851.9321	3,088.1257
Costa Rica (Colon)	856.750483	808.035925	771.006017	680.7585	667.3340
Cote d'Ivoire (CFA Franc)	770.204875	772.533083	765.028242	753.9941	757.1598
Croatia[1] (Kuna/Euro)	8.832933	8.870908	7.552633	1.1495	1.1543
Cuba (Peso)	1.371208	8.029975	15.04745	29.8362	30.0683
Cyprus (Euro)	1.174183	1.177958	1.166525	1.1495	1.1543
Czech Republic (Koruna)	29.749125	28.948308	28.474025	27.5880	27.9776

Average for year ending	31.3.22	31.12.22	31.03.23	31.12.23	31.03.24
Denmark (Krone)	8.733058	8.763033	8.678967	8.5634	8.6031
Djibouti (Franc)	243.687983	222.443008	217.152	221.2364	222.9607
Dominica (EC$)	3.702267	3.372242	3.290717	3.3578	3.3846
Dominican Republic (Peso)	77.971208	68.807925	66.773917	69.3993	70.6131
Dubai (Dirham)	5.036608	4.587583	4.476675	4.5660	4.6012
Ecuador (US$)	1.371217	1.249458	1.219267	1.2432	1.2529
Egypt (£)	21.528508	23.079258	26.458733	37.6180	38.7251
El Salvador (Colon)	11.997025	10.928442	10.664025	10.8776	10.9618
Equatorial Guinea (CFA Franc)	770.204875	772.533083	765.028242	753.9941	757.1598
Eritrea (Nakfa)	20.5646	18.734733	18.281817	18.6476	18.7921
Estonia (Euro)	1.174183	1.177958	1.166525	1.1495	1.1543
Ethiopia (Birr)	62.526067	64.426317	64.12205	67.9648	69.3770
Eurozone (Euro)	1.174183	1.177958	1.166525	1.1495	1.1543
Fiji Islands (F$)	2.862567	2.727417	2.683442	2.7782	2.8098
Finland (Euro)	1.174183	1.177958	1.166525	1.1495	1.1543
France (Euro)	1.174183	1.177958	1.166525	1.1495	1.1543
French Polynesia (CFP franc)	140.11265	140.539225	139.173942	137.1666	137.7425
Gabon (CFA franc)	770.204875	772.533083	765.028242	753.9941	757.1598
Gambia (Dalasi)	71.145883	68.751142	69.758625	76.8323	79.2517
Georgia (Lari)	4.356567	3.677642	3.462192	3.2682	3.2954
Germany (Euro)	1.174183	1.177958	1.166525	1.1495	1.1543
Ghana (Cedi)	8.246033	10.768683	12.170933	14.4005	14.7238
Greece (Euro)	1.174183	1.177958	1.166525	1.1495	1.1543
Grenada/Wind. Isles (EC$)	3.702267	3.372242	3.290717	3.3578	3.3846
Guatemala (Quetzal)	10.588517	9.658108	9.470175	9.7416	9.8035
Guinea Bissau (CFA Franc)	770.204875	772.533083	765.028242	753.9941	757.1598
Guinea Republic (Franc)	13,226.28354	11,062.409800	10,609.16913	10,704.0504	10,775.7770
Guyana (G$)	286.946792	261.310525	255.152633	261.0753	262.8011
Haiti (Gourde)	128.812592	139.630000	150.5696	176.2162	173.0467
Honduras (Lempira)	33.058825	30.702658	30.011417	30.6761	30.9045
Hong Kong (HK$)	10.665842	9.783883	9.553342	9.7270	9.8033
Hungary (Forint)	420.910308	455.204617	460.408958	440.1980	439.6469
Iceland (Krona)	173.975733	166.914933	167.687967	171.6828	171.3430
India (Rupee)	101.973617	97.560208	97.412425	102.6182	103.7034
Indonesia (Rupiah)	19,666.16168	18,416.008242	18,283.72129	18,950.1854	19,193.6594
Iraq (Dinar)	2,002.72125	1,823.344258	1,778.995433	1,690.8863	1,657.1627
Ireland (Euro)	1.174183	1.177958	1.166525	1.1495	1.1543
Israel (Shekel)	4.40695	4.137783	4.127867	4.5433	4.6611
Italy (Euro)	1.174183	1.177958	1.166525	1.1495	1.1543
Jamaica (J$)	208.703925	191.686408	186.367783	191.3193	193.5235
Japan (Yen)	152.927892	162.148108	164.193992	173.7983	179.6778
Jordan (Dinar)	0.972192	0.885917	0.864692	0.8820	0.8886
Kazakhstan (Tenge)	588.500883	571.997592	566.955258	570.9575	573.1095
Kenya (Shilling)	151.35675	146.142083	146.031758	171.3438	181.8608
Korea South (Won)	1,593.502258	1,599.895175	1,588.517933	1,620.5895	1,650.4019
Kuwait (Dinar)	0.413583	0.382142	0.374042	0.3820	0.3855
Kyrgyz Republic (Som)	116.155558	104.682758	102.446883	108.8218	110.7048
Laos (New Kip)	13,844.41001	17,129.935425	18,554.28488	22,931.9173	24,265.9316
Latvia (Euro)	1.174183	1.177958	1.166525	1.1495	1.1543
Lebanon (£)	2,077.124725	1,889.545975	3,196.5929	15,884.2902	18,815.6954
Lesotho (Loti)	20.347292	20.249583	20.356708	22.7107	23.3099
Liberia ($ pegged to US$)	1.371217	1.249458	1.219267	1.2432	1.2529
Libya (Dinar)	6.211958	5.960717	5.886467	5.9786	6.0293
Lithuania (Euro)	1.174183	1.177958	1.166525	1.1495	1.1543
Luxembourg (Euro)	1.174183	1.177958	1.166525	1.1495	1.1543
Macao (Pataca)	10.984792	10.073417	9.835958	10.0189	10.0974
Macedonia (Denar)	72.294242	72.511692	71.799833	70.7447	71.0523
Madagascar (Malagasy Ariary)	5,335.710233	5,100.389675	5,095.812367	5,513.4165	5,617.2319
Malawi (Kwacha)	1,107.938783	1,143.846642	1,183.304642	1,377.9891	1,595.2677
Malaysia (Ringgit)	5.731425	5.474008	5.397125	5.6519	5.8070
Maldive Islands (Rufiyaa)	21.182592	19.265767	18.776692	19.1291	19.2809

Average for year ending	31.3.22	31.12.22	31.03.23	31.12.23	31.03.24
Mali Republic (CFA Franc)	770.204875	772.533083	765.028242	753.9941	757.1598
Malta (Euro)	1.174183	1.177958	1.166525	1.1495	1.1543
Mauritania (Ouguiya)	49.851075	44.626108	43.547258	45.7135	47.3043
Mauritius (Rupee)	57.922183	54.860475	53.768217	55.9418	56.4477
Mexico (Peso)	27.867567	25.216475	24.0871	22.2182	21.8068
Moldova (Leu)	24.403783	23.428475	23.227242	22.6248	22.4255
Mongolia (Tugrik)	3,910.600783	3,866.233808	3,962.776383	4,323.2727	4,342.1873
Montserrat (EC$)	3.702267	3.372242	3.290717	3.3578	3.3846
Morocco (Dirham)	12.425783	12.516267	12.544617	12.6367	12.6474
Mozambique (Metical)	86.85835	79.501925	77.588642	79.4154	80.0262
Myanmar (Kyat)	2,310.2158	2,376.123875	2,420.796592	2,609.8253	2,629.7775
Nepal (Rupee)	163.158283	156.039000	155.802558	164.2149	165.9710
Netherlands (Euro)	1.174183	1.177958	1.166525	1.1495	1.1543
New Caledonia (CFP Franc)	140.11265	140.539225	139.173942	137.1666	137.7425
New Zealand (NZ$)	1.967325	1.950917	1.929425	2.0181	2.0491
Nicaragua (Gold Cordoba)	48.278775	44.677892	43.912992	45.4399	45.8794
Niger Republic (CFA Franc)	770.204875	772.533083	765.028242	753.9941	757.1598
Nigeria (Naira)	565.677667	528.036800	527.848025	763.8595	973.4864
Norway (Krone)	11.878892	11.857917	11.899383	13.0191	13.2688
Oman (Rial Omani)	0.528292	0.481300	0.469258	0.4786	0.4823
Pakistan (Rupee)	227.258283	251.475625	265.421767	341.8771	357.2271
Panama (Balboa)	1.371208	1.248967	1.218775	1.2432	1.2529
Papua New Guinea (Kina)	4.814617	4.394100	4.291908	4.4497	4.5527
Paraguay (Guarani)	9,317.166592	8,667.174108	8,583.659417	9,053.6504	9,119.2508
Peru (New Sol)	5.371342	4.808908	4.666042	4.6590	4.6648
Philippines (Peso)	68.433592	67.568508	67.30305	69.2168	69.9627
Poland (Zloty)	5.370367	5.506658	5.503558	5.2471	5.1626
Portugal (Euro)	1.174183	1.177958	1.166525	1.1495	1.1543
Qatar (Riyal)	4.992908	4.548225	4.438533	4.5260	4.5606
Romania (Leu)	5.792775	5.813208	5.749633	5.6838	5.7230
Russia (Rouble)	107.382983	92.189042	82.310275	103.6031	110.9978
Rwanda (R Franc)	1,375.6681	1,287.687250	1,274.076858	1,419.6548	1,490.0158
Saotome & Principe (Dobra)	29,136.46667	28,910.383333	28,515.875	Not published	Not published
Saudi Arabia (Riyal)	5.143233	4.691083	4.579042	4.6648	4.6992
Senegal (CFA Franc)	770.204875	772.533083	765.028242	753.9941	757.1598
Serbia (Dinar)	138.033525	138.351933	136.944642	134.7963	135.3182
Seychelles (Rupee)	21.394775	17.970425	17.397875	17.1580	17.0719
Sierra Leone (Leone)	14,576.45433	15,889.594467	13,503.47706	Not published	27.4404
Singapore (S$)	1.849633	1.722058	1.675192	1.6697	1.6844
Slovakia (Euro)	1.174183	1.177958	1.166525	1.1495	1.1543
Slovenia (Euro)	1.174183	1.177958	1.166525	1.1495	1.1543
Solomon Islands (SI$)	11.026867	10.160000	9.959233	10.3789	10.4927
Somali Republic (Schilling)	802.327075	723.207908	700.579375	707.9340	714.1673
South Africa (Rand)	20.347292	20.254450	20.363467	22.7126	23.3099
Spain (Euro)	1.174183	1.177958	1.166525	1.1495	1.1543
Sri Lanka (Rupee)	273.656017	386.788617	430.760917	411.4264	400.4216
St Christopher & Nevis (EC$)	3.702267	3.372242	3.290717	3.3578	3.3846
St Lucia (EC$)	3.702267	3.372242	3.290717	3.3578	3.3846
St Vincent (EC$)	3.702267	3.372242	3.290717	3.3578	3.3846
Sudan Republic (£)	549.858583	606.466408	635.535233	733.6370	746.5071
Surinam (Dollar)	26.606275	29.162683	31.848058	45.0423	46.7648
Swaziland (Lilangeni)	20.347292	20.249583	20.3586	22.7126	23.3099
Sweden (Krona)	11.977483	12.430433	12.495058	13.1361	13.2492
Switzerland (Franc)	1.261917	1.189767	1.161625	1.1191	1.1117
Taiwan (New T$)	38.315242	36.907833	36.874942	38.6448	39.2744
Tanzania (Schilling)	3,173.298867	2,901.870233	2,840.202058	2,995.5255	3,079.3899
Thailand (Baht)	44.561967	43.640367	42.943117	43.1671	43.9808
Togo Republic (CFA Franc)	770.204875	772.533083	765.028242	753.9941	757.1598
Tonga Islands (Pa'Anga)	1.812217	1.786317	1.759892	2.1260	2.4263
Trinidad and Tobago (TT$)	9.26325	8.435533	8.231233	8.4028	8.4794
Tunisia (Dinar)	3.85635	3.837967	3.817725	3.8508	3.8849
Turkey (Lira)	13.726917	20.249233	21.3076	28.6471	32.4102

Average for year ending	31.3.22	31.12.22	31.03.23	31.12.23	31.03.24
Turkmenistan (New Manat)	4.80555	4.376475	4.268208	4.3472	4.3818
Uganda (New Schilling)	4,887.814	4,585.370842	4,523.575567	4,627.9509	4,707.5598
Ukraine (Hryvnia)	37.438425	39.140292	41.035483	45.7249	46.4682
United Arab Emirates (Dirham)	5.036608	4.587583	4.476675	4.5660	4.6012
Uruguay (Peso Uruguayo)	60.047917	52.078017	49.221867	48.1777	48.6581
USA (US$)	1.371217	1.249458	1.219267	1.2432	1.2529
Uzbekistan (Sum)	14,632.27089	13,782.084425	13,600.38266	14,488.6476	14,942.9963
Vanuatu (Vatu)	153.041225	145.966742	143.530358	148.3724	150.1870
Venezuela (Bolivar Fuerte)	337,689.5808	310,194.693333	304,876.5683	Not published	Not published
Vietnam (Dong)	31,393.55474	29,168.755583	28,696.12768	29,537.5955	30,070.2604
Wallis & Futuna Islands (CFP Franc)	140.11265	140.539225	139.173942	137.1666	137.7425
Western Samoa (Tala)	3.527625	3.345750	3.286142	3.3922	3.4302
Yemen (Republic of) (Rial)	344.221367	312.466317	304.943708	311.1324	313.5411
Zambia (Kwacha)	26.643017	21.029708	20.912858	24.2879	26.4667
Zimbabwe (Dollar)	496.236267	452.006683	441.079283	1,558.0669	4,352.5706

1 Croatia adopted the Euro on 1 January 2023.

Rates of exchange on year-end dates

[T9.102]

	31.03.22	31.12.22	31.03.23	31.12.23	31.03.24
Australia (A$)	1.7506	1.7816	1.8464	1.8714	1.9355
Canada (Can$)	1.6401	1.6355	1.6753	1.6865	1.7088
Denmark (Krone)	8.7765	8.4033	8.4505	8.5989	8.7257
Eurozone (Euro)	1.18	1.13	1.1345	1.1528	1.1683
Hong Kong (HK$)	10.3114	9.3949	9.7190	9.9444	9.8798
Japan (Yen)	160.7428	160.5836	164.3452	179.5498	191.1198
Norway (Krone)	11.2926	11.9157	12.8824	13.0678	13.6573
South Africa (Rand)	19.0397	20.354	22.1155	23.3834	23.8340
Sweden (Krona)	12.188	12.6036	12.8252	12.8351	13.4556
Switzerland (Franc)	1.215	1.131	1.1306	1.0711	1.1391
USA (US$)	1.3174	1.2054	1.2381	1.2735	1.2625

Double taxation agreements (including protocols and regulations)

Agreements in force covering taxes on income and capital gains
[T9.103]

Country	SI/SR & O
Albania	**2013/3145**
Algeria	**2015/1888**
Antigua & Barbuda	**1947/2865**
	1968/1096
Argentina	**1997/1777**
Armenia	**2011/2722**
Australia	**2003/3199**
Austria	**2019/255**
Azerbaijan	**1995/762**
Bahrain	**2012/3075**
Bangladesh	**1980/708**
Barbados	**2012/3076**
Belarus[1]	**2018/778**
Belgium	**1987/2053**
	2010/2979
Belize	**1947/2866**
	1968/573
	1973/2097
Bolivia	**1995/2707**
Bosnia Herzegovina[2]	**1981/1815**
Botswana	**2006/1925**
British Virgin Islands	**2009/3013**
Brunei	**1950/1977**
	1968/306
	1973/2098
	2013/3146
Bulgaria	**2015/1890**
Canada	**1980/709**
	1980/1528
	1985/1996
	2003/2619
	2014/3274
	2015/2011
Cayman Islands	**2010/2973**
Chile	**2003/3200**
China[4]	**2011/2724**
	2013/3142
Colombia	**2018/377**
Croatia	**2015/1889**
Cyprus	**2018/839**
	2019/1113
Czech Republic[3]	**1991/2876**
Denmark	**1980/1960**
	1991/2877
	1996/3165
Egypt	**1980/1091**
Estonia	**1994/3207**
Ethiopia	**2011/2725**
Falkland Islands	**1997/2985**
Faroes	**2007/3469**
Fiji	**1976/1342**
Finland	**1970/153**
	1973/1327
	1980/710
	1985/1997
	1991/2878
	1996/3166
France	**2009/226**

Country	SI/SR & O
Gambia	1980/1963
Georgia	**2004/3325**
	2010/2972
Germany	**2010/2975**
	2014/1874
	2021/634
Ghana	**1993/1800**
Gibraltar	**2020/275**
Greece	**1954/142**
Grenada	**1949/361**
	1968/1867
Guernsey	**2018/1345**
Guyana	**1992/3207**
Hong Kong	**2010/2974**
Hungary	**2011/2726**
Iceland	**2014/1879**
India	**1993/1801**
	2013/3147
Indonesia	**1994/769**
Irish Republic	**1976/2151**
	1976/2152
	1995/764
	1998/3151
Isle of Man	**2018/1347**
Israel	**1963/616**
	1971/391
	2019/1111
Italy	**1990/2590**
Ivory Coast	**1987/169**
Jamaica	**1973/1329**
Japan	**2006/1924**
	2014/1881
Jersey	**2018/1348**
Jordan	**2001/3924**
Kazakhstan	**1994/3211**
	1998/2567
Kenya	**1977/1299**
Kiribati (and Tuvalu)	**1950/750**
	1968/309
	1974/1271
Korea (South)	**1996/3168**
Kosovo	**2015/2007**
Kuwait	**1999/2036**
Kyrgyzstan	**2018/525**
Latvia	**1996/3167**
Lesotho[5]	**1997/2986**
	2018/376
Libya	**2010/243**
Liechtenstein	**2012/3077**
Lithuania	**2001/3925**
	2002/2847
Luxembourg	**2022/1055**
Macedonia	**2007/2127**
Malawi	**1956/619**
	1964/1401
	1968/1101
	1979/302
Malaysia	**1997/2987**
	2010/2971

129

Country	SI/SR & O	Country	SI/SR & O
Malta	**1995/763**	Singapore	**1997/2988**
Mauritius	**1981/1121**		2010/2685
	1987/467		2012/3078
	2003/2620	Slovak Republic[3]	**1991/2876**
	2011/2442	Slovenia	**2008/1796**
	2018/840	Solomon Islands	**1950/748**
Mexico	**1994/3212**		1968/574
	2010/2686		1974/1270
Moldova	**2008/1795**	South Africa	**2002/3138**
Mongolia	**1996/2598**		2011/2441
Montenegro[2]	**1981/1815**	Spain	**2013/3152**
Montserrat	**1947/2869**	Sri Lanka	**1980/713**
	1968/576	Sudan	**1977/1719**
	2011/1083	Swaziland	**1969/380**
Morocco	**1991/2881**	Sweden	**2015/1891**
Myanmar	**1952/751**		2021/633
Namibia	**1962/2352**	Switzerland	**1978/1408**
	1962/2788		1982/714
	1967/1489		1994/3215
	1967/1490		2007/3465
Netherlands	**2009/227**		2010/2689
	2013/3143		2012/3079
New Zealand	**1984/365**		2018/627
	2004/1274	Taiwan	**2002/3137**
	2008/1793		2021/1447
Nigeria	**1987/2057**	Tajikistan	**2014/3275**
Norway	**2013/3144**	Thailand	**1981/1546**
Oman	**1998/2568**	Trinidad and Tobago	**1983/1903**
	2010/2687	Tunisia	**1984/133**
Pakistan	**1987/2058**	Turkey	**1988/932**
Panama	**2013/3149**	Turkmenistan	**2016/1217**
Papua New Guinea	**1991/2882**	Tuvalu (and Kiribati)	**1950/750**
Philippines	**1978/184**		1968/309
Poland	**2006/3323**		1974/1271
Portugal	**1969/599**	Uganda	**1993/1802**
Qatar	**2010/241**	Ukraine	**1993/1803**
	2011/1684		2018/779
Romania	**1977/57**	United Arab Emirates	**2016/754**
Russian Federation[6]	**1994/3213**	Uruguay	**2016/753**
St Christopher (St Kitts) and Nevis	**1947/2872**	USA	**2002/2848**
		Uzbekistan	**1994/770**
San Marino	**2023/841**		2018/628
Saudi Arabia	**2008/1770**	Venezuela	**1996/2599**
Senegal	**2015/1892**	Vietnam	**1994/3216**
Serbia[2]	**1981/1815**	Zambia	**2014/1876**
Sierra Leone	**1947/2873**	Zimbabwe	**1982/1842**
	1968/1104		

[1] Belarus partially suspended the UK-Belarus treaty by a resolution of the Council of Ministers on 22 March 2024. The resolution suspends the provisions relating to dividends, interest and capital gains with effect from 1 June 2024. The UK government considers the treaty to remain in force.

[2] SI 1981/1815 (former Yugoslavia agreement) treated as remaining in force between the UK and, respectively, Bosnia-Herzegovina, Serbia and Montenegro until superseded by new agreements. (SP 3/04.)

[3] SI 1991/2876 (former Czechoslovakia agreement) treated as remaining in force between the UK and, respectively, Czech Republic and Slovak Republic. (SP 5/93.)

[4] Hong Kong Special Administrative Region has its own agreement.

[5] The 2018 treaty replaces SI 1997/2986 but where, immediately before the entry into force on 18 September 2018, an individual is entitled to the benefits of the 1997 agreement and was in receipt of pensions or other similar remuneration, or pensions paid and other payments made under a public scheme which is part of the social security system of a Contracting State, a political subdivision or a local authority thereof, the provisions of the 1997 agreement will continue to apply to such pensions and payments.

[6] Russia suspended substantially all of the UK-Russia treaty by presidential decree on 8 August 2023. The UK government considers the treaty to remain in force.

Tax information exchange agreements in force
[T9.104]

Country	SI	Country	SI
Anguilla	2010/2677	Isle of Man	2009/228
Antigua and Barbuda	2011/1075	Jersey	2009/3012
Aruba	2011/2435	Liberia	2011/2434
Bahamas	2010/2684	Liechtenstein	2010/2678
Belize	2011/1685	Macao	2015/801
		Marshall Islands	2013/3153
Bermuda	2018/518	Monaco	2015/804
British Virgin Islands	2009/3013	San Marino	2011/1688
Curaçao, Sint Maarten and BES Islands (formerly the Netherlands Antilles)	2011/2433	St Christopher (St Kitts) and Nevis	2011/1077
Dominica	2011/1686	St Lucia	2011/1076
Gibraltar	2010/2680	St Vincent and Grenadines	2011/1078
	2014/1356	Turks and Caicos Islands	2010/2679
Grenada	2011/1687		2014/1360
Guernsey	2009/3011	Uruguay	2014/1358

Tax information exchange agreements signed but not in force
[T9.105]

Anguilla Exchange of Letters[1]
Brazil
British Virgin Islands Exchange of Letters[1]

[1] These will amend the existing tax information exchange agreements.

International agreements in force to improve tax compliance
[T9.106]

Isle of Man, Guernsey, Jersey, Gibraltar	2014/520
USA	2015/878

Agreements in force covering shipping and air transport profits
[T9.107]

Country	SI/SR & O	Country	SI/SR & O
Brazil	1968/572	Congo Democratic Republic	1977/1298
Brazil (aircrew)	2011/2723	Iran (air)	1960/2419
Cameroon (air)	1982/1841	Lebanon	1964/278
China (air)	1981/1119	Saudi Arabia (air)	1994/767

Agreements in force covering estates, inheritances and gifts
[T9.108]

France*	1963/1319	Pakistan*	1957/1522
India*	1956/998	South Africa	1979/576
Ireland	1978/1107	Sweden	1981/840
Italy*	1968/304		1989/986
Netherlands	1980/706	Switzerland	1994/3214
	1996/730	USA	1979/1454

* Agreements pre-date UK inheritance tax/capital transfer tax.

Overseas income – basis of assessment

[T9.109]

SEE TOLLEY'S TAX COMPUTATIONS 23.1.

From 6 April 2025 onwards

	Professions, trades, etc	Pensions	Other income
Non-residents	Exempt	Exempt	Exempt
Residents			
(1) **Foreign income and gains regime applies**[2,3]	Effectively exempt	Effectively exempt	Effectively exempt
(2) **Foreign income and gains regime does not apply**[4]	Arising	Arising[1]	Arising

[1] Pensions paid by the governments of the Federal Republic of Germany, Austria and the Netherlands, to certain victims of WW2 persecution are exempt.

[2] Individuals qualify for the foreign income and gains regime (FIG regime) for their first 4 tax years of UK residency as long as they were UK non-resident for the 10 consecutive tax years immediately prior to arrival in the UK. Foreign income and gains arising in the tax year that are covered by the FIG regime claim are effectively exempt from UK tax and can be remitted to the UK without attracting a UK tax liability. The foreign income and gains arising in the tax year are reported on the tax return for the year and a 100% deduction from taxable income is given for these amounts. Where the individual makes a claim for the FIG regime for a tax year they are not entitled to a UK personal allowance, blind person's allowance, married couple's allowance and transferable marriage allowance, and (if the claim covers gains) the annual exempt amount.

[3] Members of Parliament and the House of Lords are excluded from qualifying for the FIG regime.

[4] If the individual does not qualify for the FIG regime in the tax year or does not make a claim for it to apply, their foreign income and gains arising in the tax year are taxable on the arising basis. If the individual was non-domiciled for any years prior to 6 April 2025 and was taxed on the remittance basis in any of these years, they can elect for the temporary repatriation facility (TRF) to apply in respect of any unremitted foreign income and gains relating to those years of remittance basis. The TRF is available for three tax years from 6 April 2025 to 5 April 2028. To use the TRF, the individual must make an election for the relevant tax year, designate amounts of unremitted income and gains on their tax return for that year and pay the flat rate of UK tax on them that applies in that tax year. The individual can then remit the designated amounts at any point, even if this is after 5 April 2028. The flat tax rates of the TRF are 12% in 2025/26 and 2026/27, and 15% in 2027/28.

Up to 5 April 2025

(ITTOIA 2005 Pt 8; ITEPA 2003 ss 573–576A, 642, 642A; ITA 2007 ss 809A–809Z10)

	Professions, trades, etc	Pensions	Other income
Non-residents	Exempt	Exempt	Exempt
Residents			
(1) **Foreign domicile**[2]	Remittance	Remittance	Remittance
(2) **UK domicile**	Arising	Arising[1]	Arising

[1] Pensions paid by the governments of the Federal Republic of Germany, Austria and the Netherlands, to certain victims of WW2 persecution are exempt.

[2] Before 6 April 2025, where an individual not domiciled in the UK who has overseas income or gains in excess of £2,000 claims the remittance basis, they will not qualify for personal allowances or the capital gains tax annual exempt amount. The claim for remittance basis must be made annually. If the individual is not UK domiciled in a year and has been resident in the UK for at least seven out of the last nine tax years and has overseas income or gains in excess of £2,000, there is an additional charge of £30,000. The charge is £60,000 for non-domiciles who have been UK resident for at least twelve tax years in the previous fourteen. From April 2017 an individual who has been resident in the UK for more than 15 of the last 20 tax years is deemed UK-domiciled for tax purposes. It is also no longer possible for an individual born in the UK to parents who are UK-domiciled to claim non-domicile status if they leave but then return and take up residency in the UK.

Employment income liability of non-resident employees see T6.162.

Tax-free (FOTRA) securities

[T9.110]

(FA 1996 s 154; FA 1998 s 161; ITTOIA 2005 ss 713, 714; CTA 2009 s 1279)

Interest on all government stock is exempt from tax where the beneficial owner is not resident in the UK. Except in the case of $3^1/_2$% War Loan 1952 or after, the exemption does not apply where the securities are held for the purposes of a trade or business carried on in the UK.

Social security benefits

Taxable state benefits

[T10.101]

	Weekly 7.4.25	Total 2025–26 (52 weeks)	Weekly 8.4.24	Total 2024–25 (52 weeks)
	£	£	£	£
Bereavement benefits — deaths before 6 April 2017[1]				
Widowed parent's allowance	150.90	7,847	148.40	7,717
Carer's allowance	83.30	4,332	81.90	4,259
Employment and support allowance[6]				
– under 25	72.90	–	71.70	–
– 25 or over	92.05	–	90.50	–
Incapacity benefit[6]				
Long-term (after 52 weeks)	141.25	7,345	138.90	7,223
– Adult dependency increase	82.05	4,267	80.70	4,196
– Age increase: higher rate	14.95	777	14.70	764
lower rate	8.30	432	8.15	424
Short term				
– Under pension age: higher rate	126.10	–	124.00	–
– Adult dependency increase	63.90	–	62.85	–
– Over pension age: higher rate	141.25	–	138.90	–
– Adult dependency increase	79.00	–	77.70	–
Industrial death benefit[2]				
Widow's pension: higher rate	176.45	9,175	169.50	8,814
lower rate	52.94	2,753	50.85	2,644
Widower's pension	176.45	9,175	169.50	8,814
Invalidity allowance[3]				
Higher rate	28.90	1,503	28.40	1,477
Middle rate	18.50	962	18.20	946
Lower rate	9.25	481	9.10	473
Jobseeker's allowance[4]				
Single: under 25	72.90	–	71.70	–
25 or over	92.05	–	90.50	–
Couple: both under 18	72.90	–	71.70	–
both under 18 higher rate	110.15	–	108.30	–
one under 18, one under 25	72.90	–	71.70	–
one under 18, one 25 or over	92.05	–	90.50	–
both 18 or over	144.65	–	142.25	–
State pension — retired before 6 April 2016				
Single person (Category A or B)	176.45	9,175	169.50	8,814
Single person (Category B lower) based on spouse's or civil partner's insurance	105.70	5,496	101.55	5,281
Non-contributory pension				
– single (Category C or Category D)	105.70	5,496	101.55	5,281
Age addition (over 80) (each)	0.25	13	0.25	13
State pension — retired after 5 April 2016				
Rate	230.25	11,973	221.20	11,502
Statutory adoption pay				
Rate[5]	187.18	–	184.03	–
Earnings threshold	125.00	–	123.00	–
Statutory maternity pay				
Rate[5]	187.18	–	184.03	–
Earnings threshold	125.00	–	123.00	–

	Weekly 7.4.25	Total 2025–26 (52 weeks)	Weekly 8.4.24	Total 2024–25 (52 weeks)
	£	£	£	£
Statutory parental bereavement pay				
Rate[5]	**187.18**	–	184.03	–
Earnings threshold	**125.00**	–	123.00	–
Statutory paternity pay				
Rate[5]	**187.18**	–	184.03	–
Earnings threshold	**125.00**	–	123.00	–
Statutory shared parental pay				
Rate[5]	**187.18**	–	184.03	–
Earnings threshold	**125.00**	–	123.00	–
Statutory sick pay				
Rate	**118.75**	–	116.75	–
Earnings threshold	**125.00**	–	123.00	–

[1] Paid to widows, widowers, civil partners or cohabiting partners of the deceased with dependent children. For deaths on or after 6 April 2017 bereavement support payments replace bereavement benefits and are non-taxable (see **T10.102**).

[2] For deaths before 11 April 1988 only.

[3] When paid with retirement pensions. See note below on non-taxable benefits in **T10.102**.

[4] Where the allowance exceeds the amount shown above, the excess is not taxable.

[5] The allowance is 90% of average weekly earnings if less than the above amount. In the first six weeks the rate of SMP and SAP is 90% of average weekly earnings even if higher than the standard rate.

[6] Employment and support allowance replaces incapacity benefits for new claimants on or after 27 October 2008. Only contributory employment and support allowance is taxable. Income related allowance is not taxable.

[7] **A cap is placed on the total amount of benefit** that most people aged 16 or over and who have not reached state pension age can receive. The cap applies to the total amount that the people in a household receive from certain benefits. From 1 April 2023, the cap is £423.46 (previously £384.62) a week or £486.98 (previously £442.31) in Greater London for couples (with or without children living with them), and for single parents whose children live with them, and £283.71 (previously £257.69) a week or £326.29 (previously £296.35) in Greater London for single adults who do not have children, or whose children do not live with them. See www.gov.uk/benefit-cap/benefit-cap-amounts.

[8] **Universal credit** replaces some of the benefits above. It is intended that by 2025 most claimants currently receiving the legacy benefits will be transferred to universal credit. For current rates see table of non-taxable benefits in **T10.102**. See www.gov.uk/universal-credit.

Non-taxable state benefits

[T10.102]

Weekly rates from	7.4.25	8.4.24
	£	£
Attendance allowance		
Higher rate (day and night)	110.40	108.55
Lower rate (day or night)	73.90	72.65
Child benefit[3]		
Eldest child	26.05	25.60
Each subsequent child	17.25	16.95
Child dependency addition		
Paid with state pension; widowed mother's/parent's allowance; short-term incapacity benefit - higher rate or over state pension age; long-term incapacity benefit; carer's allowance; severe disablement unemployability supplement	11.35	11.35
Disability living allowance[2]		
Care component higher rate	110.40	108.55
middle rate	73.90	72.65
lower rate	29.20	28.70
Mobility component higher rate	77.05	75.75
lower rate	29.20	28.70
Personal independence payment[2]		
Daily living component enhanced rate	110.40	108.55
standard rate	73.90	72.65
Mobility component enhanced rate	77.05	75.75
standard rate	29.20	28.70
Guardian's allowance	22.10	21.75
Incapacity benefit (short-term)[1]		
Under pension age – lower rate (first 28 weeks)	106.65	104.85
– Adult dependency increase	63.90	62.85
Over pension age – lower rate (first 28 weeks)	135.50	133.25
– Adult dependency increase	79.00	77.70
Maternity allowance (where SMP not available)		
Standard rate	187.18	184.03
MA threshold	30.00	30.00
Severe disablement allowance[7]		
Basic rate	100.05	98.40
Age-related addition higher rate	14.95	14.70
middle rate	8.30	8.15
lower rate	8.30	8.15
– Adult dependency increase	49.20	48.40

See next page for universal credit amounts

Amount payable per assessment period[5] in:		2025–26	2024–25
		£	£
Universal credit[5]			
Universal credit amounts			
Standard allowance	single under 25	316.98	311.68
	single 25 or over	400.14	393.45
	joint claimants both under 25	497.55	489.23
	joint claimants either 25 or over	628.10	617.60
Child element[6]	first child	339.00	333.33
	second/ subsequent child	292.81	287.92
Disabled child additions	lower rate addition	158.76	156.11
	higher rate addition	495.87	487.58
Limited capability for work element		158.76	156.11
Limited capability for work and work-related activity element		423.27	416.19
Carer element		201.68	198.31
Childcare cost element	maximum for one child	1,031.88	1,014.63
	maximum for two or more children	1,768.94	1,739.37
Non-dependants' housing cost contributions		93.02	91.47
Work allowances			
Higher work allowance (no housing element)	single, no dependent children	Nil	Nil
	single, one or more children	684.00	673.00
	single, limited capability for work	684.00	673.00
	joint claimant, no dependent children	Nil	Nil
	joint claimant, one or more children	684.00	673.00
	joint claimant, limited capability for work	684.00	673.00
Lower work allowance	single, no dependent children	Nil	Nil
	single, one or more children	411.00	404.00
	single, limited capability for work	411.00	404.00
	joint claimant, no dependent children	Nil	Nil
	joint claimant, one or more children	411.00	404.00
	joint claimant, limited capability for work	411.00	404.00

[1] Incapacity benefit replaced invalidity allowance from April 1995. The benefits are taxable except those paid in the first 28 weeks of incapacity and those paid to persons already receiving invalidity benefit on 13 April 1995 so long as they remain incapable of work.

[2] Personal Independence Payment (PIP) started to replace Disability Living Allowance (DLA) for new claims by eligible people aged 16 to 64 from 8 April 2013. PIP will be introduced in stages over a number of years for existing DLA claimants.

[3] See note in **T6.108** regarding the income tax charge arising to certain child benefit claimants from 7 January 2013.

[4] **A cap is placed on the total amount of benefit** that most people aged 16 or over and who have not reached state pension age can receive. The cap applies to the total amount that the people in a household receive from certain benefits. From 1 April 2023, the cap is £423.46 (previously £384.62) a week or £486.98 (previously £442.31) in Greater London for couples (with or without children living with them), and for single parents whose children live with them, and £283.71 (previously £257.69) a week or £326.29 (previously £296.35) in Greater London for single adults who do not have children, or whose children do not live with them. See www.gov.uk/benefit-cap/benefit-cap-amounts.

[5] **Universal credit** replaces some of the benefits listed in the above tables. It is intended that by 2025, most claimants currently receiving the legacy benefits will be transferred to universal credit. An assessment period is a calendar month from effective date of claim. See www.gov.uk/universal-credit.

[6] The child element of universal credit is no longer awarded for third and subsequent children born after 6 April 2017. This also applies to families claiming universal credit for the first time after April 2017. The restriction does not apply to disabled children and multiple births.

[7] Severe disablement allowance has been replaced with employment and support allowance except for those who reached retirement age before 6 April 2014.

Bereavement support payments — deaths on or after 6 April 2017[1]	2025–26 First payment £	2025–26 Monthly £	2024–25 First payment £	2024–25 Monthly £
With children under 20 in full-time education	**3,500**	**350**[1]	3,500	350[1]
Without children under 20 in full-time education	**2,500**	**100**[1]	2,500	100[1]

[1] Paid to widows, widowers, civil partners and cohabiting partners of the deceased. For deaths on or after 6 April 2017 bereavement support payments replace taxable bereavement benefits (see **T10.101**). Monthly payments paid for up to 18 months.

Other non-taxable benefits include:
[T10.103]

Back to Work bonus
Child tax credit (see Tax Credits, **T6.202**)

Christmas bonus (with retirement pension)
Cold weather payments
Housing benefit (income related)
Income support (income related)
Industrial injuries disablement pension

Pension credit
Pneumoconiosis, byssinosis and miscellaneous disease benefits
Social fund payments
Vaccine damage (lump sum)
War pensions
Winter fuel payment
Working tax credit (see Tax Credits, **T6.202**)

Stamp taxes

Stamp duty land tax

[T11.101]

(FA 2003 Schs 2A–9; FA 2021 ss 87–89, Schs 16–17; SDLT(TR)A 2020; SDLT(TR)A 2023)

Stamp duty land tax does not apply in Scotland to transactions with an effective date on or after 1 April 2015, from which date land and buildings transaction tax applies (see table below), subject to transitional provisions in particular in relation to contracts entered into on or before 1 May 2012. Stamp duty land tax does not apply in Wales to transactions with an effective date on or after 1 April 2018, from which date land transaction tax applies (see table below), subject to transitional provisions in particular in relation to contracts entered into on or before 17 December 2014.

Land transactions from 1 April 2021 onwards							
	Residential property[5]	*Rate for residents*[3]	*Rate for non-residents*[3,8]	*Higher rate for residents*[7]	*Higher rate for non-residents*[7,8]	*Non-residential or mixed property*	*Rate*
Effective date	**1.4.25 onwards**					**1.4.25 onwards**	
	On band of consideration[2]					On band of consideration[2]	
	Up to £125,000[3]	Nil	2%	5%	7%	Up to £150,000	Nil
	£125,001–£250,000[3]	2%	4%	7%	9%	£150,001–£250,000	2%
	£250,001–£925,000[3]	5%	7%	10%	12%	£250,001 or more	5%
	£925,001–£1,500,000	10%	12%	15%	17%		
	£1,500,001 or more	12%	14%	17%	19%		
	On total consideration[1]						
Non-natural persons[1,6,8]	£500,001 or more	17%	19%	N/A	N/A		
Effective date	31.10.24–31.3.25					31.10.24–31.3.25	
	On band of consideration[2]					On band of consideration[2]	
	Up to £250,000[3]	Nil	2%	5%	7%	Up to £150,000	Nil
	£250,001–£925,000[3]	5%	7%	10%	12%	£150,001–£250,000	2%
	£925,001–£1,500,000	10%	12%	15%	17%	£250,001 or more	5%
	£1,500,001 or more	12%	14%	17%	19%		
	On total consideration[1]						
Non-natural persons[1,6,8]	£500,001 or more	17%	19%	N/A	N/A		
Effective date	23.9.22–30.10.24					23.9.22–30.10.24	
	On band of consideration[2]					On band of consideration[2]	
	Up to £250,000[3]	Nil	2%	3%	5%	Up to £150,000	Nil
	£250,001–£925,000[3]	5%	7%	8%	10%	£150,001–£250,000	2%
	£925,001–£1,500,000	10%	12%	13%	15%	£250,001 or more	5%
	£1,500,001 or more	12%	14%	15%	17%		
	On total consideration[1]						
Non-natural persons[1,6,8]	£500,001 or more	15%	17%	N/A	N/A		

	Land transactions from 1 April 2021 onwards						
	Residential property[5]	**Rate for residents**[3]	**Rate for non-residents**[3,8]	**Higher rate for residents**[7]	**Higher rate for non-residents**[7,8]	**Non-residential or mixed property**	**Rate**
Effective date	1.10.21–22.9.22 On band of consideration[2]					1.10.21–22.9.22 On band of consideration[2]	
	Up to £125,000[3]	Nil	2%	3%	5%	Up to £150,000	Nil
	£125,001–£250,000[3]	2%	4%	5%	7%	£150,001–£250,000	2%
	£250,001–£925,000[3]	5%	7%	8%	10%	£250,001 or more	5%
	£925,001–£1,500,000	10%	12%	13%	15%		
	£1,500,001 or more	12%	14%	15%	17%		
	On total consideration[1]						
Non-natural persons[1,6,8]	£500,001 or more	15%	17%	N/A	N/A		
Effective date	1.7.21–30.9.21 On band of consideration[2]					1.7.21–30.9.21 On band of consideration[2]	
	Up to £250,000[3]	Nil	2%	3%	5%	Up to £150,000	Nil
	£250,001–£925,000[3]	5%	7%	8%	10%	£150,001–£250,000	2%
	£925,001–£1,500,000	10%	12%	13%	15%	£250,001 or more	5%
	£1,500,001 or more	12%	14%	15%	17%		
	On total consideration[1]						
Non-natural persons[1,6,8]	£500,001 or more	15%	17%	N/A	N/A		
Effective date	1.4.21–30.6.21 On band of consideration[2]					1.4.21–30.6.21 On band of consideration[2]	
	Up to £500,000[3]	Nil	2%	3%	5%	Up to £150,000	Nil
	£500,001–£925,000[3]	5%	7%	8%	10%	£150,001–£250,000	2%
	£925,001–£1,500,000	10%	12%	13%	15%	£250,001 or more	5%
	£1,500,001 or more	12%	14%	15%	17%		
	On total consideration[1]						
Non-natural persons[1,6,8]	£500,001 or more	15%	17%	N/A	N/A		

Land transactions from 1 April 2021 onwards					
Lease rentals	*On net present value (NPV) of rent over term of lease (applying a discount rate of 3.5%)[4]*				
	Residential property	*Rate for residents*	*Rate for non-residents*	*Non-residential or mixed property*	*Rate*
Effective date	**1.4.25 onwards**			**1.4.25 onwards**	
	Up to £125,000	**Nil**	**2%**	**Up to £150,000**	**Nil**
	£125,001 or more	**1%**	**3%**	**£150,001–£5,000,000**	**1%**
				£5,000,001 or more	**2%**
Effective date	23.9.22–31.3.25			23.9.22–31.3.25	
	Up to £250,000	Nil	2%	Up to £150,000	Nil
	£250,001 or more	1%	3%	£150,001–£5,000,000	1%
				£5,000,001 or more	2%
Effective date	1.10.21–22.9.22 [8]			1.10.21–22.9.22 [8]	
	Up to £125,000	Nil	2%	Up to £150,000	Nil
	£125,001 or more	1%	3%	£150,001–£5,000,000	1%
				£5,000,001 or more	2%
Effective date	1.7.21 30.9.21[8]			1.7.21–30.9.21[8]	
	Up to £250,000	Nil	2%	Up to £150,000	Nil
	£250,001 or more	1%	3%	£150,001–£5,000,000	1%
				£5,000,001 or more	2%
Effective date	1.4.21–30.6.21[8]			1.4.21–30.6.21[8]	
	Up to £500,000	Nil	2%	Up to £150,000	Nil
	£500,001 or more	1%	3%	£150,001–£5,000,000	1%
				£5,000,001 or more	2%
Premiums The same tax is payable for a premium granted as for a land transaction.					

Land transactions before 1 April 2021					
	Residential property[5]	**Rate**[3]	**Higher rate**[7]	**Non-residential or mixed property**	**Rate**
Effective date	8.7.20–31.3.21			8.7.20–31.3.21	
	On band of consideration[2]			On band of consideration[2]	
	Up to £500,000	Nil	3%	Up to £150,000	Nil
	£500,001–£925,000	5%	8%	£150,001–£250,000	2%
	£925,001–£1,500,000	10%	13%	£250,001 or more	5%
	£1,500,001 or more	12%	15%		
	On total consideration[1]				
Non-natural persons[1, 6]	£500,001 or more	15%			
	Residential property[5]	**Rate**		**Non-residential or mixed property**	**Rate**
Lease rentals	On net present value (NPV) of rent over term of lease (applying a discount rate of 3.5%)[4]				
Effective date	**Residential property**	**Rate**		**Non-residential or mixed property**	**Rate**
8.7.20–31.3.21	Up to £500,000	Nil		Up to £150,000	Nil
	£500,001 or more	1%		£150,001–£5,000,000	1%
				£5,000,001 or more	2%

Premiums
The same tax is payable for a premium granted as for a land transaction.

[1] Rate applies to the full consideration.
[2] Rates are charged on the portion of the consideration that falls within each rate band.
[3] With effect from 1 April 2025, residential property purchases by first-time buyers attract a nil rate of SDLT for purchase consideration up to £300,000 (£425,000 from 23 September 2022 to 31 March 2025; £300,000 before 23 September 2022). Purchase consideration over £300,000 (£425,000 from 23 September 2022 to 31 March 2025; £300,000 before 23 September 2022) up to and including £500,000 (£625,000 from 23 September 2022 to 31 March 2025; £500,000 before 23 September 2022) attracts 5% SDLT. Where the purchase consideration is in excess of £500,000 (£625,000 from 23 September 2022 to 31 March 2025; £500,000 before 23 September 2022), no relief is due and standard rates above apply. The 2% non-resident surcharge applies from 1 April 2021 (see note 8). These provisions were suspended whilst the nil rate band was increased to £500,000 for transactions with an effective date between 8 July 2020 and 30 June 2021 inclusive.
[4] Rates apply to the amount of NPV in the slice, not the whole value.
[5] Before 1 June 2024, where a purchaser (or a connected person) of residential property acquires more than one dwelling from the same vendor (or a connected person) and makes a claim, the rate of SDLT will be calculated based on the mean consideration for each property, subject to a minimum rate of 1%. Relief may be claimed in respect of superior interests in dwellings subject to a long lease, where the transaction is the lease element of a "lease and leaseback" funding arrangement entered into by a housing association or other qualifying body. This relief is abolished for transactions with an effective date on or after 1 June 2024, except where the contract is made on or before 6 March 2024 and is not subsequently varied (F(No 2)A 2024 s 7).
[6] A 17% rate (15% before 31 October 2024) applies to certain non-natural persons (ie companies, partnerships with at least one company member, and collective investment schemes) acquiring a residential property where consideration exceeds a threshold of £500,000. The 2% non-resident surcharge applies from 1 April 2021 (see note 8). Relief is available for certain acquisitions so that the charge is at the lower percentage.
[7] A higher rate applies broadly to purchases of additional residential property by individuals, and to purchases of residential property by companies and trusts other than bare trusts and interest in possession trusts. It does not apply to purchases of property under £40,000 or to purchases of caravans, mobile homes and houseboats. If there is a period of overlap in ownership of a main residence, a refund of the higher rate can be obtained if the previous main residence is sold within 3 years following the purchase of the new. Relief is available in certain circumstances when someone gets divorced, exchanges a property with a spouse, adds to an existing interest in their main residence or is a child whose affairs are subject to the Court of Protection. For purchases on or after 1 January 2017, a taxpayer will still be able to obtain a refund if HMRC is satisfied that they were unable to sell the previous residence within 3 years due to 'exceptional circumstances'.
[8] A 2% surcharge applies from 1 April 2021 on purchases of residential property by non-residents (as defined for SDLT purposes only), including certain UK resident companies controlled by non-residents.

Exemptions and reliefs
[T11.102]

No SDLT is chargeable on:
- (1) transfers to charities for use for charitable purposes.
- (2) transfers to bodies established for national purposes.
- (3) gifts inter vivos.
- (4) certain transfers on divorce or dissolution of a civil partnership.
- (5) transfers of property to beneficiaries under a will or an intestacy.
- (6) land transfers within groups of companies.
- (7) land transferred in exchange for shares on company reconstruction and acquisitions.
- (8) certain transfers to or leases granted by registered providers of social housing.
- (9) sale & leaseback and lease & leaseback arrangements involving commercial & residential property.
- (10) certain acquisitions of residential property by house building companies or property traders from personal representatives, or when people move into a new dwelling or a chain of transactions break down, or by employers involving employee relocations.
- (11) purchases of residential property by first-time buyers for consideration of not more than £500,000 (but see note 3 under table above).
- (12) demutualisation of building societies and insurance companies.
- (13) incorporation of limited liability partnerships.
- (14) transfers of land between public bodies under a statutory reorganisation.
- (15) compulsory purchase of land facilitating redevelopment.
- (16) land transactions in compliance with planning obligations enforceable against the vendor and made within five years of the obligation where the purchaser is one of certain public authorities.
- (17) transfers by a local constituency association in consequence of a reorganisation of parliamentary constituencies.
- (18) purchases or leases of certain diplomatic or consular premises or headquarters premises of certain international organisations.
- (19) transfers of properties into an authorised PAIF or CoACS within an initial period if conditions are met.
- (20) certain transfers of securities, property and land from a failed institution to the appointed temporary holding entity under a Bank of England stabilisation power, and on transfers of securities to bondholders following exercise of the bail-in stabilisation power.
- (21) certain acquisitions of land situated in freeport special tax sites from the date the site is formally designated until 30 September 2031 (30 September 2034 in Northern Ireland). See SI 2021/1193, 2021/1194, 2021/1195 and 2021/1389; SI 2022/184, SI 2022/185, SI 2022/186, SI 2022/ 643, SI 2022/972 and SI 2022/973; SI 2024/71 for details of the current freeport special tax sites in England.
- (22) certain acquisitions of land situated in special tax sites in or connected with an investment zone from the date the site is designated until 30 September 2034. See SI 2024/383 for the current investment zone special tax sites.

Relief from SDLT may also apply on:
- (a) right to buy transactions, shared ownership leases and rent to loan transactions.
- (b) alternative property finance schemes.
- (c) exercise of collective rights by leaseholders.
- (d) crofting community right to buy.
- (e) certain arrangements relating to land transactions involving public or educational bodies.
- (f) acquisitions of interests in land by certain National Health Service bodies.

Land and buildings transaction tax (Scotland)

[T11.103]

(Land and Buildings Transaction Tax (Scotland) Act 2013; Land and Buildings Transaction Tax (Amendment) (Scotland) Act 2016; SSI 2018/372; SSI 2020/24; SSI 2020/215; SSI 2022/375; SSI 2023/280; SSI 2024/104)
Land and buildings transaction tax applies in Scotland instead of stamp duty land tax.

Land transactions					
Effective date	**Residential property**	**Rate**[2,3]	**Effective date**	**Non-residential or mixed property**	**Rate**
	On band of consideration[1]			On band of consideration[1]	
From 1.4.21	Up to £145,000[3]	Nil	**From 1.4.21**	Up to £150,000	Nil
	£145,001–£250,000[3]	2%		£150,001–£250,000	1%
	£250,001–£325,000	5%		£250,001 or more	5%
	£325,001–£750,000	10%			
	£750,001 or more	12%			
15.7.20–31.3.21	Up to £250,000[3]	Nil	15.7.20–31.3.21	Up to £150,000	Nil
	£250,001–£325,000	5%		£150,001–£250,000	1%
	£325,001–£750,000	10%		£250,001 or more	5%
	£750,001 or more	12%			
25.1.19–14.7.20	Up to £145,000[3]	Nil	25.1.19–14.7.20[4]	Up to £150,000	Nil
	£145,001–£250,000[3]	2%		£150,001–£250,000	1%
	£250,001–£325,000	5%		£250,001 or more	5%
	£325,001–£750,000	10%			
	£750,001 or more	12%			
Lease rentals					
LBTT is applied to non-residential leases. Residential leases are generally exempt from LBTT with the exception of certain long leases which are qualifying leases. Before 7 February 2020, where a lease is chargeable the amount of tax payable is 1% of the amount of net present value (NPV) of the rent above £150,000. For transactions with an effective date on or after 7 February 2020, where contracts were entered into on or after that date and subject to some exceptions for further returns, the rate is 1% of the NPV between £150,000 and £2m, and 2% above £2m[4]. Licences to occupy property are exempt interests, except licences that are of a description prescribed under Land and Buildings Transaction Tax (Scotland) Act 2013 s 53(1).					
Premiums					
The same tax is payable for a premium granted as for a land transaction, subject to the exemption for residential leases other than qualifying leases (see above). Special rules apply to a premium in respect of non-residential property where the rent exceeds £1,000 a year.					

[1] Rates are charged on the portion of the consideration that falls within each rate band.
[2] For land transactions with an effective date on or after 16 December 2022 (other than where contracts were entered into before 16 December 2022), an additional amount of LBTT of 6% (previously, 4% for transactions with an effective date on or after 25 January 2019 (other than where contracts were entered into before 12 December 2018) of the consideration applies to transactions which consist of or include the acquisition of an additional dwelling by individuals or which consist of or include the acquisition of a dwelling by certain businesses, companies and trusts. It does not apply to purchases of property under £40,000 or, in the case of jointly owned property, where the individual's share in the value of the property is under £40,000. If there is a period of overlap in ownership of a main residence, a refund of the higher rate can be obtained if the previous main residence is sold within 36 months following the purchase of the new residence. Before 1 April 2024, the period was 18 months, except that for transactions with an effective date between 24 September 2018 and 24 March 2020 inclusive, the period was extended from 18 months to 36 months. Relief is available in certain circumstances when two buyers jointly buy a new dwelling and previously lived together as a married couple, civil partners or cohabitants in a dwelling owned by either one of them solely.
[3] Relief for first-time buyers applies a nil rate to the first £175,000 of purchase consideration resulting in first-time buyers benefiting from the relief up to a maximum of £600. Note, however, that there was a temporary increase in the overall nil rate band to £250,000 from 15 July 2020 to 31 March 2021.
[4] Rates apply to the amount of NPV in the slice, not the whole value.

Exemptions and reliefs

[T11.104]

There are various exemptions and reliefs from LBTT, see 'LBTT3010 - Tax Reliefs' and 'LBTT3002 - Exempt Transactions' at www.revenue.scot.

Land transaction tax (Wales)

[T11.105]

(Land Transaction Tax and Anti-avoidance of Devolved Taxes (Wales) Act 2017; SI 2017/953; SI 2018/126; SI 2020/794; SI 2021/238; SI 2022/1027; SI 2024/791)

Land transaction tax applies in Wales instead of stamp duty land tax.

Land transactions					
Effective date	Residential property	Rate	Higher rate[2]	Non-residential or mixed property	Rate
	On band of consideration[1]			On band of consideration[1]	
10.10.22 onwards[4]	Up to £180,000	Nil	4%	Up to £225,000	Nil
	£180,001–£225,000	Nil	7.5%	£225,001–£250,000	1%
	£225,001–£250,000	6%	7.5%	£250,001–£1,000,000	5%
	£250,001–£400,000	6%	9%	£1,000,001 or more	6%
	£400,001–£750,000	7.5%	11.5%		
	£750,001–£1,500,000	10%	14%		
	£1,500,001 or more	12%	16%		
1.7.21–9.10.22[4]	Up to £180,000	Nil	4%	Up to £225,000	Nil
	£180,001–£250,000	3.5%	7.5%	£225,001–£250,000	1%
	£250,001–£400,000	5%	9%	£250,001–£1,000,000	5%
	£400,001–£750,000	7.5%	11.5%	£1,000,001 or more	6%
	£750,001–£1,500,000	10%	14%		
	£1,500,001 or more	12%	16%		
22.12.20–30.6.21[4]	Up to £180,000	Nil	4%	Up to £225,000	Nil
	£180,001–£250,000	Nil	7.5%	£225,001–£250,000	1%
	£250,001–£400,000	5%	9%	£250,001–£1,000,000	5%
	£400,001–£750,000	7.5%	11.5%	£1,000,001 or more	6%
	£750,001–£1,500,000	10%	14%		
	£1,500,001 or more	12%	16%		
27.7.20–21.12.20[4]	Up to £180,000	Nil	3%	Up to £150,000	Nil
	£180,001–£250,000	Nil	6.5%	£150,001–£250,000	1%
	£250,001–£400,000	5%	8%	£250,001–£1,000,000	5%
	£400,001–£750,000	7.5%	10.5%	£1,000,001 or more	6%
	£750,001–£1,500,000	10%	13%		
	£1,500,001 or more	12%	15%		

Land transactions					
Effective date	Residential property	Rate	Higher rate[2]	Non-residential or mixed property	Rate
1.4.18–26.7.20[4]	Up to £180,000	Nil	3%	Up to £150,000	Nil
	£180,001–£250,000	3.5%	6.5%	£150,001–£250,000	1%
	£250,001–£400,000	5%	8%	£250,001–£1,000,000	5%
	£400,001–£750,000	7.5%	10.5%	£1,000,001 or more	6%
	£750,001–£1,500,000	10%	13%		
	£1,500,001 or more	12%	15%		

Lease rentals
LTT is applied to non-residential leases and the amount of tax payable for transactions with an effective date between 1 April 2018 and 21 December 2020 is 1% of the amount of net present value (NPV) of the rent between £150,000 and £2m, and 2% above £2m. For transactions with an effective date on or after 22 December 2020 the rate is 1% of the amount of net present value (NPV) of the rent between £225,000 and £2m, and 2% above £2m^3.

Premiums
The same tax is payable for a premium granted as for a land transaction. Special rules apply to a premium in respect of non-residential property where the rent exceeds £13,500 a year on or after 4 February 2021 (£9,000 before 4 February 2021).

[1] Rates are charged on the portion of the consideration that falls within each rate band.
[2] The higher rate applies broadly to purchases of additional residential property by individuals, and to purchases of residential property by companies and trusts other than bare trusts and interest in possession trusts. It does not apply to purchases of property under £40,000. If there is a period of overlap in ownership of a main residence, a refund of the higher rate can be obtained if the previous main residence is sold within 36 months following the purchase of the new. Relief is also available where immediately before the purchase the buyer's spouse or civil partner owns a major interest in the same dwelling and that dwelling will be the buyer's only or main residence immediately before and after the purchase. For purchases on or after 12 July 2024, the 36-month period may be extended where emergency measures have a substantial adverse effect restricting the purchase or sale of the new or previous main residence.
[3] Rates apply to the amount of NPV in the slice, not the whole value.

Exemptions and reliefs

[T11.106]

There are various exemptions and reliefs from LTT, see Land Transaction Tax and Anti-avoidance of Devolved Taxes (Wales) Act 2017 Schs 3, 9–22.

Stamp duty

[T11.107]

(FA 1986 Part III; FA 1999 Sch 13; FA 2024 s 20, Sch 11)

Shares, etc	
Shares put into depository receipts or put into duty free clearance systems[5]	1.5%
Purchase of own shares by company	0.5%
Transfers of stock or marketable securities	0.5%
Takeovers, mergers, demergers, schemes of reconstruction and amalgamation (except where no real change of ownership)	0.5%

[1] Stamp duty is rounded to the next multiple of £5.
[2] Stamp duty is not chargeable where the amount or value of the consideration is less than £1,000.
[3] Transfers of interests in exchange traded funds will be exempt from stamp duty and stamp duty reserve tax.
[4] No stamp duty or stamp duty reserve tax is due on trades in 'recognised growth markets' such as the Alternative Investment Market and the ISDX Growth Market.
[5] Where UK securities are deposited with a depositary receipt issuer or clearance service following the exercise of an option, the transfer will be chargeable to stamp duty or stamp duty reserve tax (SDRT) at 1.5% of the higher of the market value or the option strike price at the date the instrument is executed (for stamp duty) or the date of transfer (for SDRT).

Fixed duties

[T11.108]

| Instruments affecting land transactions | £5 |

From 13 March 2008 fixed duties are generally abolished other than as above. The £5 rate applies to instruments effected from 1 October 1999.

Stamp Duty Reserve Tax (SDRT)

[T11.109]

(FA 1986 Part IV)

Agreements to transfer chargeable securities for money or money's worth (eg renounceable letters of allotment)[1]	0.5%
Chargeable securities put into a clearance service[2] or converted into depositary receipts where the transfer is not an integral part of an issue of share capital[4,7]	1.5%
Dealings of units in unit trusts and shares in open-ended investment companies before 30 March 2014[3]	0.5%
Transfers of foreign currency bearer shares and agreements to transfer sterling or foreign currency convertible or equity-related loan stock issued by UK companies	0.5%

[1] If the transaction is completed by a duly stamped instrument within six years from the date on which the charge is imposed, the SDRT will be cancelled or repaid.
[2] Where the operator of a clearance service elects to collect and account for SDRT on the normal rate of 0.5% on dealing within the system the higher SDRT charge of 1.5% does not apply.
[3] From 30 March 2014 exemption applies to all transfers of units in a unit trust and all surrenders of shares in open-ended investment companies, although the charge remains on non pro-rata in specie redemptions.
[4] SDRT of 1.5% is not applicable to issues of securities or stock into depositary receipt systems and clearance services and transfers of securities made in the course of capital-raising arrangements or qualifying listing arrangements. This is a statutory exemption from 1 January 2024. Previously the exemption was applied by HMRC following the cases of HSBC Holdings plc and the Bank of New York Mellon Corporation v HMRC and HSBC Holdings plc and Vidacos Nominees Limited v Commissioners for HMRC which held that the charge contravened EU law. Following the UK's exit from the EU and the end of the implementation period on 31 December 2020, the SDRT charge continued to be disapplied before it was enacted by FA 2024 (see STSM053010).
[5] Transfers of interests in exchange traded funds are exempt from stamp duty and stamp duty reserve tax.
[6] No stamp duty or stamp duty reserve tax is due on trades in 'recognised growth markets' such as the Alternative Investment Market and the ISDX Growth Market.
[7] Where UK securities are deposited with a depositary receipt issuer or clearance service following the exercise of an option, the transfer is chargeable to stamp duty or stamp duty reserve tax (SDRT) at 1.5% of the higher of the market value or the option strike price at the date the instrument is executed (for stamp duty) or the date of transfer (for SDRT).

Interest on unpaid tax

[T11.110]

Stamp duty land tax. *From 1 March 2019*: Interest runs from the end of 14 days (previously 30 days) after the effective date of transaction (normally completion), or the date of a disqualifying event, until the tax is paid. In the case of a deferred payment, interest runs from the date the payment is due until the tax is paid. A penalty carries interest from the date determined until the date of payment.

Stamp duty. Interest runs from the end of 30 days after the date the instrument is executed until the tax is paid. Amounts less than £25 are not charged.

Stamp duty reserve tax. The harmonised interest regime applies, see **T1.108**.

Rates: see **T1.108**, **T1.109**, **T1.110**.

Land and buildings transaction tax (Scotland). Interest runs broadly from the filing date of the return and is charged at the Bank of England base rate plus 2.5% and is paid to Revenue Scotland. Rates are as follows.

Period	*Rate*
13 November 2024	**7.25%**
7 August 2024–12 November 2024	7.50%
9 August 2023–6 August 2024	7.75%
28 June 2023–8 August 2023	7.50%
17 May 2023–27 June 2023	7.00%
29 March 2023–16 May 2023	6.75%
8 February 2023–28 March 2023	6.50%

Period	Rate
21 December 2022–7 February 2023	6.00%
9 November 2022–20 December 2022	5.50%
28 September 2022–8 November 2022	4.75%
10 August 2022–27 September 2022	4.25%
22 June 2022–9 August 2022	3.75%
11 May 2022–21 June 2022	3.50%
23 March 2022–10 May 2022	3.25%
9 February 2022–22 March 2022	3.00%
22 December 2021–8 February 2022	2.75%
25 March 2020–21 December 2021	2.60%
17 March 2020–24 March 2020	2.75%
8 August 2018–16 March 2020	3.25%

Land transaction tax (Wales). Interest runs broadly from the filing date of the return and is charged at the Bank of England base rate plus 2.5% and is paid to the Welsh Revenue Authority. Rates are as follows.

Period	Rate
from 13 November 2024	7.25%
7 August 2024–12 November 2024	7.50%
9 August 2023–6 August 2024	7.75%
28 June 2023–8 August 2023	7.50%
17 May 2023–27 June 2023	7.00%
29 March 2023–16 May 2023	6.75%
8 February 2023–28 March 2023	6.50%
21 December 2022–7 February 2023	6.00%
9 November 2022–20 December 2022	5.50%
28 September 2022–8 November 2022	4.75%
10 August 2022–27 September 2022	4.25%
22 June 2022–9 August 2022	3.75%
11 May 2022–21 June 2022	3.50%
23 March 2022–10 May 2022	3.25%
9 February 2022–22 March 2022	3.00%
22 December 2021–8 February 2022	2.75%
25 March 2020–21 December 2021	2.60%
17 March 2020–24 March 2020	2.75%
8 August 2018–16 March 2020	3.25%

Repayment supplement / Interest on overpaid tax

[T11.111]

Stamp duty land tax. Interest is added to repayments of overpaid stamp duty land tax and runs from the date tax was paid or an amount was lodged with HMRC, or the date a penalty was made, to the date the order for repayment is issued.

Stamp duty. Interest is added to repayments of overpaid stamp duty and runs from 30 days after the date the instrument is executed or the date of payment if later. Amounts less than £25 are not paid.

Stamp duty reserve tax. The harmonised interest regime applies, see **T1.108**.

Rates: see **T1.108**, **T1.110**.

Land and buildings transaction tax (Scotland). Interest runs from the date the tax, penalty or interest was paid or an amount was lodged with Revenue Scotland, to the date repayment is made. It is paid by Revenue Scotland and the rate is the higher of 0.5% and the Bank of England rate. Rates are as follows.

Period	Rate
from 13 November 2024	4.75%
7 August 2024–12 November 2024	5.00%
9 August 2023–6 August 2024	5.25%
28 June 2023–8 August 2023	5.00%
17 May 2023–27 June 2023	4.50%
29 March 2023–16 May 2023	4.25%
8 February 2023–28 March 2023	4.00%
21 December 2022–7 February 2023	3.50%

Period	Rate
9 November 2022–20 December 2022	3.00%
28 September 2022–8 November 2022	2.25%
10 August 2022–27 September 2022	1.75%
22 June 2022–9 August 2022	1.25%
11 May 2022–21 June 2022	1.00%
23 March 2022–10 May 2022	0.75%
17 March 2020–22 March 2022	0.50%
8 August 2018–16 March 2020	0.75%

Land transaction tax (Wales). Interest runs from the date the tax, penalty or interest was paid, to the date repayment is made. It is paid by the Welsh Revenue Authority and the rate is the higher of 0.5% and the Bank of England rate. Rates are as follows.

Period	Rate
from 13 November 2024	**4.75%**
7 August 2024–12 November 2024	5.00%
9 August 2023–6 August 2024	5.25%
28 June 2023–8 August 2023	5.00%
17 May 2023–27 June 2023	4.50%
29 March 2023–16 May 2023	4.25%
8 February 2023–28 March 2023	4.00%
21 December 2022–7 February 2023	3.50%
9 November 2022–20 December 2022	3.00%
28 September 2022–8 November 2022	2.25%
10 August 2022–27 September 2022	1.75%
22 June 2022–9 August 2022	1.25%
11 May 2022–21 June 2022	1.00%
23 March 2022–10 May 2022	0.75%
17 March 2020–22 March 2022	0.50%
8 August 2018–16 March 2020	0.75%

Stamp tax penalties

[T11.112]

Offence	Penalty
Stamp duty land tax and stamp duty reserve tax	
Inaccuracy in return or other document (FA 2007 Sch 24).	See **Penalties — modernised penalty regime**, T1.133
Inaccuracy in return or other document as a result of third party providing incorrect (or withholding) information (FA 2007 Sch 24).	See **Penalties — modernised penalty regime**, T1.134
Failure to notify HMRC of an error in an assessment (within 30 days) (FA 2007 Sch 24).	See **Penalties — modernised penalty regime**, T1.135
Failure to comply with HMRC investigatory powers with effect from 1 April 2010 (FA 2008 Sch 36).	(a) Initial penalty of £300; (b) if failure/obstruction continues, a further penalty of up to £60 per day; (c) if failure/obstruction continues after penalty under (a) imposed, a tax-related amount determined by the Upper Tribunal.
Provision of inaccurate information or document when complying with an information notice with effect from 1 April 2010 (FA 2008 Sch 36).	Up to £3,000 per inaccuracy.
Stamp duty reserve tax – for charges due and payable from 1 January 2015	
Failure to make returns on time (FA 2009 Sch 55)	See **Penalties — modernised penalty regime**, T1.137
Failure to make payments on time (FA 2009 Sch 56)	See **Penalties — modernised penalty regime**, T1.138
Stamp duty	
Failure to present instrument for stamping within 30 days after execution (or the day in which it is first received in the UK if executed outside the UK) (Stamp Act 1891 s 15B; SI 1999/2537). HMRC guidance to penalty amounts applies.	Documents submitted late for stamping: If presented within one year after the end of the 30-day period: 10% of the unpaid duty capped at £300. If presented more than one year after the end of the 30-day period but not more than two years after: 20% of the amount of unpaid duty. If presented more than two years after the end of the 30-day period: 30% of the unpaid duty. For delays of one year or more, penalty rate may be higher if there is evidence that the failure to submit documents was deliberate.
Stamp duty land tax	
Failure to deliver a land transaction return by the filing date (FA 2003 Sch 10 paras 3, 4).	£100 if return delivered within three months of filing date, otherwise £200. If not delivered within 12 months, penalty up to amount of tax chargeable.
Failure to comply with notice to deliver return within specified period (FA 2003 Sch 10 para 5).	Up to £60 for each day on which the failure continues after notification.
Failure to keep and preserve records under FA 2003 Sch 10 para 9 or Sch 11 para 4 (FA 2003 Sch 10 para 11, Sch 11 para 6).	Up to £3,000 unless the information is provided by other documentary evidence.
Failure to disclose certain SDLT proposals or arrangements (TMA 1970 s 98C).	(a) Up to £600 per day during 'initial period' (but tribunal can determine a higher penalty up to £1 million); (b) further penalty up to £600 per day while failure continues. Both the initial penalty in (a) above and the secondary penalty in (b) above can be increased up to £5,000 per day that failure continues from 10 days after the order is made.
Failure to provide prescribed information relating to disclosure certain SDLT proposals or arrangements (TMA 1970 s 98C).	(a) Initial penalty up to £5,000; (b) further penalty up to £600 per day while failure continues. This can be increased up to £5,000 per day after a tribunal has issued a disclosure order.
Failure to provide scheme reference number relating to certain SDLT proposals or arrangements (TMA 1970 s 98C);	(a) Penalty of £100 in respect of each scheme to which the failure relates;
for second failure, occurring within three years from the date on which the first failure began;	(b) penalty of £500 in respect of each scheme to which the failure relates;
for subsequent failures, occurring within three years from the date on which the previous failure began.	(c) penalty of £1,000 in respect of each scheme to which the failure relates.

Offence	Penalty
Land and buildings transaction tax (Scotland)	
Inaccuracy in return or document (RSTPA 2014 ss 182, 183)	Careless inaccuracy — maximum 30% of tax lost Deliberate inaccuracy — maximum 100% of tax lost
Failure to make returns on time (RSTPA 2014 ss 160–163)	The penalty rates applying are as for stamp duty reserve tax **Penalties — modernised penalty regime** in **T1.137**, though reductions for disclosure differ. Penalties are payable to Revenue Scotland.
Failure to make payments on time (RSTPA 2014 s 169)	The penalty rates applying are as for stamp duty reserve tax **Penalties — modernised penalty regime** in **T1.138** though for some types of payment penalty is due as soon as tax is late. Penalties are payable to Revenue Scotland.
Land transaction tax (Wales)	
Inaccuracy in return or document (TCM(W)A 2016 s 130)	Careless inaccuracy — maximum 30% of tax lost Deliberate inaccuracy — maximum 100% of tax lost
Failure to make returns on time (TCM(W)A 2016 ss 118–121)	Initial penalty £100 Failure continues for more than 6 months — greater of 5% of the tax due and £300 12 months late and return deliberately withheld — greater of £300 or up to 95% of tax due 12 months late and return not deliberately withheld — greater of 5% of the tax due and £300 Reductions for disclosure Penalties are payable to the Welsh Revenue Authority.
Failure to make payments on time (TCM(W)A 2016 ss 122, 122A)	5% of unpaid tax Further 5% of any outstanding amount 6 months after return filing date Further 5% of any outstanding amount 12 months after return filing date Reductions for disclosure Penalties are payable to the Welsh Revenue Authority.

Value added tax

Value added tax rates

[T12.101]

(VATA 1994 s 2)

	From 4.1.11	
	Rate	VAT fraction
Standard rate	20%	1/6
Reduced rate (see T12.144)	5.0%[2]	1/21
Flat-rate scheme for farmers	4.0%[1]	

[1] Flat rate addition to sale price. From 1 January 2021 there are entry and exit thresholds for the scheme of £150,000 and £230,000 respectively. These thresholds are the same as those applying to the flat-rate scheme for small businesses in **T12.110**.
[2] A temporary reduced rate of 12.5% applied to VATA 1994 Sch 7A Groups 14–16 from 1 October 2021 to 31 March 2022. See **T12.114**.

Registration limits

UK taxable supplies

[T12.102]

(VATA 1994 Sch 1 para 1, Sch 1A para 1)
A person who is UK-established[3] and makes taxable supplies is liable to be registered:
  (a)   at the end of any month, or
  (b)   at any time, if:

	(a) turnover in the past year[1] (b) turnover in the next 30 days[2] exceeds:	Unless, in the case of (a), turnover for next year not expected to exceed:
From 1.4.24–	**£90,000**	**£88,000**
1.4.17–31.3.24	£85,000	£83,000

[1] The value of taxable supplies in the year then ending.
[2] If there are reasonable grounds for believing the value of taxable supplies will exceed limit.
[3] Non-UK established businesses are required to register for VAT regardless of the value of taxable supplies made in the UK.

Supplies from EU countries ('distance selling')

[T12.103]

(VATA 1994 Sch 2)
NOTE: These rules only apply to registration in Northern Ireland from 1 January 2021. In addition, the UK distance selling threshold referenced below was abolished and replaced with an EU-wide threshold (applying also to Northern Ireland) of EUR 10,000 with effect from 1 July 2021. A business person in an EU country not registered or liable to be registered in Northern Ireland (UK before 1 January 2021) is liable to be registered on any day if, in the period beginning with 1 January in that year, the value of supplies by that person to non-taxable persons in Northern Ireland (UK before 1 January 2021) exceeds:

1.1.93 to 30.6.21	£70,000

Acquisitions from EU countries

[T12.104]

(VATA 1994 Sch 9ZA, Part 8)

NOTE: These rules only apply to registration for bringing goods into Northern Ireland from the EU from 1 January 2021. The concept of acquisitions was broadly abolished in the rest of the UK from that date. A person not registered or liable to be registered under the above rules is liable to be registered:
- (a) at the end of any month if, in the period beginning with 1 January in that year, the value of taxable goods acquired by that person for business purposes (or for non-business purposes if a public body, charity, club, etc) from suppliers in EU countries exceeds the following limits; or
- (b) at any time, if there are reasonable grounds for believing the value of such acquisitions in the next 30 days will exceed the following limits:

From 1.4.24–	£90,000
1.4.17–31.3.24	£85,000

Deregistration limits

UK taxable supplies

[T12.105]

(VATA 1994 Sch 1 para 4)

A registered taxable person who is UK-established[1] ceases to be liable to be registered if, at any time, HMRC are satisfied that the value of taxable supplies in the year then beginning will not exceed the limit below, unless the reason for not exceeding the limit during that year is that the person will cease making taxable supplies or suspend making taxable supplies for 30 days or more:

From 1.4.24–	£88,000
1.4.17–31.3.24	£83,000

[1] Non-UK established businesses are required to register for VAT regardless of the value of taxable supplies made in the UK.

Supplies from EU countries ('distance selling')

[T12.106]

(VATA 1994 Sch 2)

NOTE: These rules only apply to registration for supplies into Northern Ireland from the EU from 1 January 2021 to 30 June 2021 (they ceased to apply to the rest of the UK after 31 December 2020). From 1 July 2021 this threshold was abolished and replaced with an EU-wide threshold (applying also to Northern Ireland) of EUR 10,000. A person registered under these provisions ceases to be liable to be registered if, at any time:
- (a) relevant supplies in year ended 31 December last before that time did not exceed following limit; and
- (b) HMRC are satisfied that value of relevant supplies in year immediately following that year will not exceed following limit:

1.1.93 to 30.6.21	£70,000

Acquisitions from EU countries

[T12.107]

(VATA 1994 Schs 3, 9ZA)

NOTE: These rules only apply in repsect of registration for bringing goods into Northern Ireland from the EU from 1 January 2021. The concept of acquisitions was broadly abolished in the rest of the UK from that date. A person registered under these provisions ceases to be liable to be registered if, at any time:
- (a) relevant acquisitions in year ended 31 December last before that time did not exceed the following limits; and
- (b) HMRC are satisfied that value of relevant acquisitions in year immediately following that year will not exceed the following limits:

From 1.4.24–	£90,000
1.4.17–31.3.24	£85,000

Annual accounting scheme

[T12.108]

(SI 1995/2518 regs 49–55)
A business may, subject to conditions, complete one VAT return a year. Quarterly or monthly interim payments to be made.

	Can join if taxable supplies in next year not expected to exceed:	Must leave at end of accounting year if taxable supplies exceeded:
1.4.06 onwards	£1,350,000	£1,600,000

Cash accounting scheme

[T12.109]

(SI 1995/2518 regs 56–65)
A business may, subject to conditions, account for and pay VAT on the basis of cash paid and received. It can join the scheme at any time as follows.

	Can join if taxable supplies in next year not expected to exceed:	Must leave at end of VAT period if taxable supplies in previous year exceed:	Unless turnover for next year not expected to exceed:
1.4.07 onwards	£1,350,000	£1,600,000	£1,350,000

Flat-rate scheme for small businesses

[T12.110]

(SI 1995/2518 regs 55A–55V)
An eligible business which expects its taxable supplies in the next year to be no more than £150,000 can opt to join a flat-rate scheme. The appropriate percentage below is applied to total turnover generated, including exempt income, to calculate net VAT due. Once in the scheme a business may continue to use it until its total business income exceeds £230,000, and if income does exceed this limit, the business can still remain in the scheme if the income in the following year is estimated not to exceed £191,500.

A 16.5% rate applies to a 'limited cost trader', that is a trader whose VAT-inclusive expenditure on goods used for business purposes (excluding capital expenditure, food and drink for consumption by the business or its employees, and certain vehicles, vehicle parts and fuel) is less than 2% of turnover, or greater than 2% of turnover but less than £1,000 per year. Any trader which is not a limited cost trader continues to use the flat rate based on the categories of business detailed below.

Category of business	Appropriate %
	From 4.1.11 (except temporary rates)
Accountancy or book-keeping	14.5
Advertising	11
Agricultural services	11
Any other activity not listed elsewhere	12
Architect, civil and structural engineer or surveyor	14.5
Boarding or care of animals	12
Business services that are not listed elsewhere	12
Catering services, including restaurants and takeaways before 15 July 2020 and from 1 April 2022	12.5
Catering services, including restaurants and takeaways from 15 July 2020 to 30 September 2021	4.5
Catering services, including restaurants and takeaways from 1 October 2021 to 31 March 2022	8.5
Computer and IT consultancy or data processing	14.5
Computer repair services	10.5
Entertainment or journalism	12.5
Estate agency and property management services	12
Farming or agriculture that is not listed elsewhere	6.5
Film, radio, television or video production	13
Financial services	13.5
Forestry or fishing	10.5
General building or construction services[1]	9.5
Hairdressing or other beauty treatment services	13
Hiring or renting goods	9.5

Category of business	Appropriate %
	From 4.1.11 (except temporary rates)
Hotel or accommodation before 15 July 2020 and from 1 April 2022	10.5
Hotel or accommodation from 15 July 2020 to 30 September 2021	0
Hotel or accommodation from 1 October 2021 to 31 March 2022	5.5
Investigation or security	12
Labour-only building or construction services[1]	14.5
Laundry or dry-cleaning services	12
Lawyer or legal services	14.5
Library, archive, museum or other cultural activity	9.5
Management consultancy	14
Manufacturing fabricated metal products	10.5
Manufacturing food	9
Manufacturing that is not listed elsewhere	9.5
Manufacturing yarn, textiles or clothing	9
Membership organisation	8
Mining or quarrying	10
Packaging	9
Photography	11
Post Offices	5
Printing	8.5
Publishing	11
Pubs before 15 July 2020 and from 1 April 2022	6.5
Pubs from 15 July 2020 to 30 September 2021	1
Pubs from 1 October 2021 to 31 March 2022	4
Real estate activity not listed elsewhere	14
Repairing personal or household goods	10
Repairing vehicles	8.5
Retailing food, confectionery, tobacco, newspapers or children's clothing	4
Retailing pharmaceuticals, medical goods, cosmetics or toiletries	8
Retailing that is not listed elsewhere	7.5
Retailing vehicles or fuel	6.5
Secretarial services	13
Social work	11
Sport or recreation	8.5
Transport or storage, couriers, freight, removals and taxis	10
Travel agency	10.5
Veterinary medicine	11
Wholesaling agricultural products	8
Wholesaling food	7.5
Wholesaling that is not listed elsewhere	8.5

[1] That is, services where value of materials supplied is less than 10% of turnover of such services; any other services are 'general building or construction services'.

Partial exemption

[T12.111]

SEE TOLLEY'S TAX COMPUTATIONS **408.1, 408.2**.

(SI 1995/2518 regs 106–107)

A registered person who makes taxable and exempt supplies is partly exempt and may not be able to deduct (or reclaim) all their input tax. Where, however, input tax attributable to exempt supplies in a prescribed accounting period or tax year is within the de minimis limits below, all such input tax is attributable to taxable supplies and recoverable (subject to the normal rules).

De minimis limits	£625 per month on average and 50% of all input tax for the period concerned

Capital goods scheme

[T12.112]

SEE TOLLEY'S TAX COMPUTATIONS **402.1**.
(SI 1995/2518 regs 112–116)

Input tax adjustment following change in taxable use of capital goods

Item	Value	Adjustment period
Computer equipment	£50,000 or more	Five years
Ships, boats or other vessels[1]	£50,000 or more	Five years
Aircraft[1]	£50,000 or more	Five years
Land and buildings	£250,000 or more	Ten years

[1] Applies for goods acquired on or after 1 January 2011.

Adjustment formula where adjustment period begins on or after 1 January 2011

$$\frac{\text{Total VAT on item}}{\text{Length of adjustment period}} \times \text{adjustment percentage}$$

The adjustment percentage is the percentage change in the extent to which the item is used (or treated as used) in making taxable supplies between the first interval in the adjustment period and a subsequent interval. (The first interval generally ends on the last day of the tax year in which the input tax was incurred.) For goods acquired on or after 1.1.11 total VAT includes any non-business VAT and the extent to which a capital item is used for business purposes must be determined when ascertaining taxable use for each subsequent interval.

Zero-rated supplies

[T12.113]

A zero-rated supply is a taxable supply, but the rate of tax is nil (VATA 1994 Sch 8).

Group 1 – Food
Group 2 – Sewerage services and water
Group 3 – Books etc including e-publications from 1 May 2020
Group 4 – Talking books for the blind and disabled and wireless sets for the blind
Group 5 – Construction of buildings etc
Group 6 – Protected buildings
Group 7 – International services
Group 8 – Transport
Group 9 – Caravans and houseboats
Group 10 – Gold
Group 11 – Bank notes
Group 12 – Drugs, medicines, aids for the disabled etc
Group 13 – Imports, exports etc
Group 15 – Charities etc
Group 16 – Clothing and footwear
Group 18 – European Research Infrastructure Consortia
Group 19 – Women's sanitary products (from 11pm on 31 December 2020); reusable period underwear (from 1 January 2024)
Group 20 – Personal protective equipment (coronavirus) (from 1 May 2020 to 31 October 2020)
Group 21 – Online marketplaces (deemed supply) (from 11pm on 31 December 2020)
Group 22 – Free zones (from 8 November 2021)
Group 23 – Installation of energy-saving materials (from 1 April 2022 to 31 March 2027; Northern Ireland excluded until 1 May 2023) including additional technologies, such as water-source heat pumps, and bringing buildings used solely for a relevant charitable purpose (from 1 February 2024)

Reduced rate supplies

[T12.114]

(VATA 1994 Sch 7A)

Group 1 – Domestic fuel and power

Group 2 – Installation of energy-saving materials (zero-rated in Great Britain from 1 April 2022 to 31 March 2027; reduced rate continued in Northern Ireland until 1 May 2023 at which point treatment aligned with Great Britain)

Group 3 – Grant-funded installation of heating equipment or security goods or connection of a gas supply

Group 4 – Women's sanitary products (zero-rated from 11pm on 31 December 2020)

Group 5 – Children's car seats and bases

Group 6 – Residential conversions

Group 7 – Residential renovations and alterations

Group 8 – Contraceptive products

Group 9 – Welfare advice or information

Group 10 – Installation of mobility aids for the elderly

Group 11 – Smoking cessation products

Group 12 – Caravans

Group 13 – Cable-suspended transport systems

Group 14 – Course of catering (5% from 15 July 2020 to 30 September 2021 and 12.5% from 1 October 2021 to 31 March 2022)

Group 15 – Holiday accommodation etc (5% from 15 July 2020 to 30 September 2021 and 12.5% from 1 October 2021 to 31 March 2022)

Group 16 – Shows and certain other attractions (5% from 15 July 2020 to 30 September 2021 and 12.5% from 1 October 2021 to 31 March 2022)

Exempt supplies

[T12.115]

(VATA 1994 Sch 9)

Group 1 – Land

Group 2 – Insurance

Group 3 – Postal services

Group 4 – Betting, gaming, dutiable machine games and lotteries

Group 5 – Finance

Group 6 – Education

Group 7 – Health and welfare

Group 8 – Burial and cremation

Group 9 – Subscriptions to trade unions, professional and other public interest bodies

Group 10 – Sport, sports competitions and physical education

Group 11 – Works of art etc

Group 12 – Fund-raising events by charities and other qualifying bodies

Group 13 – Cultural services etc

Group 14 – Supplies of goods where input tax cannot be recovered

Group 15 – Investment gold

Group 16 – Supplies of services by groups involving cost sharing

Private school fees are excluded from exemption in relation to supplies of education provided after 31 December 2024.

EC Sales Lists

[T12.116]

(SI 1995/2518 regs 2, 21–23)

Before 1 January 2021, all VAT-registered businesses in the UK had to provide HMRC with details of goods and services supplied to a VAT-registered customer in an EU country. With effect from 1 January 2021 the circumstances in which returns are required are reduced and apply only to VAT-registered businesses trading or operating under the Northern Ireland protocol.

From 1 January 2021 the requirement for returns is as follows:

Supplies of		Frequency
Goods	Supplies of goods subject to acquisition tax in an EU member state are in excess of £35,000 in any of the current or last four quarters	Monthly
Goods	Supplies of goods subject to acquisition tax in an EU member state are below £35,000 per quarter in the current and previous four quarters	Quarterly on 31 March, 30 June, 30 September and 31 December
Goods supplied by a business completing annual VAT returns	Total annual taxable turnover does not exceed £145,000; annual value of supplies to EU member states not more than £11,000 (and do not include *New Means of Transport*)	On application — annual on agreed due date

| Goods only supplied | Total annual taxable turnover does not exceed the VAT registration threshold plus £25,500; annual value of supplies to EU member states not more than £11,000 (and do not include *New Means of Transport*) | On application — annual in simple format on agreed due date |

Before 1 January 2021 the requirement for returns was as follows:

Supplies of		Frequency
Goods	Supplies of goods are in excess of £35,000 in any of the current or last four quarters	Monthly
Goods	Supplies of goods are below £35,000 per quarter in the current and previous four quarters	Quarterly on 31 March, 30 June, 30 September and 31 December
Services supplied to a business where the place of supply is where the customer belongs		Quarterly as above
Goods and services where a business is required to submit monthly lists for goods		Monthly for all supplies, or monthly for goods and quarterly for services
Goods or services supplied by a business completing annual VAT returns	Total annual taxable turnover does not exceed £145,000; annual value of supplies to other EU countries not more than £11,000 (and do not include *New Means of Transport*)	On application — annual on agreed due date
Goods only supplied	Total annual taxable turnover does not exceed the VAT registration threshold plus £25,500; annual value of supplies to other EU countries not more than £11,000 (and do not include *New Means of Transport*)	On application — annual in simple format on agreed due date

The due date for returns is 21 days after the end of the period if submitted online and 14 days after the end of the period if submitted on paper.

Country	Code
Austria[10]	AT
Belgium	BE
Bulgaria	BG
Croatia	HR
Cyprus[9]	CY
Czech Republic	CZ
Denmark[2]	DK
Estonia	EE
Finland[3]	FI
France[4]	FR
Germany[5]	DE
Greece[11]	EL
Hungary	HU
Ireland	IE
Italy[6]	IT
Latvia	LV
Lithuania	LT
Luxembourg	LU
Malta	MT
Netherlands[12]	NL
Poland	PL
Portugal[7]	PT
Romania	RO
Slovak Republic	SK
Slovenia	SI
Spain[8]	ES
Sweden	SE

[1] Countries not listed in the table above are not part of the EU VAT area and so sales to those countries should not be included on the EC sales list. The following are not part of the EU VAT area; Andorra, The Channel Islands, Gibraltar, Mount Athos, San Marino, and Vatican City.
[2] Does not include the Faroe Islands and Greenland.
[3] Does not include Aland Islands.

[4] Includes Monaco; excludes Martinique, Guadeloupe, Reunion, St Pierre & Miquelon, and French Guiana.
[5] Does not include Busingen and Isle of Heligoland.
[6] Does not include communes of Livigno and Campione d'Italia and the Italian waters of Lake Lugano.
[7] Includes the Azores and Madeira.
[8] Includes the Balearic Islands but excludes Ceuta, Melilla, and the Canary Islands.
[9] Includes British sovereign base areas of Akrotiri and Dhekelia, but excludes those areas in United Nations buffer zone and to the north of that where the Republic of Cyprus does not have effective control.
[10] Includes Jungholz and Mittelberg.
[11] Excludes Mount Athos.
[12] Excludes Antilles (now Curaçao, Sint Maarten and BES Islands).

Intrastat

[T12.117]

(SI 1992/2790)

Intrastat is the name given in the UK to the system for collecting statistics on the trade in goods between Northern Ireland and EU member states. Until 31 December 2021 it was also used (in certain circumstances) to report trade between Great Britain and EU member states. Whether a business is required to submit Intrastat 'supplementary declarations' will depend on the total value of goods supplied to EU member states (dispatches) and acquired from EU member states (arrivals). Businesses exceeding certain dispatches and/or arrivals thresholds must make supplementary declarations containing further information each month.

Thresholds are set for each calendar year and recent thresholds are shown below. If a person's dispatches or arrivals in the previous calendar year exceeded the current year's threshold, supplementary declarations must be made for the full current year. If the cumulative total of dispatches or arrivals in a year exceeds that calendar year's threshold, supplementary declarations must be made for the rest of the year, starting in the month in which the threshold is exceeded. Additional delivery terms information must be provided on the supplementary declaration only if the annual value of arrivals or dispatches exceeds the delivery terms threshold, and the information must be submitted from the start of the next calendar year. If the delivery terms threshold for arrivals is exceeded, but not that for dispatches, delivery terms must be provided for arrivals only, and vice versa. Declarations must be submitted electronically and will be due 21 days after the end of the month in which there is EU trade to declare.

Year	Supplies (dispatches) threshold per calendar year[1]	Acquisitions (arrivals) threshold per calendar year[2]	Delivery terms threshold per calendar year
From 1.1.22	**£250,000**	**£500,000**	**£24,000,000**
From 1.1.15 to 31.12.21	£250,000	£1,500,000	£24,000,000

[1] From 1 January 2021 dispatches refers only to 'exports' from Northern Ireland to EU member states. Prior to that date it included 'exports' from the UK as a whole to other EU member states.
[2] Until 31 December 2021 arrivals included arrivals from the EU to Great Britain and to Northern Ireland. From 1 January 2022 arrivals refers only to arrivals from the EU to Northern Ireland.

Some of the EU country codes and the areas included for intrastat purposes differ from those used for EC sales list purposes. The intrastat codes are as follows.

Country	Code
Austria	AT
Belgium	BE
Bulgaria	BG
Croatia	HR
Cyprus[9]	CY
Czech Republic	CZ
Denmark[2]	DK
Estonia	EE
Finland[3]	FI
France[4]	FR
Germany[5]	DE
Greece[10]	GR
Hungary	HU
Ireland	IE
Italy[6]	IT
Latvia	LV
Lithuania	LT
Luxembourg	LU
Malta	MT
Netherlands	NL
Northern Ireland	XI
Poland	PL
Portugal[7]	PT

Country	Code
Romania	RO
Slovak Republic	SK
Slovenia	SI
Spain[8]	ES
Sweden	SE

[1] Andorra and Liechtenstein are both outside the customs territory (and therefore the statistical territory) of the EU.
[2] Does not include the Faroe Islands.
[3] Includes Aland Islands.
[4] Includes Monaco, but excludes all French Overseas departments and territories. Martinique, Guadeloupe, Reunion, Mayotte, and French Guiana are part of the statistical territory of France but because customs documentation is still required for exports to, or imports from, these territories HMRC continue to collect trade statistics from that documentation and it must not be declared on the intrastat.
[5] Includes Isle of Heligoland but excludes Busingen.
[6] Does not include communes of Livigno and Campione d'Italia, the Italian waters of Lake Lugano and the Vatican. Livigno is part of the statistical territory of Italy but because customs documentation is still required for exports to, or imports from, this territory HMRC continue to collect trade statistics from that documentation and it must not be declared on the intrastat.
[7] Includes the Azores and Madeira.
[8] Includes the Balearic Islands but excludes Ceuta, Melilla, and the Canary Islands. The Canary Islands are part of the statistical territory of Spain but because customs documentation is still required for exports to, or imports from, these territories HMRC continue to collect trade statistics from that documentation and it must not be declared on the intrastat.
[9] Includes UK sovereign base areas but excludes Northern Cyprus.
[10] Includes Mount Athos.

VAT Mini One Stop Shop (VAT MOSS)

[T12.118]

(VATA 1994 Sch 4A paras 15, 16; SI 2018/1194; HMRC Brief 46/2014)
The following rules no longer apply from 1 January 2021.
From 1 January 2015 the place of supply for business-to-consumer (B2C) supplies of broadcasting, telecommunications and e-services (digital services) was determined by the location of the consumer unless, between 1 January 2019 and 31 December 2020, such annual supplies across the EU were less than €10,000. This applies to all businesses that supply digital services above that threshold to consumers (ie private individuals), whether or not they are registered for UK VAT. Any business supplying digital services above the €10,000 limit to a consumer in another member state therefore was required to charge VAT on the supply in that member state and register for VAT in that member state. Supplies of digital services to businesses only (including the self-employed) are not affected by these rules.

To avoid having to register for VAT in every EU member state where digital services were supplied, it was possible (prior to 1 January 2021) for a business to opt to use the VAT Mini One Stop Shop online service (VAT MOSS). Using the VAT MOSS online service meant a business was able to submit a single calendar quarterly VAT MOSS return and payment covering all its EU digital service supplies.

Car fuel

[T12.119]

SEE TOLLEY'S TAX COMPUTATIONS **406.1**.

(VATA 1994 ss 56, 57, Schs 4, 6)

Where an employer pays mileage allowances, it may use the advisory fuel rates at **T6.123** to calculate the input VAT to reclaim on the fuel element. Receipts must still be retained.

VAT-inclusive scale figures can be used to assess VAT due on fuel provided at no cost for private journeys by registered traders or their employees, where the fuel has been provided from business resources. The figures represent the tax-inclusive value of the fuel supplied to each individual and relate to return periods beginning on the dates shown. If the trader or employer opts to use the scale figures it must use them for all supplies of fuel for private use made for no consideration in the prescribed accounting period. The scale charge may also be used as an alternative to accounting for VAT on the required open market value where the fuel is supplied for a consideration below that value.

	12 months £	3 months £	1 month £
From 1 May 2024–30 April 2025: CO_2 band			
120 or below	702	174	58
125	1,050	263	87
130	1,123	279	92
135	1,191	297	98
140	1,263	315	105
145	1,331	332	110
150	1,404	350	116
155	1,471	368	122
160	1,544	385	127
165	1,612	403	134
170	1,685	420	139
175	1,752	437	145
180	1,825	455	151
185	1,893	473	157
190	1,965	490	163
195	2,033	508	169
200	2,106	526	174
205	2,174	544	180
210	2,246	560	186
215	2,314	578	192
220	2,387	596	198
225 or above	2,454	613	203

	12 months £	3 months £	1 month £
1 May 2023–30 April 2024: CO_2 band			
120 or below	737	183	61
125	1,103	276	91
130	1,179	293	97
135	1,250	312	103
140	1,327	331	110
145	1,398	349	115
150	1,474	368	122
155	1,545	386	128
160	1,622	405	134
165	1,693	423	140
170	1,769	441	146
175	1,840	459	152
180	1,917	478	159
185	1,988	497	164
190	2,064	515	171
195	2,135	534	178
200	2,212	552	183
205	2,283	571	190
210	2,359	588	195

	12 months £	3 months £	1 month £
215	2,430	607	202
220	2,507	626	208
225 or above	2,578	644	214

	12 months £	3 months £	1 month £
1 May 2022–30 April 2023: CO_2 band			
120 or below	700	174	58
125	1,048	262	87
130	1,121	279	92
135	1,188	296	98
140	1,261	314	104
145	1,329	332	110
150	1,401	349	116
155	1,469	367	122
160	1,542	385	127
165	1,609	402	133
170	1,682	419	139
175	1,749	437	145
180	1,822	454	151
185	1,889	472	156
190	1,962	490	163
195	2,030	507	169
200	2,102	525	174
205	2,170	543	180
210	2,242	559	185
215	2,310	577	192
220	2,383	595	198
225 or above	2,450	612	203

	12 months £	3 months £	1 month £
1 May 2021–30 April 2022: CO_2 band			
120 or below	585	145	48
125	875	219	72
130	936	233	77
135	992	247	82
140	1,053	262	87
145	1,109	277	91
150	1,170	292	97
155	1,226	306	102
160	1,287	321	106
165	1,343	336	111
170	1,404	350	116
175	1,460	364	121
180	1,521	379	126
185	1,577	394	130
190	1,638	409	136
195	1,694	423	141
200	1,755	438	145
205	1,811	453	150
210	1,872	467	155
215	1,928	481	160
220	1,989	496	165
225 or above	2,045	511	169

	12 months £	3 months £	1 month £
1 May 2020–30 April 2021: CO_2 band			
120 or below	581	144	48
125	870	218	72
130	930	231	76
135	986	246	81
140	1,047	261	87
145	1,103	275	91
150	1,163	290	96
155	1,219	305	101
160	1,279	319	106
165	1,335	334	111
170	1,396	348	115
175	1,452	362	120
180	1,512	377	125
185	1,568	392	130
190	1,628	406	135
195	1,684	421	140
200	1,745	436	144
205	1,801	450	149
210	1,861	464	154
215	1,917	479	159
220	1,977	493	164
225 or above	2,033	508	168

	12 months £	3 months £	1 month £
1 May 2019–30 April 2020: CO_2 band			
120 or below	592	147	49
125	886	222	73
130	947	236	78
135	1,004	250	83
140	1,066	265	87
145	1,123	280	93
150	1,184	296	98
155	1,241	310	103
160	1,303	325	107
165	1,360	340	113
170	1,421	354	117
175	1,478	369	122
180	1,540	384	128
185	1,597	399	132
190	1,658	414	137
195	1,715	429	143
200	1,777	444	147
205	1,834	458	152
210	1,895	473	157
215	1,952	487	162
220	2,014	502	167
225 or above	2,071	517	172

Value added tax interest and penalties

Default interest and late payment interest
[T12.120]

(VATA 1994 s 74; FA 2009, s 101)

For VAT periods starting on or after 1 January 2023 the VAT default interest regime was replaced by the harmonised late payment interest regime contained in FA 2009. In general terms (and subject to exceptions) interest accrues:
- from the date a payment is due
- until the date of payment

For periods starting before 1 January 2023 default interest broadly runs on the amount of any VAT assessed (or paid late by error correction):
- from the reckonable date (normally the latest date on which a return is required from the period in question)
- until the date of payment

The rates of interest are as follows:

Period	Rate
from 26 November 2024	**7.25%**
20 August 2024–25 November 2024	7.50%
22 August 2023–19 August 2024	7.75%
11 July 2023–21 August 2023	7.50%
31 May 2023–10 July 2023	7.00%
13 April 2023–30 May 2023	6.75%
21 February 2023–12 April 2023	6.50%
6 January 2023–20 February 2023	6.00%
22 November 2022–5 January 2023	5.50%
11 October 2022–21 November 2022	4.75%
23 August 2022–10 October 2022	4.25%
5 July 2022–22 August 2022	3.75%
24 May 2022–4 July 2022	3.50%
5 April 2022–23 May 2022	3.25%
21 February 2022–4 April 2022	3.00%
7 January 2022–20 February 2022	2.75%
7 April 2020–6 January 2022	2.60%
30 March 2020–6 April 2020	2.75%
21 August 2018–29 March 2020	3.25%

Note: As a result of the COVID–19 (coronavirus) pandemic businesses were not required to make a VAT payment during the period from 20 March 2020 until 30 June 2020. They could instead pay any liabilities which accumulated during the deferral period in full by 31 March 2021 and interest and penalties were not charged. Alternatively, they could pay in interest-free instalments if they opted-in between March and June 2021 or sought specific help from HMRC. Penalties were due if none of the options were taken by 30 June 2021.

Interest on VAT overpaid in cases of official error and repayment interest
[T12.121]

(VATA 1994 s 78; FA 2009 s 102)

For VAT periods starting on or after 1 January 2023 the VAT interest regime for overpayments in cases of official error was replaced by the harmonised repayment interest regime contained in FA 2009. In general terms, interest accrues:
- from the repayment start date (which will depend on the circumstances and in particular whether the amount in question has already been paid to HMRC or represents a credit owed to the taxpayer)
- until HMRC repays the VAT or sets it off against a different amount

For VAT periods starting prior to 1 January 2023 where VAT has been overpaid or underclaimed due to an error by HMRC, then on a claim HMRC must pay interest:
- from the date they receive payment (or authorise a repayment) for the return period in question;
- until the date on which they authorise payment of the amount on which interest is due.

This provision does not require HMRC to pay interest on an amount on which repayment supplement is due (repayment supplements were abolished for periods starting on or after 1 January 2023).

The rates of interest are as follows:

Period	Rate
from 26 November 2024	**3.75%**
20 August 2024–25 November 2024	4.00%

Period	Rate
22 August 2023–19 August 2024	4.25%
11 July 2023–21 August 2023	4.00%
31 May 2023–10 July 2023	3.50%
13 April 2023–30 May 2023	3.25%
21 February 2023–12 April 2023	3.00%
6 January 2023–20 February 2023	2.50%
22 November 2022–5 January 2023	2.00%
11 October 2022–21 November 2022	1.25%
23 August 2022–10 October 2022	0.75%
29 September 2009–22 August 2022	0.50%

Repayment supplement – VAT

[T12.122]

(VATA 1994 s 79; FA 2021 Sch 29)

The VAT repayment supplement was abolished with effect for VAT periods beginning on or after 1 January 2023.

Where (in relation to a VAT period beginning before 1 January 2023) a person is entitled to a repayment the payment due is increased by a supplement of the greater of:
- (i) 5% of that amount; or
- (ii) £50.

The supplement will only be paid if:
- (a) the return or claim is received by HMRC not later than the last day on which it is required to be made;
- (b) HMRC do not issue a written instruction making the refund within the relevant period; and
- (c) the amount shown on the return or claim does not exceed the amount due by more than 5% of that amount or £250, whichever is the greater.

The 'relevant period' is 30 days beginning with the receipt of the return or claim or, if later, the day after the last day of the VAT period to which the return or claim relates.

Penalties and surcharges

[T12.123]

Offence	Penalty
Inaccuracy in return or other document (FA 2007 Sch 24).	See **Penalties — modernised penalty regime**, T1.133.
Failure to notify obligation to register for VAT, change in supplies made by person exempted from registration, acquisition affecting exemption, acquisition of goods from another member state and unauthorised issue of an invoice (FA 2008 Sch 41).	See **Penalties — modernised penalty regime**, T1.136.
Inaccuracy in return or other document as a result of third party providing incorrect (or withholding) information (FA 2007 Sch 24).	See **Penalties — modernised penalty regime**, T1.134.
Failure to inform HMRC of an error in an assessment within 30 days of the date of the assessment (FA 2007 Sch 24).	See **Penalties — modernised penalty regime**, T1.135.
Failure to comply with HMRC investigatory powers (FA 2008 Sch 36).	(a) Initial penalty of £300; (b) if failure/obstruction continues, a further penalty of up to £60 per day; (c) if failure/obstruction continues after penalty under (a) imposed, a tax-related amount determined by the Upper Tribunal.
Provision of inaccurate information or document when complying with an information notice (FA 2008 Sch 36).	Up to £3,000 per inaccuracy.
Failure to submit a return electronically if required to do so by SI 1995/2518 reg 25 (SI 1995/2518 reg 25A).	Annual VAT exclusive turnover of: £22,800,001 or more — £400 £5,600,001 to £22,800,000 — £300 £100,001 to £5,600,000 — £200 £100,000 or under — £100

Offence	Penalty
For VAT periods beginning before 1 January 2023. Failure to submit return or pay VAT due within time limit (where a return is late but the VAT is paid on time or no VAT is due, a default is recorded but no surcharge arises) (VATA 1994 s 59). Failure to pay tax due under the payment on account scheme on time (VATA 1994 s 59A).	The greater of £30 and a specified percentage of outstanding VAT for period, depending on number of defaults in surcharge period: first default in period 2%, second default 5%, third default 10%, fourth and further defaults 15%. (Surcharge assessments are not issued for sums of less than £400 unless the rate of the surcharge is 10% or more.) **The default surcharge system was replaced by a harmonised system of penalties for late payment / submission of returns for accounting periods beginning on or after 1 January 2023 (see below). They will also apply for income tax self-assessment from a later date. See notes in T1.137, T1.138.**
For VAT periods beginning on or after 1 January 2023. Failure to submit a return on time (FA 2021 Sch 24).	£200 when maximum number of penalty points have been awarded.
For VAT periods beginning on or after 1 January 2023. Failure to make a payment on time (FA 2021 Sch 26).	(a) First penalty if failure is between 16 days and 30 days and '15-day time to pay condition' is not met — 2% of amount outstanding after 15 days If failure is more than 30 days and '30-day time to pay condition' is not met, first penalty is penalty in (a) above plus 2% of amount outstanding after 30 days (b) Second penalty if failure is more than 30 days (but subject to any time to pay arrangements in place) — 4% per annum for period outstanding
Issuing incorrect certificate stating that certain supplies fall to be zero-rated or taxed at the reduced rate (VATA 1994 s 62).	Difference between tax actually charged and tax which should have been charged.
Material inaccuracy in EC sales statement (or prior to 1 July 2022 a reverse charge statement) (VATA 1994 s 65, Sch 9ZA para 73).	£100 for each material inaccuracy in two-year penalty period (which commences following notice of second material inaccuracy).
Failure to submit EC sales statement (or prior to 1 July 2022 a reverse charge statement) (VATA 1994 s 66, Sch 9ZA para 73)).	Greater of £50 or a daily penalty (maximum 100 days) £5 for the first, £10 for the second, £15 for the third or subsequent failure in the default period.
Breach of walking possession agreement (VATA 1994 s 68).	50% of VAT due or amount recoverable.
Failure to preserve records, including digital records, for prescribed period (VATA 1994 ss 69, 69B).	£500.
Failure to preserve records specified in HMRC direction (VATA 1994 ss 69, 69B).	£200 for each day of failure (maximum 30 days).
Breaches of regulatory provisions, including failure to notify cessation of liability or entitlement to be registered, failure to keep records and non-compliance with any regulations made under VATA 1994 (VATA 1994 s 69).	Greater of £50 and a daily penalty (maximum 100 days) of a specified amount depending on number of failures in preceding two years: £5 per day if no previous failures; £10 per day if one previous failure; £15 per day if two or more previous failures.
Where failure consists of not paying VAT or not making a return in the required time.	*1/6, 1/3 and 1/2 of 1% of the VAT due respectively, if greater.
Breaches of regulatory provisions involving failure to pay VAT or submit return by due date (VATA 1994 s 69).	Greater of £50 and a daily penalty (for no more than 100 days) of a specified amount depending on number of failures in preceding two years: greater of £5 and 1/6 % of VAT due if no previous failures; greater of £10 and 1/3% of VAT due if one previous failure; greater of £15 and 1/2% of VAT due if two or more previous failures.
Failure to comply with the requirements of the investment gold scheme (VATA 1994 s 69A).	17.5% of the value of transactions concerned.
Import VAT (FA 2003 ss 24–41):	
– failures relating to non-compliance	maximum penalty of £2,500
– evasion.	maximum penalty equal to VAT sought to be evaded.
Evasion of VAT: conduct involving dishonesty (VATA 1994 ss 60, 61). Does not apply to acts or omissions relating to an inaccuracy in a document or failure to notify HMRC of an under-assessment (to which penalties under FA 2007 Sch 24 apply).	Amount of tax evaded or sought to be evaded (subject to mitigation).
Transactions connected with fraudulent evasion of VAT (VATA 1994 ss 69C–69E).	30% of potential lost VAT.
Failure to notify details of, or notify use of, a notifiable proposal which enables a person to obtain a tax advantage within 31 days of the making of the proposal (F(No 2)A 2017 Sch 17).	Penalty up to £600 per day in 'initial period' A continuing penalty not exceeding £600 for each day on which the failure continues after imposition of initial penalty (but a tribunal can determine a higher penalty up to £1 million).

Offence	Penalty
Failure to provide HMRC with the reference number and related information in relation to notifiable arrangements above (F(No 2)A 2017 Sch 17).	Penalty not exceeding £5,000 in respect of each scheme to which the failure relates
For second failure within three years of first, penalty not exceeding £7,500 in respect of each scheme
For subsequent failures within three years of previous, penalty not exceeding £10,000 in respect of each scheme.

Index

A

Accounts, inheritance tax
  due dates 110
  excepted estates 110
Advisory fuel rates 84
Advisory electricity rate 86
Age allowance 76
Aggregates levy 63
Agricultural property relief 112
Air passenger duty 63
Alternative finance investment bonds 33
Annual accounting scheme, VAT 157
Annual exempt amount, capital gains tax 43
Annual exemption, inheritance tax 112
Annual tax on enveloped dwellings 59
Apprenticeship levy 98
Approval applications 34
Authorised mileage rates 86
Average exchange rates 125

B

Bank base rates 1
Bank levy 60
Bank corporation tax surcharge 59
Basic rate of income tax 71
Basis of assessment
  employment income 92
  overseas income 132
Benefits, employee 87–91
Benefits, social security 135–139
Blind person's allowance 76
Bus services 81, 87
Business asset disposal relief 46
Business property relief 112

C

Capital allowances
  cars 37
  claims, time limits 30
  dredging 37
  elections, time limits 30
  enterprise zones 39
  know-how 37
  mineral extraction 37
  patent rights 37
  plant and machinery 38–40
  rates 37–40
  research and development 41

Capital allowances – *cont.*
  structures and buildings 41
Capital gains tax
  annual exempt amount 43
  ATED properties 59
  business asset disposal relief 46
  chattel exemption 43
  claims, time limits 28
  due date 1
  elections, time limits 28
  employee-ownership trusts 46
  employee shareholder shares 48
  enterprise investment scheme (EIS) 48
  entrepreneurs' relief 45
  exemptions 43
  high value UK residential property 45
  hold-over relief for gifts 48
  incorporation relief 50
  indexation allowance 52–53
  investors' relief 49
  late payment interest 4
  leases 56
  non-resident CGT 1, 12, 45
  payment of tax 1
  penalties 13–26
  personal representatives 43, 44, 50
  rates 44
  reliefs 46
  retail prices index 54–55
  returns, penalties 13–18
  roll-over relief 49
  seed enterprise investment scheme (SEIS) 49
  share identification rules 46
  social investment tax relief 49
  trustees 43, 44, 51
  venture capital schemes 49
Capital goods scheme, VAT 158
Capped income tax reliefs 103
Cars
  advisory fuel rates 84
  advisory electricity rates 86
  authorised mileage rates 99
  benefit 78
  capital allowances 37
  capital gains exemption 49
  fuel for private use
    taxable benefit 81
    VAT 164
  hired: restricted allowances 81
  mileage allowances 84
  private use 78
Carbon price floor 65
Cash accounting scheme, VAT 157

Certificates of tax deposit 9
Charities and CASCs
   capital gains exemption 48
   gift aid 75
   gift aid small donations 75
   gifts in kind 75
   gifts to, inheritance tax relief 112
   payroll giving scheme 75
Chattels, capital gains exemption 43
Cheap loans to employees 87
Child benefit income tax charge 74
Child tax credit 107
Claims, time limits
   capital allowances 30
   capital gains tax 28
   corporation tax 29
   income tax 28
Clearance applications 34
Clearing houses 32
Climate change levy 65
Community investment tax relief 98
Company share option plans 107
Compensation, capital gains exemption 46
Computer equipment 91
Construction industry scheme
   deduction of tax 74
   security, failure to provide 27
Corporation tax
   annual tax on enveloped dwellings 59
   bank corporation tax surcharge 59
   bank levy 60
   claims, time limits 29
   cultural sector reliefs 60
   disincorporation relief 58
   digital services tax 61
   diverted profits tax 60
   due date 2
   elections, time limits 29
   gifts of pre-eminent objects 58
   instalments of tax 1
   interest on overdue tax 6
   interest on overpaid tax 8
   marginal relief 57
   patent box 58
   payment of tax 1
   penalties 13–26
   rates 57
   real estate investments trusts 58
   reliefs 58
   research and development expenditure 58
   restitution interest 61
   returns, penalties 13–17
   security, failure to provide 27
Cultural sector reliefs 72
Cycles and cycle safety equipment 81

D

Default interest, VAT 167
Default surcharge, VAT 168
Deregistration limits, VAT 156

Digital services tax 61
Direct recovery of debt 9
Disabled employees, equipment 88
Disincorporation relief 58
Diverted profits tax 60
Dividends 73
Dividend allowance 73
Double taxation agreements
   air transport profits 131
   capital taxes 131
   income and capital gains 129
   shipping profits 131
   tax compliance agreements 131
   tax information exchange agreements 131
Dredging allowances 37
Due dates of tax 2–3

E

Economic crime (anti-money laundering) levy 66
Elections, time limits
   capital allowances 30
   capital gains tax 28
   corporation tax 29
   income tax 28
Employees
   accommodation, supplies etc used in employment duties 87
   amounts which would be otherwise deductible 87
   assets given to employees 87, 122
   bus services for 81, 87
   car benefits 78
   cheap loans 87
   childcare 88
   Christmas parties, annual functions 88, 122
   clothing and uniforms 122
   computers provided for private use 91
   credit cards and tokens 88 122
   cycles and cycle safety equipment 81
   disabled, equipment etc 88
   electricity for an electric car 81
   emergency vehicles 81
   employees' liability insurance 88
   entertaining 122
   eye tests 88
   fixed-rate expenses 95
   flat rate expenses 95
   fuel benefits 82, 123
   holidays 123
   homeworkers 89
   incidental overnight expenses 89
   living accommodation 89
   living expenses 89
   loan benefits 87, 123
   long service awards 89
   meals 90, 123
   medical check-ups 90
   medical insurance, etc. 90, 123
   medical treatment 90
   mileage rates 84, 86

Employees – *cont.*
  mobile phones 91, 123
  national living wage 93
  national minimum wage 93
  notional payments 123
  parking facilities for 81, 123
  payments in kind 123
  pensions advice 90
  personal expenses 90, 123
  relocation benefits 103, 131
  round sum allowances 123
  scholarships and school fees 90, 123
  share schemes 106
  shareholder status 44, 101
  subscriptions 91
  tax paid for 123
  telephone costs 123
  third party gifts 91
  trivial benefits 91
  use of employer's assets 91
  van benefits 81
  vouchers 91, 124
Employee shareholder status 48, 101
Employment benefits and expenses payments 87–91
Employment exemption 91
Employment income 92
  basis of assesment 93
  due dates of tax 2
  fixed rate expenses 95
  termination payments 94
Employee-ownership trusts 46, 91
Enterprise investment scheme (EIS)
  capital gains exemption 48
  income tax relief 98
Enterprise management incentives (EMIs) 106
Enterprise zones 39
Entrepreneurs' relief 45, 46
Environmental taxes and other levies 63–67
Excepted estates, inheritance tax 110, 111
Excepted transfers 110
Exchange rates
  average 125
  year end 128
Exchanges
  alternative finance investment bonds 33
  recognised foreign exchanges 32
  recognised futures exchanges 32
  recognised investment exchanges 32
  recognised stock exchanges 30
Exempt supplies, VAT 160

F

Filing dates 11
Fixed rate expenses 95
Flat rate scheme for small businesses, VAT 157
Flat rate scheme for farmers, VAT 155
Flexible benefit arrangements 90
Foreign exchange rates
  average 125

Foreign exchange rates – *cont.*
  year end 128
Foreign income
  basis of assessment 132
  employment income 93
Foster carers 101
FOTRA securities 133
Fuel duty 66
Fuel for private use
  income tax 81
  VAT 164
Futures exchanges 32

G

Gift aid 75
Gift aid small donations 75
Gifts in kind 75
Gifts of land, shares etc 75
Gifts of pre-eminent objects 48, 58, 101

H

Harmonised interest regime 4
Help to buy: ISAs 100
High value UK residential property 44, 58, 141
Hired cars and motorcycles 81
Hold-over relief for gifts 48

I

Income tax
  capped reliefs 103
  claims, time limits 28
  due dates 2
  elections, time limits 28
  late payment interest 4
  lease premiums 56
  payment of tax 2
  penalties 13–26
  personal allowances 76
  rates 71
  reliefs 76, 101
  repayment interest 5
  returns, penalties 13–26
Incorporation relief 50
Indexation allowance 52
Individual savings accounts (ISAs) 100
Inheritance tax
  agricultural property relief 112
  annual exemption 112
  business property relief 112
  charitable gifts, exemption 112
  due dates for accounts 110
  due dates for tax 3
  excepted transfers estates and settlements 110
  gifts, reliefs 112

Inheritance tax – *cont.*
    interest on overdue tax 7
    marriage/civil partnership gifts, exemption 112
    national purposes, gifts exemption 112
    nil rate bands 109–110
    non-domiciled spouse/civil partner 113
    payment of tax 3
    penalties 13–25
    political parties, gifts exemption 112
    potentially exempt transfers 112
    quick succession relief 113
    rates 109
    reliefs 112
    small gifts exemption 113
    tapering relief 113
Insurance premium tax 66
Insurance premiums, life 101
Interest rates
    bank base rates 1
    capital gains 4
    certificates of tax deposit 9
    corporation tax 6
    default, VAT 167
    digital services tax 7
    income tax 4
    income tax on company payments 6
    inheritance tax 7
    land and buildings transaction tax (Scotland) 146
    land transaction tax (Wales) 147
    late payment interest 5
    national insurance contributions 5
    official, cheap loans 87
    overpaid tax 7
    repayment interest 4
    stamp duties 5
    unpaid tax 5, 6
    VAT 167
Investment exchanges 32
Investment reliefs
    community investment tax relief 98
    enterprise investment scheme (EIS) 98
    help to buy: ISAs 100
    individual savings accounts (ISAs) 100
    junior ISAs 100
    lifetime ISAs 100
    seed enterprise investment scheme (SEIS) 98
    social investment tax relief 99
    urban regeneration companies 100
    venture capital trusts (VCTs) 99
Investment zones 38, 40, 41, 115, 143
Investors' relief 46

J

Junior ISAs 100

K

Know-how, capital allowances 37

L

Land and buildings transaction tax (Scotland) 146
Land transaction tax (Wales) 147
Landfill disposals tax (Wales) 67
Landfill tax 67
Landfill tax, Scottish 67
Late payment interest 4
Leases
    depreciation table 56
    premiums 56
    stamp duties 141–147
Lifetime ISAs 100
Local authority members, travel expenses 86
Loans to employees 87
Loans to participators
    payment of tax 1
    tax charge 61

M

Machinery and plant allowances 38–41
    cars 37
    rates 38
Maintenance payments 101
Managed services companies 92
Marginal relief, corporation tax 57
Marriage/civil partnership gifts, inheritance tax relief 112
Married couple's allowance 76
Mileage allowances 84
Minimum wage, national 93
Misdeclarations, VAT 168
Mobile phones 91
Motorcycles 81

N

National insurance contributions
    apprentices under age 25 115
    Class 1 115, 122
    Class 1A, 1B 122, 123
    Class 3 121
    Classes 2 and 4 3, 121
    employees under age 21 115
    employers' contributions on benefits 122
    employment allowance 115
    interest on overdue contributions 5
    interest on overpaid contributions 7

National insurance contributions – *cont.*
  payment of 3
  rates 115
  weekly and monthly thresholds 92
National living wage 93
National minimum wage 93
Nazi persecution, pensions to victims 132
Non-domiciled individuals
  employment income 93
  overseas income 130
  spouses/civil partners, inheritance tax 113
Non-residents
  employment income 93
  overseas income 132
  stamp duty land tax 141
Non-resident CGT
  filing date 12
  payment of tax 1
  rate of tax 44

O

Official rate of interest, employee loans 87
Offshore matters, penalties, territory categories, transfers 13, 14, 16–20
Optional remuneration arrangements 91
Overseas income, basis of assessment
  employment income 92
  overseas income 132

P

Parking facilities 81
Partial exemption, VAT 158
Participators, loans and benefits to
  payment of tax 1
  tax charge 61
Patent rights, capital allowances 37
Patent box 58
Payment dates of tax 1–3
PAYE
  payment of 3
  penalties 13–25
  security, failure to provide 27
  settlement agreements 92
  weekly and monthly thresholds 92
Payroll giving scheme 75
Penalties
  asset-based for offshore inaccuracies etc 21
  deliberate enablers of offshore evasion etc 21
  generally 13–26
  interest on 4, 26
  mitigation of 26
  offshore matter asset moves 20
  offshore matter, territory categories 19, 20
  special information returns 22
  stamp taxes 152
  VAT 167
Pension provision 103
Personal allowances 76

Personal pension schemes 103
Personal representatives 43, 44, 50
Personal savings allowance 71
Personal service companies 92
Pillar 2 global minimum tax 61
Plant and machinery allowances
  rates 38–40
Potentially exempt transfers 112
Premiums on leases
  capital gains tax 56
  income tax 56
  stamp taxes 145, 147
Property allowance 101
Publishing details of
  deliberate tax defaulters 26
  enablers of offshore evasion 26
  persistently uncooperative large businesses 27
  serial tax avoiders 27

Q

Qualifying corporate bonds 49
Qualifying care relief 101
Quick succession relief 113

R

Rates of tax
  annual tax on enveloped dwellings 59
  capital gains tax 43
  corporation tax 57
  digital services tax 61
  diverted profits tax 60
  environmental taxes and other levies 63–67
  income tax 71
  inheritance tax 109
  non-resident CGT 44
  stamp taxes 141–149
  VAT 155
Real Estate Investment Trusts 58
Recognised clearing houses 32
Recognised futures exchanges 32
Recognised investment exchanges 32
Recognised stock exchanges 30
Reduced rate supplies, VAT 160
Registration limits, VAT 155
Reliefs
  capped income tax reliefs 103
  capital gains 45, 46
  corporation tax 57
  income tax 76, 98, 101
  inheritance tax 109
Remission of tax 9
Rent, stamp duties 141–147
Rent-a-room relief 101
Repayment interest 5
Repayment supplement, general 5
Repayment supplement, stamp duty 153
Repayment supplement, VAT 168

Research and development 41, 58
Restitution interest 61
Retail prices index 54–55
Retirement pensions 103
Return filing dates 11
Roll-over relief 50

S

Salary sacrifice arrangements 90
Save as you earn (SAYE) share option schemes 106
Scottish income tax 71
Scottish landfill tax 67
Scottish VAT 155
Seafarers' deduction 93
Securities, tax-free for non-residents 133
Security, failure to provide 27
Seed enterprise investment scheme (SEIS) 49, 98
Share identification rules 46
Share incentive plans 106
Share schemes 106
Shared lives carers 101
Small gifts relief 113
Simple assessment 10
Simplified fixed rate deductions 103
Social investment tax relief 49, 99
Social security benefits
  cap on benefits 136, 134
  non-taxable 137
  taxable 134
Special relief 8
Stamp taxes
  exemptions 145
  fixed 149
  interest 5, 6, 149
  land and buildings transaction tax (Scotland) 146
  land transactions 141, 147
  land transaction tax (Wales) 147
  leases 145, 146
  penalties 152
  premiums 145, 146, 147
  rates 141–149
  reliefs 145
  rent 141–147
  repayment supplement 5, 150
  stamp duty 152
  stamp duty land tax 141
  stamp duty reserve tax 149
  stock transfers 148
State benefits
  cap on benefits 136, 138
  non-taxable 137
  taxable 135
Stock exchanges 30
Structures and buildings 41
Student loans 10
Subscriptions 32, 91

Supplement VAT 168

T

Tapering relief, inheritance tax 113
Tax credits 107
Tax information exchange agreements 131
Termination payments 94
Time limits, claims and elections 27
Trading allowance 101
Travel expenses, local authority members 86
Trustees
  capital gains annual exempt amount 43
  expenses allowable for CGT 51
Trusts
  capital gains tax rates 44
  income tax rates 71

U

Universal credit 138
Urban regeneration companies 100

V

Van, employee benefit 81
VAT
  annual accounting scheme 157
  capital goods scheme 158
  car fuel advisory rates 164
  car fuel for private use 164–166
  cash accounting scheme 157
  default interest 166
  default surcharge 168
  deregistration limits 156
  EC sales lists 160
  EU country codes 161, 162
  evasion 18
  exempt supplies 160
  failure to notify liability 168
  flat-rate scheme for farmers 155
  flat-rate scheme for small businesses 157
  interest on overpaid tax 167
  intrastat 162
  Mini One Stop Shop (MOSS) 163
  partial exemption 158
  penalties 168
  rates 155
  reduced rate supplies 160
  registration limits 155
  repayment supplement 168
  Scottish VAT 155
  zero-rated supplies 159
Vehicle excise duty 68
Venture capital trusts (VCTs)
  capital gains exemptions 49

Venture capital trusts (VCTs) – *cont.*
  income tax reliefs 99

Withdrawal of self assessment 12
Working tax credit 107

W

Welsh income tax 72

Z

Zero-rated supplies, VAT 159